Del-Aware
Lenape Legacies

Jay Miller, PhD

Contents

Please Help Obliterate Typo Gnomes!

Cover: Nahkoman (p136) by George Catlin

Preface

Gathering together my articles and drafts concerned with Lenapei ~ Delaware Culture allows for corrections of typos, revised correct spellings of terms such as "struckon", and updating facts and opinons perculating and pulsating since 1970. Now, almost 50 years later, we mourn the passing of Nora Thompson Dean, Lillie Hoag Whitehorn, Esther Hoag Homovich, Lucy Parks Blalock, and other esteemed elders. Esther, in particular, was uniquely qualified by being both a native speaker of Lenape and Caddo, who served as a WAC in the homeland, where she could better understand indigeous place names and topography.

Delawares persist in communities in Oklahoma, Wisconsin, Ontario, and even in the homeland. My updated articles are mostly in chronological order, from short treatments to long analyses, with studies of the October Gamwing Rite in the Big House drawn togething in their own section, considering times, places, and traumas.

Delaware Integrity is my analystical synthesis of Lenapei over time and space. *Del-Aware* retraces the steps that took me there. To aid further scholarship, original page numbers of my published works appear between [square brackets].

Again, *wanishi* ~ my thanks to those already thanked in the various chapters, heart felt from start to finish.

Thanks

Interweaving documents, interpretative devices, Oklahoma visits, and Delaware memories has occupied my life. Nora Thompson Dean, an extraordinary woman well versed in Unami Delaware traditions guided my efforts, along with Charlie, Louise, Jim, Edward Leonard, and others of the Wolf clan. Lucy Parks Blalock, Jake ~ Rosemary, Sonny, Sissy, Jerald, Ruthe, and their own families also advised, along with Tom and Irene Wilson, and Annie Brown Parks. Support around Anadarko came from Linda Poolaw, Lillie Hoag Whitehorn, Esther Hoag Homovich, Willie and Bessie Snake, Lawrence and Dorothy Snake, Georgia Chisman Gallegos, and Edgar French. At the Bartlesville Public Library, Wilma Berry, Ruby Cranor, and Susan Box encouraged.

Helpful colleagues were Drs Lorraine Williams, Janet Pollak, Sue Roark, Duane Hale, and Bruce Pearson. Others were Bob Grumet, Mel Thurman, Ives Goddard, Fritz Jennings, CA Weslager, Fred Gleach, Marshall Becker, Ray Fogelson, and William Fenton.

For aid with research, it is a pleasure to thank Vi and Don Hilbert for all their help and encouragement, along with their family of Lois, Ron, Jay, Bedelia, Jill, John, and all the grandchildren. Within the larger Lushootseed family, thanks go to Peggy Dunn, Alf Shepard, Robbie Rudine, Janet Yoder, Pam Cahn (*wiw'isu*), Carolyn Marr, Brad Burns, Carolyn Michael, Barbara Iliff Brotherton, Dean Reiman, and many more.

Among other degreed members, appreciation goes to Drs. Thom Hess, Pam Amoss, Dale Kinkade, Laurel Sercombe, William Seaburg, Dawn (ƛup) Bates, Andie Palmer, Robin Wright, Bill Holm, Greg Watson, Bob and Laura Dassow Walls, Mary Laya, John Adams, Sally Anderson, Astrida Blukis Onat, Ann Bates, Carol Eastman, Fr Patrick Touhy, Viola Garfield, and Erna Gunther.

Among the native community, while they cannot all be named, or wish to be, I single out the late Isadore Tom, Ed Davis, Lawrence Webster, Martin Sampson, Susie Sampson Peter,

Morris Dan, Theresa Willup, Helen Ross, Lottie Sam, Walter Sam, and Dewey Mitchell. Younger members include Lona Wilbur, Dobie Tom, and the families of Andy Fernando and Jack and Deborah Fiander. Blue, Sherry, and Sanger Clark provide strong support.

Many people have helped me to understand the complexities of Tsimshian culture. In particular, at Hartley Bay, these were Chief John and Helen Clifton, Ernest, Lynne, Cameron, and Jodie Hill, Ernest and Margie Hill, Sr, and Mildred Wilson. At Klemtu, my teachers were Violet and Peter Neasloss, Chief Tom Brown, and others. Other colleagues include John and Luceen Dunn, Susan Marsden, Marjorie Halpin, Margaret Seguin, Carol Sheehan, Bill Holm, Robin Wright, Viola Garfield, Amelia Susman Schultz, Jean Mulder, Marie-Lucie Tarpent, Bruce Rigsby, Dale Kinkade, Jay Powell, Vickie Jensen, Guy Gibeau, and Stanley Newman.

Students in the Simon Fraser University, Native Language Teacher Program at Prince Rupert clarified and expanded my thinking: Cameron and Eva-Ann Hill, Nadine Robinson, Mel Tait, Maureen Yeltatzie, Beatrice Skog, Isabelle Hill, Pansy Collison, Deborah Schmakeit, Marilyn Bryant, Karla Gamble, and Shani Heal. Mary Tomlinson, Mercedes de la Nuez, and Thomas Perry helped me smooth out complications with Canadian bureaucracy.

At the beginning, support came from James and Charlotte Toulouse, Carmie Lynn, Laura Lee, Charlotte Mary, Jeremy Alan, Tamaya Lynn, Trent, Marie, Ella Mae, and others. As an undergraduate at the University of New Mexico, Stanley Newman, WW "Nibs" Hill, Philip Bock, Bruce Rigsby, and, especially, Florence Hawley Ellis and Mary Elizabeth Smith set my academic course. Outside the classroom, Cynthia Irwin-Williams and the Anasazi Origins Project gave me first-hand experience as an archaeologist on Sia Pueblo Land. Later as an advisor at Salmon Ruin, I was introduced to Chaco outliers and reoccupations.

As a graduate student at Rutgers and Princeton, my teachers were Robin Fox, Yehudi Cohen, Warren Shapiro, and Mark Leone. Margaret Bacon, Jane Lancaster, and Martin Silverman gave encouragement. Alfonso Ortiz, Esther Goldfrank, and Karl Wittfogel, Elizabeth Brandt, Wick Miller, Tom Windes, Anna Sofaer, and John Stein provided insights.

My parents and siblings aided as needed, as did fellow students Janet Pollak, Michele Teitelbaum, Cheryl Wase, Edward Deal, Nina Versaggi, Nancy Trembly, Kenneth Wilkie, Corinne Black, Karen and Tom Reynolds, John and Luceen Dunn and family, Glenn and Dorothy Williams and family, Andrew and Nancy Core, Joanne, and family, and Roland Wildman. Support also came from Darby Stapp, Kara Powers, Julia Longenecker, James Knobb, Marilyn Richen, Tammy Jackson, Ann Schuh, Bob and Christine Keyes-Back, Tom and Donna Steinburn, Ellen Lowe, Nancy Griffin, and, especially, Monday Nite.

Why the World Is on the Back of a Turtle
Correspondence

Sir,

During his visit to the New World, between 1678 and 1680, Jaspar Danckaerts recorded the most quoted account of the Origin Myth of the Delaware Indians (Newcomb 1950: 72) of the Eastern United States. I will paraphrase it: First there was only water, then the Great Turtle gradually rose above water level and the Creator placed mud on his shell. The mud dried and the Great Tree grew in the middle of the earth. As the Tree grew towards the sky a sprout became a man, then the Great Tree bent down and in touching the earth caused a sprout to become a woman. From this man and woman all of humanity descended.

'The traditional Delaware belief that the earth rests on the back of a turtle' (Tantaquidgeon 1950: 25) is also shared by other tribes of the Northeastern Woodlands, most notably the Iroquois (Hewitt 1928). Originally, I viewed the turtle as a logical choice for this atlantean burden because its shape and appearance were appropriate to this role. But that was before I understood Delaware culture and the choice of natural symbols.

The turtle is more than it appears. Speck (1931: 44) noted that 'the turtle is the earth, is life.' Speck saw this assertion based on qualities of the turtle that the Delaware admired in life: perseverance, longevity, and steadfastness. Also the Delawares viewed all life, time, and turtles as continuously moving from east to west.

My own conversations with Delaware indicate that life and the earth would have been impossible without the turtle supporting the world. In recognition of its importance for survival, turtles have come to symbolise life itself and the earth that nourishes life. Among the Delaware, one quality of life has priority. This is the quality of consciousness.

The Delaware word for consciousness (*pɛnayindʌməswakʌn*) also translates as thoughts of the mind. So important is this quality for life as a whole that anyone born with a mental defect is said to be *mɛčiʌmgəl* (now he is already dead). A strong consciousness can survive the death of its body and continue to affect the earth as a spirit. The significance of consciousness for my argument will emerge later.

The qualities of the Great Turtle are attributed to a particular genus, the box turtle (Speck 1931: 46). Its shell was used for the rattle during the major Delaware ceremonial: the gamwing ~ Big House. When I sought the position of the box turtle within the Delaware ethnozoological taxonomy, an important point was noticed. The Delaware ethnozoology shows a pervasive distinction between land and water animals. For example, the Delaware language has two words for turtle: *taxkok* means land turtle ~ tortoise while the more obscure term *tulpe* may be used for water turtles ~ terrapins. The box turtle is anomalous to this division for two reasons. First, it is more aquatic when young and more terrestrial when old and, second, its feet, especially the hind feet, are partially webbed and thus intermediate between aquatic and terrestrial forms (Babock 1971: 90, 91). As the box turtle mediates between land and water forms in the taxonomy, so the Great Turtle mediates between land and water in the Origin Myth.

In Delaware society the turtle also figures prominently as the eponym of one of three matriclans: turtle, fowl, and canine (Miller 1975). The leader of the turtle clan was also the chief of all the Delawares and the protector of their traditions (Herman 1950: 60). Again the turtle figures as a mediator because the fowl are viewed as vegetarian and the canine as carnivorous. But 'the box turtle subsists on a mixed diet, consisting of vegetable matter on the one hand, and animal matter ... on the other' (Babcock 1971: 92).

Speck (1937: 24) also reported a general division of the Delaware into male and female categories.   The Origin Myth also includes a man / woman opposition.   Since the Turtle represents life and thereby consciousness, it also mediates between man and woman who also share consciousness between them.

The other opposition in the Origin Myth is that of Earth and Sky. The mediator for this pair is not the Turtle, but rather is the Great Tree. In the gamwing ~ Big House Ceremony, the centre post represents this Great Tree, linking earth and sky. Since the Big House itself represents the Delaware universe (Speck 1931: 22), the turtle shell rattle and the centre post [307] refer to the Turtle and Tree of the Origin Myth. This opposition between Turtle and Tree is mediated by (lie mind. The Turtle has already been shown to symbolise[1] consciousness. The Delaware also believe that trees have consciousness. They are the only plants considered to be animate and are called "kins people" in recognition of this consciousness they share with humanity. In the Origin Myth the mind itself is represented by the Creator, who places mud on the Turtle's back. The Creator is the embodiment of all consciousness. He is said to spend eternity sitting and thinking.

With intensive research, the above analysis should also apply for other societies who place the world on the back of a turtle. Parker (1912: 611) provides the tantalising report that members of the False Face Society among the Seneca Iroquois 'rub their turtle rattles on pine tree trunks, believing that thereby they become imbued with both the earth-power and the sky-power, ... a recognition of the connection between the turtle and the world-tree that grows upon the primal turtle's back.'

It now remains to discuss these examples of natural symbols of mediation. I had originally believed that it was the appearance of the turtle that led to its use as a mediator. However, given the structure of Delaware culture, the behaviour of the turtle emerged as crucial. In fact, what is important about natural symbols is that they cannot be predicted before the culture is known. The turtle was important for the Delaware because it served to mediate the important land / water and vegetarian / carnivore oppositions; the Tree because it mediated between earth and sky. But most important of all was the conscious mind, which was attributed to both turtles and trees. The mind also mediated the man / woman opposition.

The three Delaware clans use natural symbols to express the three elements and three oppositions of the Delaware universe − turtle : canine : fowl :: water : land : air. Here the referents are the omnivorous Great Turtle floating in the water, the carnivorous canines on the land, and the vegetarian fowl roosting in trees.

While the Delaware cosmos can be viewed as structured by the land / water, earth / sky and man / woman oppositions and the mediation of turtles and trees, all are subsumed by the ultimate natural symbol of mediation: the Mind. More generally, I suggest that the more culturally inclusive a mediator is, the closer it will reflect the overarching importance of the mind. [308]

---

[1] British English spellings have been retained throughout.

Triads in Delaware Culture

I want to discuss recent developments in the concept of culture and conceptual models of society, using the Lenape or Delaware Indians as my example. Some of my data and insights on the Delaware are the result of the generous help of Mrs Nora Thompson Dean, the last articulate Lenape speaker. However, she is not to be held directly responsible for this interpretation.

When I speak of culture I am being very specific: Culture is a conceptual system of organization, a mental construct. Stripped to its essentials, culture can be considered a framework for ordering the world of a human society. Therefore, when I discuss Lenape clans and tribes I am not concerned with them per se, but rather with what they can tell me about the form of Lenape culture. I have found the methodologies of structuralism and ethnoscience particularly effective for delimiting this view of Lenape culture. Structuralism provided a sense of the dynamic oppositions that unified Lenape culture, and ethnoscience, particularly as it pertains to zoological taxonomy, gave an insight into the Delaware's conceptualization of the world around them. When both approaches have shown redundancies, I have assumed that these are due to the structure of Lenape culture.

Part of my fascination with the Delaware steins from what I call the "Delaware Paradox." This paradox relates to the discrepancy between the accounts of the Moravian missionaries, David Zeisberger and John Heckewelder. The relevant facts of the paradox have been presented by Clinton Weslager in his new book. The Delaware Indians, A History. Zeisberger cited three Lenape clans – wolf, turtle, and turkey – and three Lenape tribes – Munsi, Yunami, and Unalachtigo. Later Heckewelder took this a step further and equated the tribes and the clans: The Munsi were wolves, the Yunami were turtles, and the Unalachtigo were turkeys. But Mrs Dean is emphatic on the independence of Lenape tribes and clans, as well she might be since her tribe is Yunami and her clan is wolf. Weslager also cites historical sources to this effect. Before someone wants to credit this mutual independence to the disruption of Lenape society, I must remind you that this separation makes good anthropological sense. A basic knowledge of human society demands that political and social units must cross-cut each other if that society is to be functionally integrated and survive.

Given this separation, how then could Heckewelder, who was much closer to a functioning Lenape society than we are, have equated tribes and clans? Let me make a suggestion based on part on what I have recently learned about Delaware zoological taxonomy.

Remember that the zoological taxonomy taught in biology courses was largely developed by one man, Karl Linneus. Nature has not supplied man with any inherent taxonomy. Each society must develop a taxonomy for its own environment, imposing order on the natural world and the creatures in it. It is clear from the Lenape taxonomy that the clan names are meant to be generic and not specific terms.

The turkey clan is actually -pəle^e, which means "fowl." -pəle^e- belong to the family -čulens- ("birds") and are opposed to -biahele- = "water birds". In other words, pəle^e signifies "ground birds". Wolf is actually -tuksi•t-, which translates as "round foot" but means "canine." Tuksiit are part of the family xʌm-, "quadruped." Turtle is -pukuangu-, which translates "hollow in the heel" and means *taxok* = "turtle' or perhaps "webbed foot."

These three generic terms are important for the Lenape's conception of themselves and their world, for each shares some human attribute. *pəle^e* are ground-dwelling bipeds, *tuksiit* are meat-eaters, and *pukuangu* are swimmers. Note that the terms are structured as a triad or threesome, two of which (fowl and canines) are very similar (terrestrial) and one of which (turtle) is very different (aquatic).

Munsi is said to mean "People of the Hilly ~ Stoney Country." They were known as great warriors. Yunami is said to mean "People Down River" and they were outstanding healers. Unalachtigo seems to mean "People of the Waves ~ Seacoast." I do not know positively what they were known for, but I would like to make a guess that they were the obverse of warriors and healers, in other words Sorcerers of War Magic. I base this guess on the fact that the Lenape structured their world in threesomes, two of which were similar and the third different. Warriors and Healers are positive and similar, while War Sorcerers would be negative and different. Further, modem Delaware remember the Nanticoke as war sorcerers, and I therefore concur with Brinton and others in assuming that the Unalachtigo were Nanticokes. At least that is what the internal structure of Lenape culture suggests.

While the clan terms indicate behavioral differences, the tribal names signify differences in terrain: The Munsi are on land, the Yunami on the river, and the Unalachtigo on the sea. Here land is the different member, and the aquatic locations are similar. Note the clear possibility of cross-cutting divisions. For tribal attributes or specialties, the Munsi and Yunami are similar, and the Unalachtigo are different. But for terrain differences in the tribal names, the Yunami and Unalachtigo are similar, and the Munsi different. This is what I mean by cross-cutting ties which serve to unify a society.

Moving away from the Delaware paradox, we can find other threesomes in Lenape culture. The supernaturals in their myths are the Thunderers in the sky, the Water Serpent in bodies of water, and the Giants on the land. In this triad, the earthly supernaturals are similar and the sky beings are different. I suspect that threesomes pervaded all of Lenape culture.

Although Heckewelder was an intimate of the Lenape, his mistake came from assuming that there was only one threesome in Delaware culture. In fact there were probably many, each of which intersected the others and structurally integrated the Delaware. Zeisberger seems closer to the truth, but even he lacked a holistic approach.

Just as political and social divisions must intersect in a human society, so must the economic sphere transect both of them. It is these economic features that are most susceptable to archaeological recovery. Future work throughout the former Delaware area should reveal regionally specialized tool kits and evidence of exchange networks. One hypothesis in this regard comes from Speck who noted that the Nanticoke of the eastern shore had to import stones for their lithics, and according to my model the "People of the Stoney Country" would be logical suppliers. In addition, once Delaware society had evolved to its present form, that is one based on intersecting threesomes, it should be archaeologically definable as three distinct but interrelated complexes, two of which are more similar to each other than to the third. The areas around the upper Delaware and middle Delaware seem to represent the different complexes, but I have been unable to recognize the missing one. My guess is that these complexes will largely be defined on the basis of ceramics.

The Unalachtigo?

Abstract

This article considers the anthropological evidence against the use of the term Unalachtigo for the third Delaware tribe and presents evidence for the substitution of the term "Winetkok" which is used by the Delaware themselves.

HISTORIANS say that the Delaware Indian Nation was divided into 3 tribes: Munsi, Unarm, and Unalachtigo. However, each time anthropologists go to the Delawares they fail to find any evidence of the last tribe named. This in itself is not all that unusual. Many American Indian tribes are known by names given them by Whites but continue to identify themselves by an indigenous designation that all but ignores the given one. Thus the Delawares are known among themselves as "*Lenapeawk*" or "*Awɛnik*" (both mean people) or as "*mexkesihkesichik*" ~ Indiens ~ Red People.

Among modern Oklahoma Delawares the terms Munsi (pronounced nasally as *monsi*) and Unami (pronounced as *wenami*) are used to label separate tribes. But with one exception the Unalachtigo are unknown. The one exception is Nora Thompson Dean who recalled that her mother had once referred to a group called the -*wenilaxteku*-. The term itself is interesting. It literally means "those who were detached from where there are waves". The Brinton-Anthony dictionary (1888: 85) tries to derive Munsi from "*min-achsi-ink*" = "where the stones are gathered together", but this is post hoc folk etymology. In the same way others have tried to derive Unami from "*nahi*" = "down river". Actually Munsi and Unami have become abreviated and have lost their original meaning. They survive only as tribal names and cannot be used to support contentions that they are only geographical, not political, designations. They are political!

It is also revealing that the term Unalachtigo was first committed to Delaware ethnohistory by Reverend David Zeisberger, whose work served as the basis for the accounts of Loskiel, Heckewelder, and others (Gray 1956: 62). Zeisberger worked among the Delawares in Ohio after they had all been detached from where there are waves.

The discussion would be stalemated here but for the consistent use of another tribal term by contemporaneous Delaware speakers. This is the term "*winetkok*" which is presently translated as the Nanticoke. As with the terms Munsi and Unami, Winetkok has no literal translation. Brinton suggested that the Unalachtigo were actually Nanticokes by another name; however, this assertion is too facile. We know of close ties between Delawares and Nanticokes historically and at present.

But the historical records also indicate that the Nanticoke are a recent tribe, formed by the aggregation of survivors of closely related Algonquian tribes (Weslager 1950).

The modern Delaware use of the term Winetkok for the Nanticoke suggests to me that a tribe called the Winetkok merged with others to form the Nanticoke. The extension of the [8] term Winetkok for the new tribe suggests that a primary identification with the Winetkok was transfered to the Nanticoke. I also suspect the new tribe may have been referred to descriptively as the Unalachtigo because detachment from the waves was a trait all Nanticokes shared.

To test the possibility that the Winetkok were in fact the third Delaware tribe, I used a sociogram. The purpose of a sociogram is to learn how individuals feel about and relate to each other. In this case, I was probing how Dean felt about the Winetkok. To do this I asked her if she would consider marrying into the Munsi, Unami, Winetkok, Unalachtigo, or Iroquois. Her answers were revealing because traditional Delawares insist upon marriage outside of all blood lines and clans but still within the Delaware Nation. These were her responses:

Munsi	Unami	Winetkok	Unalachtigo	Iroquois
No	Yes	Yes	Unsure	Never

Dean is herself a Unami and this was her first marriage choice, but the Winetkok were second choice and this indicates a subjective closeness between Unami and the Winetkok.

Another interesting datum about the Munsi, Unami, and Winetkok tribes is that Unami can still specify crucial differences between the funeral rites of each. The Munsi and Unami in [b] Oklahoma still observe them. The Nanticoke have given up their Skeleton Dance with the bones of the dead.

In summary, I suggest that anthropologists interested in social realities should consider designating the 3 tribes of the Delaware Nation as the Munsi, Unami, and Winetkok. Historians shackled to the written word will have to mention the Unalachtigo but hopefully only as a descriptive term for the Winekok. It is important to consider all of the evidence on this, but it is more important to give first priority to evidence duplicated from many sources and recognized by the Delaware themselves.

K^w ulakan:
The Delaware Side of Their Movement West

Abstract
The movement of the Delawares from their East Coast homeland to their present locations has been much discussed by Whites. The usual explanation given is the pressure of European colonists. This paper offers another version of the events derived from modern Delaware in northeastern Oklahoma.

THE movement of the Delaware Indians from the Delaware River Valley through Pennsylvania, Ohio, Indiana, Missouri, and Texas to their present homes in Kansas, Oklahoma, and Ontario, has been the subject of much historical research. The recurrent pattern was for the Delaware to meet the vanguard of European settlers amiably but then to be inundated by European colonists and to move on. The usual explanation given is European pressure. While this was certainly a factor in the Delaware migrations, contemporary Delaware suggest that another reason may have been primary. Nora Thompson Dean, a fluent Delaware speaker, insisted that a traditional Delaware will leave an area if it "becomes a *k^w ulakan*."

Frank Speck has called attention to the ritual use of this word, writing it as "*kwula^a an*" (1931: 51, note 1) and as "*kula^a an*" (1937: 61, note 1). He translates it as something forbidden, feeling that the core of the meaning was strict adherence to taboo regulations prescribed by ancient rulings. However, as described by Dean, things become *k^w ulakan* or they might already be *k^w ulakan*. Only in the latter sense is there a static concept. Property is especially vulnerable to becoming *k^w ulakan*, as the following stories reveal. Some of the details of the stories have been changed to assure anonymity.

A local game reserve was to supply a deer for the birthday of a nonagenarian. Part of the venison was to go for the birthday party and part for a peyote meeting. However, the reserve administrator first hedged and then argued against giving the deer. Because of the unpleasantness that developed, the deer became a *k^w ulakan* and was later refused by the family. It became a *k^w ulakan* because the hostility generated was sure to anger the deities {*manituwak*} who would punish everyone by affecting the deer. The deer would then harm not only the participants to the fight but anyone else indirectly involved, such as the peyote meeting participants.

Since the Dawes Severally Act was approved by some Delaware, the Delaware have been given individual allotments, and intense land disputes have developed over the inheritance of these. In 1 case 3 family members were contending for an allotment after a personal will was declared illegal. One member was acutely aware that the allotment was becoming a k^w ulakan, and he had to decide on either of 2 possible settlements. The first was to sustain an appearance of complacence and harmony so as to placate the deities. The second was to sell the land to remove the reason for contention and to transfer any harmful associations to the new owner. [46]

The last is a story I heard from a Delaware about the Osage, a neighboring tribe in Oklahoma. A wealthy Osage man built a fine house, and after his death his children fought long and bitterly for its ownership. In the pitch of the fight the deities struck the house with lightning and it was destroyed. This story is interesting because it shows that a k^w ulakan can affect people other than Delawares.

As these incidents reveal the *k^w ulakan* is not so much a taboo as it is a threshold. When something becomes a *k^w ulakan* a line has been crossed, and, the deities are roused to action. As such the *kʷulakan* is different from the correction or injunction (*kwitələtəwakan*). Corrections include young people not eating gizzards to prevent them from becoming wrinkled, not asking a dog a question for if it answers you will die, and not eating the skin of a fowl to keep your skin from becoming loose. Each of these corrections relies heavily on analogy: an act and its consequences are observably related.

This is not the case with the *kʷulakan*. Here there is a breach in the harmony that the deities expect. To restore order the deities punish the guilty by destroying or altering the source of the contention. Their anger is such that bystanders might also be harmed. Although this seems like a biblical Christian notion, I suspect that it is also a Delaware one. The deities are described in human terms, and anger is a human emotion. However, there does seem to be a parallel to the *kʷulakan* concept in the landing of the Pilgrims. Recent historical research, indicates that the original Pilgrims left Europe to escape the disastrous consequences of the Second Coming of Christ which they believed imminent (Maier 1971). I mention this possibility but still believe that the *kʷulakan* concept is especially Delaware.

The relationship of the *kʷulakan* concept and the colonial situation should be clear. Contact between Delaware and Whites within an area would move gradually towards unpleasantness. The focus of the contention was the land upon which the Delaware were living. As harmony broke down traditional Delaware would have feared their land was becoming a *kʷulakan* and that their lives and well-being were in jeopardy. Since the Whites could not be contented the hope was to move on. Delaware still say that when they move to the Pacific the entire continent will become a *kʷulakan* and will be destroyed.

Playing Cards

Conversations [145] with Mary Haas originally encouraged me to try to collect the Delaware (Lenape) terms for playing cards from Unami Delaware speakers living in northeastern Oklahoma in 1976. The task proved to be more complicated, but, in the process, I was able to add the Dutch terms for playing card suits to those from French supplied by Haas[2]1 for Chipewyan and Menomini and those from Spanish supplied by Greenfeld[3]2 for Western Apache.

Initially, the three most fluent Unami speakers could not name all the playing cards, instead supplying the single term *škəp* for any card in the deck and specifically *spade*. Goddard[4]3 gave a similar term from Monsi Delaware, derived from Dutch, and noted that the name of one of the suits applied to the entire deck among the Western Abnaki (club = card) and Fox (spade = card). Haas added Menomini (spade = card).

I began to think that the other names for playing cards would have to be sought among [146] Unami speakers around Anadarko, Oklahoma or perhaps the Canadian Monsi. This was not necessary because of the foresight of James Rementer, a student of the Delaware living among them for over a decade. He recalled that he might have collected the terms from one of the speakers now deceased. As luck would have it, Rementer had collected these terms from the late Fred Falleaf in 1970, who names for all four suits, but was sure only of the terms for hearts and spades. I hoped that once the European source for these card terms was located, the correct equations of clubs and diamonds would become apparent, as indeed it has.

A recent encounter with a Dutch speaker from the Delft region enabled me to collect the Dutch terms for playing cards and thus to establish the source for the Delaware terms. On the slight chance that the early Swedish colonists living near the aboriginal Delaware might have influenced the terms, I also collected the Swedish terms from a colleague at the University of Washington, although Seattle is not noted for its paucity of Swedish speakers.

According to Falleaf, Unami terms for playing cards are: *halət* = heart (Dutch hart, harten; lit. heart), *liš* = diamond (Dutch ruit, ruiten; lit. window), *kwʌlas* = club (Dutch klaver, klaveren; lit. clover), and *škəp* = spade (Dutch schop, schoppen; lit spade, shovel). Dutch has a distinct term for card (kaat, kaaten). Note the substitution of Delaware "1" for Dutch "r".

For more general theoretical problems concerned with Algonquian card terms, Haas reported that Bloomfield found that most of the Menomini terms were classed as animate nouns. At least one Unami speaker thought that the plural spades should be *škəpa*, an inanimate noun, but that the term for cards should be *škəpak*, the animate plural.

For comparison, if a Middle [b] Atlantic slope native language borrowed their terms from Swedish, they are: hjarter = heart (lit. heart), ruter = diamond (lit. window pane, square), klover = club (lit. clover), spader = spade (lit. shovel), and kortlek = card deck (lit. card play).

---

2 Mary Haas, Notes on a Chipewyan Dialect, *IJAL* 34: 169-70 1968; Menomini Terms for Playing Cards *IJAL* 34: 217 1968.

3 Philip Greenfeld, Playing Card Names in Western Apache *IJAL* 37: 196-96 1971.

4 Ives Goddard, Dutch Loan Words in Delaware 1974.

Delaware Colors and Culture
Making Best Connections

Abstract

Greater cultural values learned from listening to two of the last speakers of Unami Delaware (Lenape) as they divided a color chart serve as caution and tribute to fieldwork.

On July 21, 1974, two Delaware elders, fluent speakers of the Unami dialect who spent their lives in Northeastern Oklahoma, taught me a valuable lesson in the academics of cultural analysis. Nora Thompson Dean (died 29 November 1984), her family, and I had driven several hours from Dewey to visit with Lucy Parks Blalock (died 11 February 2000) in Quapaw. My research then focused on the fashionable "ethnoscience" and our goal that day was to mark a color chart with the intensities and limits of the eight color terms I had already assembled for the Lenape language.

These 8 words, in simplest form and translation, followed by < indicating the root of the word, are

black	*səke* ≈ "it is black" < *sək-*	BPR 94: 61
blue	*aone* ≈ "it is blue" < *aon-*	BPR 94: 61
green	*æskæskw*e ≈ "it is green" < *æskæskw-*	BPR 94: 65
grey	*wipunkwe* ≈ "it is grey" < *wipunkw-*	BPR 94: 65
purple	*čʌkinkwɛm* ≈ "pokeweed" <	BPR 94: 68
red	*mʌxke* ≈ "it is red" < *mʌxk-*	BPR 94: 68
white	ɔpe ≈ "it is white" < ɔp-	BPR 94: 72
yellow	wisæ ≈ "it is yellow" < wisɔ-	BPR 94: 72

Twenty years later, a Delaware grammar with lessons by Lucy Blalock as first alphabetical author (Blalock, Pearson, and Rementer 1994: 21, cited herein as BPR 94) lists nine color terms in Chapter Four on Intransitive Verbs, in both the Inanimate (II) and Animate (AI) sections, yet only seven overlap with mine since they also list (BPR 94, 21, 22)

spotted:	*səsʌəpe* it is spotted	*sesʌp-*
striped:	*mamale* it is striped	*mamal-*

The single term that I use that they do not is purple, clearly meaning "like the color of pokeweed and berries," but since it was distinctive and derived from their natural landscape, I include it as an example of creative color derivations and applications that are often overlooked in narrow analyses.

My only publication to include the results of these chart blockings remarks

Delaware colors are classified much like those in English, with these exceptions. Black tends to include the spectrum from dark purple to dark red. This means that Delaware colors tend to be slightly lighter than their English values. Yellow includes most of the orange shades. For example, /wisawpales/ yellow apple means a Golden Delicious to Mrs Dean but an orange to

Mrs Blalock (Miller 1975, 440).

For comparison, the extensive and recent dictionary (O'Meara 199:, 422; herein O96) of Munsee (Munsi), the other surviving dialect, though called Delaware by its speakers in Ontario, lists these colors [colours] in adjective, noun, and verb forms.

black   *nzukeew* ≈ "be black" O96, 403

blue   *oolihkaapamukwat* ≈ "be blue coloured" O96: 404

green   *askaskwaapamukwat* ≈ "be green coloured" O96: 480

red   *maxkaapamukwat* ≈ "be red coloured" O96: 568

white   *waapaapamukwat* ≈ "be white coloured" O96:652

yellow *wiisaawaapamukwat* ≈ "be yellow coloured"

grey   *wiipongwaapamukwat* ≈ "be grey~brown coloured" O96: 480
~brown

Interesting additions include "be bright coloured" (O96: 408), "see through (clear)" (O96: 422), and overlap among white, grey, and brown, especially in terms of a whitish grey beard, and this familiar pair.

Spotted *papsakeew* O96: 603
Striped *maamaaleew* O96: 612

As used in this research, covered in clear plastic overlays, the Berkeley color chart represents 8 x 40 squares in a colored loop with pinks on the ends grading through the spectrum. In devising numbering to reflect these squares, the first one refers to one of the 8 vertical rows and the others refer to the long horizontal rows, thus 827-30 means the 8th row down and the 27th to 30th squares across. Along one side, a distinct column of 9 squares from black through greys to white is numbered separately.

Both speakers used the chart with the address upside down (reversing the acronym ROY G BIV) so that the pinks blended, left to right, into the violets, indigos, blues, greens, yellows, oranges, and reds, with light to dark shades going from bottom to top. On the right side, a separate panel of 9 squares shaded from white to black. Each speaker was asked to mark with a circled X the best examples of that color, then draw a line around all the squares with that same color. The result was a set of colored islands far from each other.

For example, Lucy marked

black   ~ with three Xs (833-36) in a line of 8 squares (829-36) at the top of the yellow to orange
      section;
blue   ~ with two rows of 4 Xs (511-14 611-14) each within three rows, upper to lower, squares
      410-17 510-15 610-15;
green   ~ in two rows of 520-27 620-26 including 5 Xs (522-26);
grey~ a line of the upper 7 squares in the 9 of the white to black section, with Xs on 3-5;
      purple ~ double row of lower 3 (67-9) and upper (75-9), with Xs on 75-8.
red ~ was marked at both ends (31 41 51 61 71; 436-40 536-40 636-40 736-40), with the upper

row (536-40) marked by 5 Xs.

white ~ also at both ends, though Lucy initially wanted to mark the stark white border itself, before she chose two squares on the left (11 12) and 7 on the right (34-40) as well as put Xs on the two bottom squares in the separate white to black column.

yellow ~ with a double row of 2 upper (229 230) and 3 lower squares (129 130 131), with each of the 3 Xed.

Nora wanted to mark a single square for each color as I said it, then decided that we should use color terms modified by the -tɛk ending to expand the range of each term. Nora had a special fondness for red, a color linked to her Roundfoot-Canine-Wolf clan, so she drew a circle instead of lines around it.

black ~   811-35 and the top 4 of the black to white column, with an X at 811

blue ~   313-17 413-18 with an X at 416

green ~   322-26 421-26 520-26 with an X at 524

grey ~   27-10 37-10 and 2-5 of white to black column with an X at 310

purple ~ 57 61-8 71-8 with an X at 75

red ~ a circle with arcs through 436 440 736 740 and an X at 537

white ~ the single Xed square at the bottom of the white to black column

yellow ~ 128-31 228-229 with an X at 130

The extender (-tɛk), suggesting a meaning of -ish (e.g. greenish) was also used for the joint session, where these old friends, encouraged by Jim Rementer, tried to show me what I should have been asking. When I thought we were done, however, an new extender -kɔt meaning "it looks like the color X" was introduced (compare with Munsee terms above) which effectively filled all the spaces. The result, of course, was a complete chart, without the free floating, isolated island of each color that made their understanding of colors seem disjointed. Each woman, however, marked her own sense of color range with an X, red for Nora or black for Lucy, that indicated they had separate but overlapping perceptions of color intensity. Nora, in particular, wanted to indicate the flux and fluidity of colors, so by this time she had taken to marking intensities at the intersections of squares if she thought that was where the typical color belonged, rather than solidly within a square as others might expect.

This filling in will be listed from left to right across the chart. After lines were drawn around each color, the intervening spaces were filled in by writing the first letter of the appropriate Lenape color term within each designated square.

Black ~ across the top from 81-16 833-40 629-34 733-35 and 3-7 of the column Nora Xed 817 and the column at 3 and between 5-6, Lucy Xed between 87-8 and between 7-8 of the column

White ~ 11-13 134-40 and 1-2 of the column, with Nora placing Xs at 11 and 1 of the column, as well as between 16-7 and between 111-12

Red ~ fills both ends from 21-6 234-40 31-6 332-40 41-6 433-40 51-5 531-40 61-5 635-40 71-5

737-40, with Nora putting Xs between 63-4 73-4 and at 52; Lucy between 53-4

Purple ~ 37-8 47-8 56-9 65-9 75-9, with Nora's X at 67 and Lucy's at 68

Grey ~ in the dark range of 817-31 718-23 and light of 27-10 37-10 49, with Nora Xing at 826 and between 817-18, between 728 828, with Lucy Xing between 730-31 830-31

Blue ~ 114-19 211-18 311-20 410-19 510-17 610-17 710-17, with Nora Xing 514 and the intersection of 318-19 4-18-19; Lucy Xed 515

Green ~ 120-27 219-28 321-29 420-29 518-29 618-28 718-26

Yellow ~ 128-33 225-33 330-32 430-32 530 with Nora marking Xs at 225 233 between 227-28 and 131-32 231-32; Lucy at the intersection of 131-32 231-32

In addition to showing how one has to be careful and expansive in what is asked, this experience also indicates the valued character of good rapport since both Nora and Lucy, when together, decided to answer what I should have asked instead of what I did.

If I had kept to my original intention, my view of Delaware culture would have been considerable limited (and lamed), but, instead, by listening carefully and being willing to alter course at the direction of informed elders, we have all benefited from a fuller and more complete understanding. In all, Delaware culture was revealed as a full pattern rather than a disjointed artifact of methodological strait jackets and scholarly ignorance.

Thanks

Pamela Amoss, twenty-five years apart, loaned me her chart to collect the terms and then to write this paper. Such archiving ability deserves praise. Jim Rementer urged me to write up our experiences, now as an employee of the finally recognized Delaware Tribe of Eastern Oklahoma. It has all taken a long time, but the results have been worth it.

Bulletin of the Archaeological Society of New Jersey # 56: 31-32 2001

Delaware Language and Culture

The Delaware settled in Oklahoma after an arduous and heroic trek which took them through periodic settlements in Pennsylvania, Ohio, Illinois, Indiana, Wisconsin, Missouri, Texas, and Kansas in the United States and into the province of Ontario in Canada. Before European contact and during the early Colonial period, the Delaware were resident in the Delaware River drainage where at least 2 divergent dialects were spoken. In the northern area near the common border of New York, New Jersey, and Pennsylvania were the northern or Monsi speakers and toward the south along the New Jersey, Pennsylvania and Delaware State borders were the southern or Unami speakers. A third group, called the Unalachtigo in the writings of Moravian missionaries, has never been satisfactorily verified ethnographicall although there is some historical evidence that the term referred to Delaware who had originally lived in New Jersey. As the vast majority of Mousi speakers settled in Ontario, so the majority of Unami speakers settled in northeastern Oklahoma in 1867 (throughout present-day Washington, Craig, Nowata, and Delaware counties). Another small group of Unami speakers adopted a Plains bison-hunting life style in Texas and joined the Caddo. They too now live in Oklahoma, around Anadarko where they settled after leaving an increasingly inhospitable Texas in 1859. It may seem something of a paradox that Oklahoma became the haven for the East Coast tribe which many other tribes called "Grandfather" out of respect and homage to the cultural standards they set; yet in Oklahoma the main body of Unami speakers around Bartlesville became identified with the Cherokee and the Anadarko Delaware are linked with the Caddo and Wichita. As we shall shortly see, such identities and allegiances are more the result of political expedience and BIA bureaucracy than they are of any loss in the grammar and cultural logic of the Delaware. Although, the present state of the language and logic suggests that such loss is imminent. For the remainder of this paper, I will focus on the Unami speakers of [2] northeastern Oklahoma both because my own fieldwork has been concentrated there and also because they were the largest and most traditional Delaware group, especially in terms of perpetuating the central or key ritual of the Big House Rite (*Xingwikawn*).

My intent is to discuss the isomorphic relationships between Delaware language and culture, as revealed in the grammatical genders common to languages of the Algonkian stock and in the biological taxa and symbolic genders that pervade the Delaware cosmos. I might anticipate my conclusion by indicating that I will assert that such isomorphism derives from the importance of "marking" in human thought as expressed in language and in culture.

Language

In his classic statement on Proto-Algonkian grammar and reconstruction, Leonard Bloomfield (1946: 94) noted that both nouns and verbs were inflected for animate and inanimate gender classes and that verbs were further inflected for transitive and intransitive, creating 4 verb classes: animate transitive (AT), animate intransitive (AI), inanimate intransitive (II), inanimate transitive (IT). While in most Central Algonkian languages animate nouns end in -*(a)k* and inanimate nouns in /-*(a)n*/, in Delaware animate nouns end in /-*(a)k*/ but inanimate nouns end in a vowel /-*a*/. This gives the impression that the Delaware inanimate has Zero expression. The animate / inanimate distinction is complex because as Bloomfield (same: 94) noted the animate

"includes all persons, animals, spirits, and large trees, and some other objects, such as tobacco, maize, apple, raspberry (but not strawberry), calf of the leg (but not thigh), stomach, spittle, feather, bird's tail, horn, kettle, [3] pipe for smoking, snowshoe."

Further light was shed on the animate when Charles Hockett (1966: 62 # 10) noticed that in one of the Swampy Cree sacred stories, the term for the skull of a witch, that rolled after and spoke to some children, was given an animate ending while ordinarily the word for "skull" is inanimate. Hockett inferred from this that the distinctive feature of the animate gender was the ability to communicate. Later in this presentation, after a discussion of Delaware taxonomy and culture configuration, I will present another interpretation of the animate gender based on work by myself and others that better accounts for these and other data.

Culture

Continuing fieldwork since 1972 established 8 alternative classifications recognized by Unami speakers around Bartlesville, Oklahoma. These alternative classifications include Form (*ɛlhʌkatčik*) "their shapes", Habitat (*ɛndalawsitčik*) "where they live", Coloration (*ɛliksitčik*) "their colors", Behavior (*ɛlayhasitčik*) "their actions or movements", Calls (*ɛlixsitčcik*) "their sounds, Utility (*ɛli hnʌkalwəsitčik*), "the way they are used", Kinship (*ɛlʌŋumʌtčik*) "our relatives", and Appearance (*ɛllinakwsitčik*) "the way they look."   Yet underlying these 8 classifications and their many taxa are 3 semantic oppositions which are hierarchically ranked in terms of their pervasiveness. These 3 semantic pairs are wildness / tameness (*awsuwakʌn / tkawsuwakʌn*), terrestrial / aquatic (Ø / *bi* "water"), and man / woman (*lənu / xkwe*). The wild / tame pair has the most restricted usage, generally being limited to individual members of a species even domesticated ones, in accordance with a judgement made about the behavior of an individual. For example, bears may be "wild" [4] but a pet bear cub is "tame"; cows are "tame", but an aggressive or "ornery" cow is "wild"; Algonkian-speaking tribes closely related to the Delaware are "tame", but distant tribes are "wild." The terrestrial / aquatic (or land / water) pair is more generally applied to whole species and taxa depending upon the observed preferences for, and familiarity with, water by various species. Thus there are snakes /*xkukʌk*/ and water snakes /*biaxkukʌk*/; birds/-*ehileyok*/ and water birds /*biya'ehileyok*/. The most ubiquitous semantic opposition, however, is that between man / woman; such that everyone, everything, and every grouping in the Delaware cosmos might be identified as Man or Woman. I must emphasize that these terms really are "man" /*lənu*/ and woman"/*xkwe*/ in Delaware, rather than being some general masculine ~ male or feminine ~ female qualities. Fish, fowl, and flesh each have Man and Woman members, as do some plants.

This recognition of the ubiquity of the Man / Woman opposition led to the further discovery that this human metaphor was the all-pervading property of the Delaware cultural configuration. Frank Speck (1937: 26) made a similar observation but did not comprehend or explore the full consequences of this anthropomorphic outlook for the Delaware. In a manuscript currently in preparation, I am trying to do just this: explore the extensions of the Man / Woman categories throughout the Delaware Cosmos. In doing so, I am in a better position to discuss the isomorphic relation between Delaware language and culture. This isomorphism derives from the concept Greenberg (1966, 1975) has called "marking" in language. In order to emphasize the fact that language and culture are not fully isomorphic in and of themselves, I have chosen to call the analogous cultural concept "exclusivity." Hence, when treating the linguistic realm I will refer to marked / unmarked oppositions, but when discussing the [5] cultural realm, I will use exclusive / inclusive as the parallel terms. In short, the linguistically "marked" is to the culturally "exclusive" as the linguistically "unmarked" is to the culturally "inclusive."

Isomophic Marking

In his classic, extended treatment of marking, Joseph Greenberg (1966: 25ff), provided a definition and 8 criteria for evaluating this phenomenon. Following Greenberg, Roman Jakobsen and the Prague School, the marked and exclusive categories state the delimited, specific presence of a certain entity A, while the unmarked and inclusive categories state the ambiguous, general presence of either the opposite member (not ~ A) to the marked entity or the entire category inclusive of the specified entity and its opposite (A + not-A). As Greenberg indicates, many societies use a term for themselves that serves both as the tribal name and also as the term for "human beings." This is an unmarked term which both specifically delimits that tribe from all other societies and also generally applies to all humans, including the tribe members. The 8 criteria discovered by Greenberg for establishing marking are:

1) Zero expression of the unmarked category (cf. Delaware terrestrial / aquatic where land has Zero (Ø) expression and water is marked by /bi-/).

2) Syncretization: Distinctions present in the unmarked form are often neutralized in the marked one (cf. English singular is unmarked and includes "he, she, it" in the third person singular, but "they" in the marked plural.) [6]

3) Facultative expression (par excellence interpretation): the unmarked form often requires interpretation of its meaning from the context of its use.

4) Contextual neutralization; In some contexts the opposition of unmarked / marked is suppressed and the unmarked is used as the generic form for the entire category.

5) Marked regularity: There is a lesser degree of morphological irregularity in marked forms.

6) Defectivation: Marked forms lack certain categories present in the unmarked. (Similar to #2)

7) Dominance: In the category of number, the unmarked form serves for a heterogeneous collection (cf. Spanish *los padres* ("the fathers") for "parents."

8) Text frequency: In spoken and written usage, unmarked forms are much more numerous than marked forms.

From these criteria and Greenberg's (same: 56ff) discussion of common "marking" characteristics in phonology, grammar, and lexicon; we can derive 4 criteria for exclusivity:

1) Zero expression of the inclusive

2) Defectivation of the exclusive

3) Contextual neutralization of the exclusive

4) Greater use frequency of inclusive

While Greenberg (same: 40) reports that the animate is unmarked in Algonkian languages, one could argue that Delaware marks the plural with a final vowel and the animate is even more marked with a final /-k/ added to this plural. While the animate does have greater text frequency, I think it significant that the animate nonetheless has the marked ending. Of related interest is the observation of Bruce Pearson (:23) that Delaware requires a semantic unit he called "feminine" for the selection of some lexicals, even though the language does not otherwise require the "feminine" in any process of grammatical agreement, nor does the language distinguish between masculine and feminine pronouns.

In Delaware culture, Man is the inclusive category and Woman the exclusive one.

1) Man has Zero expression in that the Manliness of the world is assumed or taken for granted with the specific exceptions of Mother Earth, Mother Maize, and the female members of various taxa and groups which require Pearson's "feminine" unit.

2) Woman has defectivation because the wide range of careers and activities permitted to men, from chief ship to speaking in council, were forbidden to females except in extraordinary circumstances.

3) The Man / Woman opposition is often contextually neutralized, as it is in English, in that the unmarked, Man terms can stand for the whole category, as for example in the tribal name "Lenape" derived from the word for "man" /lənu/.

4) In terms of visibility, interest, and sustained discussion, the inclusive Man has greater use frequency. This is all the more fascinating because the Delaware were matrilineal. I will return to this apparent paradox shortly.

For the present, it remains for me to tie up my argument about the isomorphism between language and culture with regard to "marking" by attempting to locate the common principal behind the animate / inanimate and the Man / Woman pairs.

In the course of doing research with Nora Thompson Dean on the Delaware partonomy of anatomy (Miller 1977), I learned of at least 11 terms for body parts which had animate endings. This was at variance with my expectation that animate forms would refer to whole entities and inanimate forms to piecemeal ones. These animate terms refer to blood, to sex organs, or to the knees and neck (body parts which mobilize, motivate, or move substantial parts of the body.)

Hockett thought that the key feature of the animate gender was the ability to communicate, but Mary Black (1969), working among the Ojibwa, found that the key feature of the animate was movement, especially self-propulsion. Much to my surprise, I discovered that in the late 1800's John Heckewelder, a Moravian missionary among the Delaware, noted that the Delaware characterized animate nature as "endowed by the Creator with the power of volition and self-motion(quoted in Miller 1975: 442). In this regard, the animate body terms make sense since the blood circulates in the body and is considered a type of soul by the Delaware, the sex organs could be conceived to move of their own accord, and the knees and neck serve to move the body and the head. The evidence of the animate plural ending on the word for "knees" seemed especially compelling to me that Delawares, and probably other Algonkians, animate gender actually was characterized by volition and self-motion. [10]

What I would like to suggest, in conclusion, is that, for the Delaware, the marking of the animate was related to the exclusivity of Woman in the culture. My reasoning runs thusly: the marking of the animate, the exclusivity of Woman, and the matrilineal descent system were of a piece. The exclusivity of the Woman category directly Influenced Delaware women in that when women were being their most distinctive selves, namely during birthing and menstruation, they were expected to restrict themselves to birth huts and menstrual lodges. I have found nothing analogous to this exclusion that applied to men. The careful circumscription of women suggests to me that the Delaware matriclans may have become empirically distinguished because women were so delimited. In other words, Delaware matrilineality may be derived from an extension of the exclusivity of the Woman category. (Gary Witherspoon (1975) has made a similar argument for the Navaho kinship system.)

Permutations of this argument should also work for the Central ~ Great Lakes Algonkians and for the Iroquois. Charles Callender (1962) discusses patrilineal descent among the Sauk, Fox, Kickapoo, Potawatomi, Shawnee, Miami, Illinois, and Menomini. The reconstruction of Harold Hickerson (1970) would allow us to include the Ojibwa among these patrilineal tribes. Among all of these tribes, the animate seems to be unmarked and the inanimate is marked. In these patrilineal societies, the marking of the inanimate may be significant because it suggests a consistent equation of Man and the inanimate, and of Woman and the animate. If the matrilineal Delaware mark the animate, then the patrilineal Great Lakes Algonkians should mark the inanimate. These variations seem plausible to me because during a recent analysis of "exclusivity" among Amerind tribes associated with language isolates, I found that Man was exclusive and Woman inclusive for the Yuchi, Keres, and Kootenay; but that Man was inclusive and Woman exclusive for the Yuki and Quileute. Thus we should not be surprised to find transpositions or metathesis of relationships from one tribe to another, or from one language to another, both in terms of anthropomorphization and in terms of genders.

For example, Floyd Lounsbury (as reported by Greenberg (same: 39)) suggests that in Oneida and other Iroquoian languages, the feminine is the unmarked gender. Similarly, in Iroquois culture Man is exclusive and Woman is inclusive; as revealed by the careful translation by JNB Hewitt of the terms for Iroquoian deities as Man-Beings (males) and Man-Woman Beings (females). Possibly, an Iroquois matriclan might be considered inclusive because it would recognize both men and women as members who are related through females.

If both language and culture are reflections of human thought processes interacting with environments, then both should be characterized by the phenomenon of "marking". The exact quality of this characterization would have to depend on the exact relationships drawn or recognized by the speakers-cum-culture bearers. I think it important to consistently distinguish language from culture, as I have done in referring to "marking" and to "exclusivity", (both referring to marked terms, strangely enough), because while they can be isomorphic or parallel, they are by no means identical. I am still some distance from fully articulating the relationships between Delaware language and culture, but in the interests of stimulating an exchange and discussion of information, I have tried to be as provocative as possible in this paper.

Delaware Alternative Classifications

This article is intended to augment the extensive literature on Delaware (Lenape), and more generally Algonkian, species designations and taxonomies which has been developing over the past two centuries. After a review of the earlier sources and my own fieldwork, I will present eight classifications of taxonomies by form, habitat, color, movement, sound, use, relationship, and appearance. Finally, the regularities found in these classifications and taxa will be discussed. Throughout the paper 'classification' will refer to a collection of taxa sharing at least one attribute in common and 'taxon' will refer to a class or group of individuals and species presumed by Delaware speakers to be related.

Concern with Delaware ethnoscience can be said to have begun with Peter Kalm, a student of Carl von Linne, sent to America by the Swedish Academy of Sciences in 1747 to record Delaware plant usage (Herman 1950: 46). A long list of Delaware biological terms was recorded by David Zeisberger in his diary of 1781 (1910) and appeared in his dictionary (1887). However, by this time the Delaware had left their East Coast homeland and the new Ohio ecology may have altered some of the species terminology but probably not the taxa. In a letter, John Heckewelder (1876: 399-400) included four words that continue to serve as form taxa: gook from /xkuk/ <u>snake</u>, names from /nʌamɛs/ <u>fish</u>, chum from / -xʌm/ <u>animal</u>, and wehellen from / -ehəle / <u>bird</u>. Modern field workers can appreciate the frustrations that Heckewelder (1876: 319) experienced in collecting such terms:

> Whenever I found the Indians disposed to attend to my enquiries, I would point to particular objects and repeat my formulary, and the answers that they. gave I immediately wrote down in a book which I kept for the purpose; at last, when I had written about half a dozen sheets, I found that I had more than a dozen names for "tree," as many for "fish, " and so on with other things, and yet I had not a single generic name. What was still worse, when I pointed to something, repeating the name or one of the names by which I had been taught to call it, I was sure to excite a laugh; and when, in order to be set right, I put the question…. I would receive for answer a new word or name which I had never heard before.

Unlike Heckewelder however, most observers concentrated on species names. Many of these species names are included in a Delaware dictionary assembled from various sources by Brinton and Anthony (1888). Chamberlain [p435] (1901) included some Delaware species in his discussion of Algonkian animal names. Most recently, Mahr (1949, 1954, 1959, 1960, 1961, 1962) has subjected all of the biological terms recorded by Zeisberger to analysis by historical and comparative linguistic methods in order to produce a semantic analysis which showed that each name reflected the particular use of the species. In other words, he gives utilitarian reasons for many of the species names. Speck (1931, 1937) included species and taxa names in some of the texts he recorded from Charles Webber. However, some of these terms are unknown to my sources and others they translate differently. Tantaquidgeon (1972) and Hill (1971) discuss Delaware plant usage. Weslager (1973) summarized Delaware herbal use for a popular audience. But all of these sources group the species by English and not Delaware classifications.

The details of the eight classifications about to be presented have been worked out with Mrs Nora Thompson Dean, a most meticulous, knowledgeable, and concerned speaker of the

Unami dialect of Delaware. Many of the terms she gave me have been checked with Mrs Lucy Parks Blalock, a fluent and careful speaker of the same dialect.

I began the research in 1972 by asking Mrs Dean every term that seemed biological in the Zeisberger and Brinton-Anthony dictionaries. Although a start, this procedure was largely unrewarding. Beginning with the few words she substantiated, I expanded the list by asking for analogies or contrasts for each term through correspondence and visits to northeastern Oklahoma. While there I could also listen to Mrs Dean use the terms, ask her for the taxon and name of an animal we had just seen, and occasionally try to use an appropriate term myself.

In addition to Mrs Dean and Mrs Blalock, who both supplied terms and served to cross-check each other, some taxa were also checked with Edward Leonard Thompson, Tom Wilson, and Mrs Anna Brown Parks. All of these Unami speakers are also fluent in English so that it was always possible to supply intuitively satisfying English equivalents for the Unami terms. While English and Unami speakers can recognize the same taxonomic distinctions, there seem to be important semantic differences behind the two systems. I will discuss the semantics of the Unami system in the conclusion.

While there is a phonemic system for Delaware (Voegelin 1946: 130), 1 have chosen to present the forms phonetically using a transcription checked .by James Rementer to conform to one he has been using informally for the past ten years (Hill 1972: 17). His system is already familiar to several Unami speakers. Although length is phonemic in Delaware, I have tended to ignore it in the surface phonetics. The 1anguage also has an important inanimate / animate grammatical distinction, which can be clearly seen in plurals. The inanimate plural ends in a vowel, while the animate ends in a vowel and final /-k/. All taxa but <u>plants</u> /skiko/ are animate. Mrs Dean has translated the single third person animate form as <u>one(s)</u> or <u>one(s)</u> who. Plurals are given in parentheses.

3.0.   While I am unable to show the five or six taxonomic levels suggested [p436] by Berlin, Breedlove, and Raven (1973) for folk classifications generally, there are two terms, which serve as what they call a unique beginner, which subsume the eight classifications and their taxa. Mrs Dean and Mrs Blalock regard the two words as synonyms, however, persistent questioning revealed a fine distinction:

    lehəlexɛt(čik) <u>alive one(s)</u> derived from the word for breath or breathing

    pəmawsit(čik) <u>living one(s)</u>

The species and taxa under these unique beginners can have any of four attributes:

    pənaylɪndamʌweit(čik) <u>one(s) with the ability to think</u>

    lixsuwakʌnit (čik) <u>one(s) with language</u>

    nɪhənitcanit(čik) <u>one(s) who can reproduce themselves</u> which includes all form taxa but deities.

    kãsɪləsit(čik) <u>one(s) with spiritual power to do great things on earth</u> These are mostly deities although some of this power can also be conferred on humans by specific ' deities.

Species and taxa might also possess both, one, or none of two spirits. The first is a soul which resembles a spark and the second is a ghost which resembles a transparent skeleton. The former journeys to the Creator after death and the latter remains on earth. I refrain from giving the terms for these because they are sensitive to Delaware traditionalists.

The Delaware seem to recognize at least eight alternative classifications based on form, habitat, color, movement, sound, use, relationship, and appearance. These will now be described.

3.1. Form: ɛlhʌkat(čik) or ɛlčɛsit(čik) their shape(s), is the primary classification of living things among the Delaware, as it is in all folk taxonomies. It is divided into seven major taxa.

A ~ manitu(wʌk) deities As a group they are immortal, have the ability to alter things and events by their thoughts, can confer powers on humans, and possess both a body soul and language.

kišelamukɔŋ the one who created us by his thoughts, the Creator who alone can create things
   and events by his very thoughts. He is described as eternally sitting in the twelfth or
   highest heaven.
mahtantu bad spirit, the Evil One or Devil.
pɛthakhuwe(yok) the thunderer(s) Large birds with the heads of old or young men who live
   in the sky and control thunder and lightning.
məxaxkuk red snake An enormous, horned red snake who lived in the ocean until he was
   killed and pieces of him divided among various tribes as tribal palladia.
wewtunəwɛs(ʌk) drawer(s) under. Serpentine male spirits who live in all bodies of water.
   They were born of a girl who neglected to cover her genitals when she bathed.
wemahtekənis all over the woods one A leather-clad man about three feet high who is very
   agile and lives wherever he can find a wooded area. He confers powers of strength and
   stamina.
tehtɔŋələmhaləwes the one who leads people astray, the will-o-the wisp. [p437]
məsingʷ A bear-like being who is guardian of game animals and vegetation.
ɔhtas(ʌk) dolls These are represented by carved wooden dolls formerly inherited in certain
   families and believed to be alive.
ɔwiyalahsu a whirlwind
kaoxən a cyclone or tornado
manitutət(ʌk) little people. They are about a foot high and can either cause painful injuries or
   grant the power of great stamina or the ability to cure without the aid of medicines.
ilawənɪtu war spirit, any comet.
Jupiter (kečipənɛs) and Mars (mʌxalʌŋw) might be considered deities but Mrs Dean was not
   positive that they were.
ãsisktayɛsʌk bunched together ones. The Pleiades, who were originally seven Delaware boys
   lifted into the sky by their purity or innocence.
ɛlantuwiɛkʷ Vocative name for the four directional spirits.
luwanʌntu Grandfather North, who is closely associated with snow and icicles. When these
   are bothered, he sends more snow and cold weather.
šawnaxawəš Grandmother South. Alternating warm and cold blasts of wind mean that South
   and North are trying out their powers.

wɛhɛnjiopvŋ Grandfather East.
ehəliwsikakw Grandfather West.

B ~ awɛn(čik) person(s), having the attributes of thought, language, reproduction, soul, ghost, and bipedalism.

Neutral Terms:
mɛxkeɔkəsit(čik) Red(s), subdivided by tribes
weɔpsit(čik) White(s), subdivided by European countries
nɛskəsit(čék) Black(s), not subdivided
wisawsit(čik) Yellow(s), not subdivided

Deprecating Terms:
awɛnhakɛ(ɔk) wild tribes for Indians
šəwʌnʌkw(ɔk) salt person(s) for Whites
səkahkolɛs(ak) black person(s) for Blacks

Derogatory Terms:
ɔping^w opossum, literally white face, for Whites
kvmhɔkw(ɔk) cloud(s) for Blacks

Mrs Dean also includes three characters from Delaware mythology within this taxon:

hmuwe A giant cannibal.
məkihape pimply face. An orphan finally taken in by an old couple who watched him grow into a wise hunter and scout.
wɛhixamukɛs A humorous but wise man who is noted for the fact that he always took metaphors literally.

C ~ xʌskwim corn. Usually called Mother Corn, it possesses thoughts, a language, and a soul.
Five species are named:

puhwɛm white flour corn
sɛhsapsiŋ blue corn [p438]
pisim sweet corn
pɛphɔksiŋ popcorn
šəwanʌhkwim White Man corn, field corn.

D ~ -xʌm animal, with the attributes of thought, reproduction, four legs and fur. Animals can take pity on people and ask deities to give these people powers. Some species (such as dogs, eagles, crows, otters) were singled out by Mrs Dean as having languages, powers, and souls of their own.

awsit (čik) wild one(s)
lənwexʌm(uk) male animal(s)

xkwexʌm(uk) female <u>animal(s)</u>

nusexʌm (uk) <u>nursing female(s)</u>

wəskxʌm(uk) <u>young animal(s)</u>

kikexʌm (uk) <u>old animal(s).</u>

tkawsit(čik) <u>tame one(s)</u>

lənuwexʌm(uk) <u>castrated male animal (s)</u>

wɛlxus(ʌk) <u>intact male animal (s)</u>

The rest of the terms duplicate those listed above under the awsitčik.

The list of the subtaxa of animals is as follows:

ayɛsəs(ʌk) <u>land mammal(s)</u> specifically, although the term can be stretched to include
      animals generally.

tahkox(ʌk) <u>turtle(s)</u>

xkuk(ʌk) <u>snake(s)</u>

kəkahtaliakwe(yok) <u>lizard (s)</u>

čahkol(ʌk) <u>frog(s)</u>

kaxkxʌkəs(ʌk) <u>toad(s)</u> literally <u>dry waist.</u>

nʌmə̌s(ʌk) <u>fish(es), sea mammal(s), shellfish(es)</u>

muxwɛs(ʌk) <u>bug(s)</u>

piskewəni muxwɛsʌk <u>night bugs.</u>

E ~ -ehɪle <u>bird</u> is characterized by thought, reproduction, wings, feathers, and a language of their own. As noted above, some bird species can take pity on humans and ask deities to transfer powers to these people.

lənuwehɪle <u>male bird (s)</u>
xkwehəle(yok) <u>female bird (s)</u>
wəskihɪle(yok) <u>young bird(s)</u>
kikehəle(yok) <u>old bird(s).</u>

Two bird subtaxa have been identified:

pale•(ok) <u>fowl</u>, gallinaceous birds

čulə̌ns(ʌk) <u>migratory</u> and <u>predatory birds</u>

piskewəni čulə̌ns(ʌk) <u>night birds</u>, especially

kukhus(ʌk) <u>owl(s)</u>

pipisilvŋɔn (ʌk) <u>bat(s)</u>, literally <u>wrinkle wing.</u>

F ~ hɪtukw (hɪtkuk) <u>tree(s)</u> which have the attributes of thought, reproduction, kinship with the

Delaware, leaves, and a language and powers of their own. As the example of rosinweed indicates, Mrs Dean seems to regard any plant over human height as a tree. This taxon can be sub-divided on the basis of two suffixes: [p439]

-akw is used for trees with straight trunks that do not bear fruit, with the exception of peach trees.

kələkənikʌnakw <u>common sumac</u>

puhwɛsənakw <u>elderberry</u>
pkuwakw <u>rosinweed</u>
xaxakw <u>sycamore</u>
pilkəšakw <u>peach tree</u>
-mə̂ši is used for branching trees which bear fruit:

mwɩmə̂ši <u>excrement tree</u>, wild black cherry

tɩtpanɩmə̂ši <u>bitter nut tree</u>, hickory

ɔkhatimuši <u>mulberry</u>

tʌkwimə̂ši i <u>round fruit tree</u>, black walnut.

G ~ skikw (skiko) <u>plant (s)</u>, <u>grasses</u>, <u>weeds</u>. Except for <u>medicine plants</u>, this taxon lacks thought, language, and powers. Its attributes are ubiquity and being shorter than a human adult. Mrs Dean translates this label as <u>plants</u>, but acculturated speakers preferred the term <u>weeds</u>. This label does in fact serve as the basis for the translation borrowing /skikwimiŋ/ <u>hayseed,</u> which is a term Delaware speakers apply to many rural Whites. There are two subtaxa:

čəphɩk (a) <u>root(s)</u>
bisuni skiko <u>medicine plants</u>, which have the ability to think, speak their own language, cure the sick, and alter events for good or evil.

The separation of corn, trees, and plants was consistently made by three Delaware speakers in each of two card sortings. I placed the species names given in the Hill (1971) ethnobotany on index cards. The Delaware word was written in black and the English translation in red; because of the eight colors named by the Delaware, these two are aesthetically and ritually preferred. Each speaker sorted the cards, first to divide them into whatever groupings they wished and, second, to place them in groups that had Delaware names. In both cases, each speaker distinguished corn and trees. Plants were also regarded as distinct but were always further sub-divided into root and medicine subtaxa. The category of 'food' also emerged in these sortings and eventually led to the use classification.

Species are placed in one of the following taxa on the basis of preferred or usual habitat, ɛndalawsitčik <u>where they live</u>, although an individual could be placed in another taxon during its appearance in a different ecological context from that it normally inhabited.

hukweyuŋ ɛndalawsit(čik) one(s) who live above

xkwithakamika ɛndalawsit(čik) <u>one(s) who live on the earth.</u>

This form alternates with the more literal form:

pəmhakamit(čik) <u>earth liver(s)</u>.

Both of these forms include the following:

bi ɛndalawsit(čik) <u>ones who live in the water</u>
bixʌm <u>water animal</u>, specifically whales.
biyaehiɬe <u>water bird</u>
tekənɪŋ ɛndalawsitčik <u>ones who live in the woods</u>
ɛ•kwi hakiŋ ɛndalawsitčik <u>ones who live underground</u> [p440]

Species are placed in the color taxa (ɛliksitčik <u>their colors</u>) by their predominant color /likte/. Delaware colors are classified much like those j English, with these exceptions. Black tends to include the spectrum from dark purple to dark red. This means that Delaware colors tend to be slightly lighter than the English values. Yellow includes most of the orange shades. For example, /wisaɔpalɪs/ <u>yellow apple</u> means a Golden Delicious to Mrs Dean but an orange to Mrs Blalock. There are eight color taxa:

mʌxksit(čik) <u>red one(s)</u>
səksit(čik) <u>black one(s)</u>
askaskwsit(čik) <u>green one(s)</u>
wisawsit(čik) <u>yellow one(s)</u>
aonsit(čik) <u>blue one(s)</u>
weɔpsit(čik) <u>white one(s)</u>
wipuŋwsit(čik) <u>grey one(s)</u>
čʌkingwɛmiktɛit(čik) <u>the color of pokeberry one(s)</u>, <u>purple</u>.

The movement classification, ɛlayhɔsitčik <u>their actions or movements</u>, is limited to beings capable of movement, especially animals. Inclusion is based on the characteristic movements of the species. However, it is the particular movement that is important and as such an individual can be temporarily placed in an untypical taxon during its distinctive behavior.

pəmuxsit(čik) <u>crawler(s)</u>
ɛlakihəlat(čik) <u>hopper(s)</u> or <u>jumper(s)</u>
kənthwit(čik) <u>flier(s)</u>
pəməsksɛt(čik) <u>walker(s)</u>
ahkusit(čik) climber(s)
lɛmbamehəlat(čik) <u>trotter(s)</u>
kɛšamehəlat(čik) <u>runner (s)</u>
ašuwihəlat(čik) <u>swimmer(s)</u>
činktɛhwɛt(čik) <u>sunner(s)</u>, <u>one sunning itself</u>.

On several occasions while eliciting for the form classification, Mrs Dean gave me the crawlers term as meaning <u>reptiles</u> (turtles, snakes, lizards, and toads). I think this is an instance of English affecting Delaware usage. However, by asking for analogies and contrasts for the crawlers this movement classification filled out, This may mean that Delaware terms with closer English equivalents have remained in use while those uniquely Delaware have faded from use but are not unrecoverable.

The placement of animals in the sound classification, ɛlixsitčik their sounds depends first on their distinctive cries or sounds, although if a particular animal happens to be physically present it will be temporarily classed on the basis of its current utterances. A species might also overlap several taxa if it can make a range of sounds,

> kənjimwit(čik) crower(s)
> məkikɛt(čik) bark(ers)
> məlimwit(čit) crier(s), sobber(s), lower(s)
> whulit(čik) howler(s)
> asuwit(čik) singer(s)

The use classification, ɛli hnʌkalwəsitčik the way they are used, [p441] emphasizes the possible usefulness of all or part of various species, especially of plants:

> bison medicine
> mehʌmičiŋ food
> məneokʌn (a) potables
> wehupɔŋ smokeables especially tobacco (kwsatay)
> mɛhəmanitasik that from which something is made, raw materials
> kwʋlakʌn(a) forbidden or taboo one(s)
> nučkwe useless one(s).

In the relationship classification, ɛlʌəŋumʌtčik our relatives, the Delaware have extended most of their lineal kinship terms with associations of authority to the natural and supernatural world:

> muxomsənanʌk our grandfathers: tobacco, the Thunderers, fire, məsingw, male turtles,
>> the male wooden dolls, whirlwind, and the directions north, east, and west. Also included are male bears together with water in large bodies or running free.
> nuhʌmənanʌk our grandmothers: female turtles and bears, female wooden dolls kept
>> formerly in certain families.
> kahɛsɪnanʌk our mothers: corn, the earth, and water in wells, springs, or containers.
> kuxəna our father: used only for the Creator
> xãsəna our elder brother: the sun
> nitis male friend with a male speaking: trees and medicines
> ničus my female friend with a woman speaking: trees and medicines.

Mrs Dean explained these terms for friend in the classification by saying that over time a friend comes to be considered a relative. Formerly friends of different sexes used sibling terms.

In the appearance classification, ɛl•inakwsitčik the way they look, we find taxa derived from surface coverings and physical features of the species. Because each taxon concentrates on a visual detail, species generally overlap several of them. The list of taxa remains incomplete because Mrs Dean could not recall the term for <u>scaled ones</u>:

mikwənit(čik) <u>feathered one(s)</u>

wixʌwɛsit(čik) <u>furred one(s)</u>

olʌxʌkayit(čik) <u>skin shedder(s)</u>

xɛsit(čik) <u>hide skinned one(s)</u>
supsit(čik) <u>naked ones</u>: humans and worms
wipit•it(čik) <u>one(s) with teeth</u>
hwιkʌšsit(čik) <u>one(s) with nails, claws, hooves</u>

wɛšəməwit(čik) <u>one(s) with tails</u>

kəmbʌhkwit(čik) <u>one(s) with leaves</u>

This completes the description of the eight classifications and their representative taxa.

It now remains to find the regularities which characterize the Delaware taxonomic system. These are the recurrence of three contrasts, which are increasingly more general: <u>wildness</u> / <u>tameness</u> (awsuwakʌn / tkawsuwakʌn), <u>land</u> / <u>water</u> (Ø / bi), and <u>man</u> / <u>woman</u> (lenu / xkwe). [p442]

The wild / tame contrast applies more to individuals and species than to taxa. The contrast is most obvious in the animal form taxa, but it can be extended to others. Tameness has more to do with frequent proximity to humans than with domestication. Wildness has to do with remoteness or unfamiliarity to humans. For example, any animal kept as a pet or which is remarkably docile around humans is considered to be tame: bears are wild but a pet cub is tame, dogs are tame but a dog which shuns humans is wild, and while fish are wild, a goldfish is tame. Indian tribes distant from the Delaware are also considered wild. The Delaware concept of wildness is close to the English one, but that of tameness is broader than that of English speakers.

The land / water contrast applies to taxa and subtaxa. The land taxa are linguistically unmarked, while the water taxa are marked by the initial /bi/. While there are distinct terms for <u>water animals</u> and <u>water birds</u>, the word /bi/ can also be added to the names of other taxa, species and individuals providing that a preference or familiarity with water justifies the addition.

The most general contrast in Delaware taxonomy is that of man / woman Every taxon of the Delaware either includes both male and female members or is recognized as consisting of only one sex; for example, Mother Corn. In fact, the man / woman contrast can be considered the semantic core of the entire taxonomy. This is shown by an analysis of the words and concepts used by the Delaware. It is the terms that specifically mean man and woman which are used to express sex differences: /lənuwexʌm/ actually means <u>man animal </u>as /*xkwehιle*/ literally means <u>woman bird</u>. In other words, the Delaware recognize 'living ones' by analogy to humans, specifically adult Delaware. After I had reached this conclusion, I found a similar observation made by Heckewelder (1876: 254):

All beings endowed by the Creator with the power of volition and self-motion, they
[the Delaware] view in a manner as a great society of which they are the head, whom

they are appointed, indeed, to govern, but between whom and themselves intimate ties of connection and relationship may exist, or at least did exist at the beginning of time. They are, in fact, according to their opinions, only the first among equals, the legitimate hereditary sovereigns of the whole animated race, of which they are themselves a constituent part. Hence, in their languages, these inflections of their nouns which we call genders, are not, as with us, descriptive of the masculine and feminine species, but of the <u>animate</u> and inanimate kinds. Indeed they go so far as to include trees and plants within the first of these descriptions. All animated nature, in whatever degree, is in their eyes a great whole, from which they have not yet ventured to separate themselves. They do not exclude other animals from their world of spirits, the place to which they expect to go after death. (*emphasis original*)

The recognition that the animate refers to 'the powers of volition and self- motion' has recently also been made by Black (1969: 18) for the animate in Ojibwa, a related Algonkian language: "Movement, especially self-propelled, is the most heavily stressed feature in these [Ojibwa] reactions to gender choices in novel situations." The reference to the Creator is instructive since he is ultimately the source of all life and thought. The thoughts of the Creator are his most powerful attribute, possessed in lesser ability by deities, people, [p443] corn, animals, trees, and medicine plants. With thought seems to go the possession of spiritual powers. A proper regard for these powers requires the selective avoidance of reproduction, which is considered to be contaminating. This injunction specifically applies to humans since the rest of nature seems better able to control powers. Languages are also recognized for most taxa. While some use the Delaware language, others have their very own. However, I have the impression that with proper ritual preparation and intent, a human could be taught any and all of these languages by a sympathetic natural speaker. Many taxa also have a soul. While I have not given the actual Delaware word, it is important to note that it is derived from the Delaware name for themselves (*lenape*). Thus we can see a metaphorical human existing within these beings. As these data indicate Delaware adults did serve as the nexus or mediation of the animate world. In addition to the classifications and taxa, Delaware speakers also recognize a few songs or sayings as characteristic of particular species. The sound of a cat purring is described in Delaware as təl, təl, etc., but the purring itself represents a sentence: "I killed a mouse this long (sɔkɛn pukwɛs nɪhəla)." The robin says "I have repeatedly sewn my former husband a breech cloth." The sound of the cry of horned owls is described as hu, hu, hu' but they are saying "Kweshkweletis will eat all of you (kwəškwəltis muhukuwa)" in order to frighten children. Blackbirds have a complete song, appropriate only for winter telling, that says they like to steal from fields and they feel strong all winter long. Weslager (1973: 75) reports a song from Mrs Dean used to call rattlesnakes to do harm. Delaware traditionalists also have several sayings about the eating or behavior of chickens. For example, gizzards and eggs should not be eaten by the young, and if a hen crows it must be killed immediately. People are also told not to mock a crow or their quilts and blankets will burn up.
These are most of the examples told to me by Mrs Dean, Mrs Blalock, and Thompson. I conclude with them in order to show the richness of the folk biology still used by the Delaware.

Originally published:
Anthropological Linguistics 17 (9): 534-544   1975

Delaware Anatomy
Linguistic, Social, and Medical Aspects

The members of any human society will vary with regard to their control and understanding of different areas of knowledge because of factors such as intelligence, interest, curiosity, and profession. Specialized careers in hunting, fishing, trapping, foraging, and farming will require detailed knowledge of relevant aspects of the natural world. However, it has been my experience both in fieldwork and in reading, that medical personnel generally possess a fuller understanding and comprehension of the system of folk science than most other members of their society. A career in a native medical system seems to require a more expansive view of the world than other, more economically oriented, careers.

But it is also the case that no feature of nature, biology, or general knowledge is ever accepted in its own right. Initially it must be something culturally recognized and thus incorporated into a logical system. One of the vital tasks of human culture and of the human mind is to filter human experience and to code empirical knowledge. Both the empirical knowledge and the logical system, as reflected in the psychological consequences of the training, self-assurance, and routine behaviors of specialists, contribute significantly to the confidence that others have in their effectiveness. Medical specialists in the native and the industrial worlds are particularly good examples of this.

While an important function of such specialists is to provide a systematic portrait of the order in the world, this order is already suggested by vocabulary items and sociolinguistic usages. As discussed by Brown and others (1976), this understanding takes the forms of taxonomies and partonomies. A taxonomy is a system based on the hierarchic inclusion of conventually named segregates (taxa), while a partonomy is a system based on a hierarchical relationship among inclusions (parta). McClure (1975), among others, distinguishes [p145] a taxonomy as typically characterized by 'kind of' relationships and partonomies as typically characterized by 'part of' relationships.

Miller (1975) has presented the complex taxonomy of all 'living or alive ones' preserved by the few remaining speakers of Unami Lenape or Delaware living in northeastern Oklahoma.[5] The taxonomy consists of eight overlapping classifications based on form, habitat, color, movement, sound or cry, use, kinship, and appearance; each of which are cross-cut by the contrasts of men / women, wild / tame, and land / water.

The present paper will present the comprehensive partonomy of anatomy as provided by a modern Unami specialist, Mrs Nora Thompson Dean, and checked with another fluent speaker, Mrs Lucy Parks Blalock. The primary referent is the human body, but some comparative terms referring to animals and plants will also be provided. My Lenape sources were also

---

[5] The Delaware or Lenape Nation originally occupied the valley of the Delaware River on the mid-Atlantic slope. They were divided into at least two political divisions: the Munsi in the north and the Unami in the south. A third group, sometimes called the Unalachtigo in the historical records, may have been further south than the Unami. Most Lenape had left the East Coast by 1700. Alter passing through Pennsylvania, Ohio, Indiana, and Kansas, the Unami settled north of Tulsa, Oklahoma. A splinter Unami group had joined the Caddo and adopted a Plains lifestyle in Texas before they settled near Anadarko, Oklahoma. Most Munsi fled to Canada and are presently located in several Ontario communities.

conscientious enough to discuss with me other linguistic, social, and medical applications which will be provided in separate sections.

Other anthropologists have remarked that modesty usually prohibits anatomical knowledge from crossing sex lines. Therefore, some discussion of my fieldwork and these Delaware data seems to be necessary.

Over the past five years, I have been increasingly more convinced that Mrs Dean is the most articulate and knowledgeable source for things Delaware, at least in northeastern Oklahoma, if not also elsewhere. She is one of the last practicing herbalists. Earlier in her life, she worked as a health professional in a small Kansas clinic and then later in an Oklahoma old age home. Her even earlier interest in anatomy was the result of growing up on a farm, where she participated in the butchering of livestock. Her data were later checked with Mrs Blalock, who is a fluent and careful Unami speaker, although not a native specialist.

The data were actually collected several times with different methods. The terms were first elicited in Lenape without careful attention to details. Later I collected as full a list of parta as possible, read them back to Mrs Dean, and asked her to mark the location and limits of each term on diagrams of male and female bodies from a general health text xeroxed through the generosity of the Bartlesville Public Library and Mr Gene Winn. Over the intervening winter, I improved my own knowledge of human anatomy and pathology before I analyzed the partonomy and returned to the field with an earlier version of this paper.

At that time, Mrs Dean was ill and seeking several medical opinions. I had also recently been exposed to the dehumanizing and singularly uninformative role that Western medicine reserves for its patients. With these common experiences, our conversations would sometimes turn to medical topics. The slang and obscene uses of anatomical terms were known to me, but it was not until I found a list of them in the field notes of Frank Speck that I could comfortably raise the topic. Mrs Dean had mentioned various of the social aspects several years previously. I reviewed them with her when we went over the final version of this paper. I was also able to ask specific question based on my knowledge of autopsies, only to learn that Mrs Dean was unaware of some features of human anatomy: for example, a size [p146] difference of the lungs.

Several factors account for Mrs Dean's willingness to ignore our sex differences and to provide me with Delaware anatomical knowledge. Among them are her general concern that the record on the Delaware be as accurate as possible, her clinical training in Western medicine, the age difference between us, and our own personal relationship of trust and kinship. As my clan mother, I sometimes address her by the Lenape term which literally means <u>little mother</u> but which is usually translated into English as <u>aunt</u>.

Mrs Dean and I were initially concerned that someone might misconstrue the references to 'ringworm' and other diseases associated with uncleanliness or to obscenities, but we have decided that an accurate record, no matter how human, is preferable to an edited or a biased one.

As taxonomies are divided into taxon (*taxa*), so, following Brown and others (1976), the partonomy will be divided into parton (*parta*). Brown and others have argued that the general principles of biological folk classification presented by Berlin and others (1973) actually have the status of universal principles of classification. These can be used for such non-biological taxonomies as those for American 'automobile' and 'tool', for Finnish 'winter vehicle', for Thai 'spirit-ghost', for Huasteca 'male body', for the diagnosis of ' skin disease' among the Subanun of Mindanao, for 'beer' in Munich, and for the 'Bucket' or city jail of Seattle tramps.

These taxonomies and partonomies rarely exceed five hierarchical levels in depth. Berlin and others (1973) call these levels, in decreasing inclusiveness: unique beginner, life form, generic, specific, and varietal. Corollary with these levels are principles of nomenclature. The higher levels have 'primary lexemes' or unitary labels, which can be productive or unproductive. A productive primary lexeme can usually be linguistically analyzed or literally translated to show a category subordination. Unproductive primary lexemes can not be analyzed unambiguously. Lower levels have 'secondary lexemes', which can be analyzed as derivative of primary lexemes. Brown and others (1976: 75) provide this chart:

HIERARCHIC LEVEL	TAXONOMIC CATEGORY	NOMENCLATURE STATUS
Level 0 – L0	Unique Beginner – UB	unanalyzable primary lexeme
Level 1 – L1	life form – lf	productive primary lexeme
Level 2 – L2	Generic – gn	unproductive primary lexeme
Level 3 – L3	Specific – sp	secondary lexeme
Level 4 – L4	Varietal – vr	

While we must be extremely cautious in using these categories for fear of skewing or biasing or forcing the data, I will accept them as heuristic devices to be accepted or rejected on the basis of available data.

For example, my finished partonomy was compared to the paper on Delaware anatomical terms by Mahr (1960), who painstakingly used the dictionary composed by the Reverend David Zeisberger in about 1782 as the source for his etymologies of anatomical parta in conjunction with his general interest in semantic analysis. While many of my parta also occur in Mahr, indicating a long time depth for the Unami terms, the entire body of Zeisberger terms appears to me to be a hopeless jumble of several Delaware [p147] dialects and inept transcriptions. Mahr also errors in imposing English (and German) categories on the Delaware system. For example, Mahr (1960: 5, 6) assumed the Lenape recognized only five senses and divided the body parta into head and neck, trunk and extremities, and internal organs. I also find unlikely (1960: 26) his conclusion that several etymologies indicate that the Delaware had an ideal model of the human body as squatting and bent forward. Mrs Dean told me she visualizes the human body as standing with arms at the sides. On the other hand, Mahr is correct with both his observations that the heart is the seat both of human emotion and of human reasoning (1960: 6) and that "Hunters as they we re, the Delaware frequently cut open an animal, thus becoming acquainted with the various tissues and substances of the mammalian body; and also with the fact that these were essentially the same in the body of man (sic)" (1960: 2). Both of these observations accord with my field data.

For reasons discussed below, each Lenape parton is given in the singular with the plural in parenthesis). English translations will usually be given in the singular. Delaware has a very important animate / inanimate grammatical distinction best seen in plurals. Inanimate forms are linguistically unmarked, ending with a vowel in the plural; while animate forms are marked by a final -k in addition to the plural vowel ending. Delaware also has only one third person form, which I will translate as someone or someone who for the animate and as something or it for the inanimate.

1 ~ L0 hɔkay(a) body
 LI wil head
    L2 təm(bʌ) brain
        xayʌndep(a) scalp, not to be confused with manukɔla someone was scalped

L3 milʌxk (mixɛkɛna) <u>hair</u>

ɔlɛk^w <u>dandruff</u>

lawxkalay <u>forehead</u>

hwɪtawk(a) <u>ear</u>

wəškiŋ^w(ɔ) <u>face</u>

mamawn(a) <u>eyebrow</u>

weškiŋ^w (ɔ) <u>eyes</u>, the <u>face</u> term seems to have replaced an archaic form

nataɛpi(a) literally, <u>something for looking,</u>

L4 rnilxiŋɔn(a) <u>eyelash</u>

biŋ čan(a) <u>eyeball</u>

L5 məlišeŋɔkʌn matter in the eye

səpiŋ (o) <u>tear</u>, literally, <u>sap from the eyes</u>

wanʌnuw(a) <u>cheek</u>

hwikiyɔn(a) <u>nose</u>

sʌnik^w <u>snot, nasal mucus</u>

kwəskwɪnɛ <u>to sneeze</u>

3L tun(a) <u>mouth</u>

4L šɛtun(a) <u>lips</u>

wilanu(wa) <u>tongue</u> [p148]

kɛhkəndakhwikʌn <u>uvula</u>, literally, <u>something that pushes</u>

5L sukwinakʌn(a) <u>spit, sputum</u>

kɔxsəma to <u>snore</u>

kšapaɛ to <u>yawn</u>

pɔikham to <u>hiccup</u>

muxkčila to <u>belch</u>

dušəwilɛxɛ <u>I gasp, irregular respiration</u>

wipit(a) <u>tooth</u>

ɛnda tuŋanikea• <u>incisors</u>, literally, <u>where my teeth are small</u>

ɛnda•hkin•anikea• <u>canines</u>, literally, <u>where my teeth are sharp</u>

ɛnda pahk•anikea• <u>molars</u>, literally, <u>where my teeth are flat</u>

6L ɔlanike <u>cavities</u>, literally, <u>someone has holes in the teeth</u>

tawmbikʌn(a) jaw

witunay(a) <u>whiskers, insect antennae</u>

hwɪkwi(a) <u>chin</u>

xkwɛk•ʌŋʌn(ʌk) <u>neck</u>

ǩ^wəndakʌn(a) <u>throat</u>

1L tuhwɛpi (a) <u>trunk</u>

2L nikani tuhwɛpiŋ <u>front of the trunk</u> (grammatical form not in common use)

3L tulhay <u>chest</u>, a triangular area with its base at the neck and apex in the upper belly region

4L tulhaixhʌn(a) <u>sternum</u>, literally, <u>chest bone</u>

3L nunakʌn(a) <u>breasts</u>, literally, <u>milk bone</u>, also occurs as a bound form -nɛ

xkelixʌn(a) <u>rib, side</u>

ahsiluŋɔn(a) <u>armpit</u>

təlamʌŋʌn(a) <u>shoulder and upper arm</u>

naxk(a) <u>forearm and hand</u>, from elbow to finger tips

4L wiskɔn(a) <u>elbow</u>, an exclusively human parton

mayayələnj(a) <u>right hand</u>, literally, <u>true, exact hand</u> [6]

amɛmʌndələnj(a) <u>left hand</u>

5L ɛnda siak^wələnj(a) <u>finger</u>, literally, <u>where my hand splits</u>

6L kitələnj(a) <u>thumb</u>, literally, <u>big finger</u>

7L kithuk^wələnj(a) <u>palmar aspect of thumb</u>

lɛlawələnj(a) <u>middle finger</u>

mɛkələnj(a) <u>pinky</u>, literally, <u>last finger</u>

hwikʌš(a) <u>nails, hooves, claws</u>

8L lənapeokʌni sʌhkihələnj(a) <u>lunula</u>, literally, <u>soul finger</u>. These are the lighter semicircles at the base of the nails, which are closely watched as [p149] the more faded they are, the sicker someone is until they disappear at death.

mutay(a) <u>belly, stomach</u>

4L wilhwi <u>navel</u>, an area with a two inch diameter

pɛhpamapisia my <u>waist</u>, also the bound form -hakɛ as in

xiŋhɔkɛ <u>pregnancy</u>, literally, <u>big waist</u>

2L ^wtɛŋ tuhwɛpiŋ <u>back of the trunk</u> (grammatical form not in common use)

3L upxkɔn(a) <u>back</u>, also occurs as the bound form -ipxkone, includes from the back of the neck to the base of the spine.

4L dəki <u>shoulder blade area</u>

ɔwikan(a) <u>spine, backbone</u>

5L pəpɛk^wsu(ʌk) <u>kidney</u>, because it is attached to the spine.

sukʌn(a) <u>lower back, small of the back</u>

2L lamuŋwi tuhwɛpiŋ <u>inside of the trunk</u> (grammatical form not in common use)

3L tɛh(ak) <u>heart</u>

hopʌn(a) <u>lung</u>

mutay(a) <u>stomach, bowels generally</u>, for humans and most animals.

hɔkahtɛs <u>stomach of a pig</u>

winaxaxkay <u>cow tripe</u>

4L wɛlʌkši (a) <u>intestines</u>

xɔy (a) <u>spleen</u>

xkwən (a) liver

---

[6] When I began fieldwork in Oklahoma, none of the six fluent Unami speakers could remember the term for the right hand. The term I was given translated as "not left." Then, in a series of visits between Anadarko Delaware and the Unami, during which words and cultural data were exchanged and shared, this word for the right hand was reintroduced from Anadarko.

wishwitakʌn (a) <u>gall bladder</u>, literally, <u>bile container</u>

      5L wishwi <u>bile</u>. A Delaware wrote to the anthropologist Frank Speck (APS: 932) to say that deer do not have a gall bladder and as a result sleep only once a year. Actually, however, while deer do lack a gall bladder, they sleep quite regularly.

1L ɛnda tahčəsia <u>crotch</u>, literally, <u>where I am divided</u> (ɛkɔktiɛ under the buttocks is a slightly vulgar form, not used in mixed company)

   2L wixa (wixʌk) <u>pubic hair</u>

  škitakʌn (a) <u>bladder</u>, literally, <u>urine container</u>

    3L škɪh <u>urine</u>

    ləxutakʌn(a) <u>scrotum</u>, literally, <u>testicle container</u>

     ləxu(ak) <u>testicles</u>, in Unami slang: hopənis(ak) <u>potato.</u>

škiyɔn(ak) <u>penis</u>, in Unami slang: sikhay <u>salt</u> and kɛkunəm(a) <u>someone's thing</u>. Related terms are nipʌhtasu it has been made to stand erect and nipʌhta someone has an <u>erection</u>. Goddard (1974: 175 #35) lists <u>Jew's harp</u> as Munsi Delaware slang for penis. Brinton-Anthony (1888: 81) list mengwe <u>foreskin</u> but this term has lapsed except as a designation for the enemy Iroquois people.

   spəlaš semen [p150]

   ma•x(ak) <u>female genitalia</u>, including the vulva, vagina, womb.

    kɛkunəm(a) literally <u>someone's thing</u> used in slang.

     min(a) <u>clitoris</u>, literally, <u>berry</u>

     a1awixənəwakʌn <u>menstruation</u>, literally, <u>can not cook</u> (an abstract state)

1L hwɪkat (a) <u>leg</u>, from hip to ankle

  2L pom(a) thigh, ham

    3L wasiti(a) buttock

     4L sputi anus, with the bound form -šɛti

      5L mwɪčti <u>feces</u>, with the shortened to form mwih and bound form –či(a).

      5L pukti <u>fart, flatus</u>

       6L piskk̊ʷti <u>silent fart</u>, literally, <u>like a night hawk</u>

  2L gətuk̊ʷ (k̊ʷəntkuʌk) <u>my knee</u>, exclusively human parton

  wiču(ʌk) <u>calf</u>

  hnikxkɔn(a) <u>shin</u>

  ɛnda tʌŋk•ata• <u>ankle</u>, literally, <u>where my leg is small</u>

1L sit (a) foot

  2L ʌŋɔn (a) heel

   ɛnda kɛntsita• <u>where the ball of my foot is</u>

   ɛnda pʌksita• <u>where my sole is</u>

   ɛnda puksita• <u>where my foot bends or breaks, instep</u>

   ɛnda siak̊ʷsita• <u>where my foot splits, toes</u>

    3L kithukwɛsit(a) <u>big toe</u>

     4L hwikʌš(a) <u>nails, hooves, claws</u>

1L lamuŋwi hɔkay(a) <u>inside of the body</u> (grammatical form not in common use)

  2L ʷčɛt(a) <u>muscle</u>

  hatəs(a) <u>ligaments, tendons</u>

wilsu <u>fat</u>

mukəm(ʌk) <u>blood vessels</u>

   3L mɛxkilək mukəm(ʌk) <u>aorta</u>, literally, <u>biggest vessel</u>

     xkʌn(a) <u>bone</u>, with the bound form: -ikʌne. The word for skeleton will not be given for religious reasons. The word also refers to ghost and mentioning it 'makes the spirits cry' and may even draw someone from the afterworld to cause the death of a loved one.

     pahkʌsun <u>marrow</u> (no plural)

  2L tšpʌtke•ɛk <u>joint</u>, literally, <u>place of separation</u>

  hmuk̓ᵂ <u>blood</u>, itself a spirit which leaves the body at death to form a spheroid which wanders the earth forever.

  lənapeokʌn <u>soul</u> or <u>body spirit</u>. The most powerful medical specialists have seen it as a spark or a miniature person. Death is caused when this soul leaves the body.

  čičʌŋᵂ(a) <u>image</u>, a word used by Christian missionaries to refer to souls of converted Delaware. Mrs Dean and Mrs Blalock know this as the word for <u>mirror</u>. [p151]

1L kɔtčʌmiŋ hɔkay(a) <u>outside of the body</u> (grammatical form, uncommon use)

  2L xɛs(a) <u>skin</u>

     3L milʌxk (mixɛkena) <u>hair</u>

     taptiksəwakʌn <u>sweat</u>

These Delaware parta conform to the principles of nomenclature outlined above, even with the occasional six or seven levels of depth. More generally, these terms bear upon two linguistic considerations: our understanding of the animate / inanimate distinction and the sociolinguistic use of insults.

In one sense, the animate / inanimate distinction is suggestive of the taxonomy / partonomy contrast. As a general rule, animate forms refer to wholes and inanimate ones to parts or to pieces. Yet a closer look at the anatomical parta show that some of these have animate plurals: <u>body</u>, <u>neck</u>, <u>knee</u>, <u>calf</u>, <u>pubic hair</u>, <u>penis</u>, <u>testicles</u>, <u>female genitalia</u>, <u>heart</u>, <u>kidney</u>, and <u>blood vessel</u>. Miller (1975: 442), following Heckewelder and Black, has argued that the animate specifically refers to the ability of self-motion or self-propulsion. These parta further strengthen this contention. While the entire body is self-propelled, the means of propulsion seems to be localized in the lower leg. As Mrs Dean told me, the Delaware words for <u>leg</u> and <u>foot</u> apply to both people and animals, while those for <u>elbow</u>, <u>knee</u> and <u>ankle</u> apply only to humans. Of these, the animateness of the <u>knees</u> seems to be particularly related to their ability to mobilize the entire body. Similarly the <u>neck</u> has the ability to move the <u>head</u>. The animateness of the <u>genitals</u> seems also to be related to movement and the creation of life. Mahr (1960: 46,45) saw the Delaware for testicles as "primarily meaning moving inside the body, by means of breath, [which] quite naturally presented itself as the perpetual slow- rhythm up-and-down movement of the testicles in the scrotum." His etymology for <u>female genitalia</u> is "copulating (movement) device." The muscular action of the penis seems related to its animateness. Pubic hair is probably animate because of its proximity to the genitals. The animateness of <u>kidneys</u> and of <u>blood vessels</u> seems to be related to their contiguity with the blood spirit and the beat of the pulse. The <u>heart</u> is animate because of the heart beat, especially obvious during the butchering of freshly killed animals.

In short, the animateness of these parta seems to be related to rhythmic actions of breath, blood, and muscle in the body. White medicine attributes much of this rhythmic mobility to muscular action, even of the testicles; while the Delaware seem to regard this and all mobility as the ultimate result of willful action on the part of spiritual entities, such as the mind and the soul.

There is an unconfirmed but general impression that Native American languages lack either proverbs or profanity. While I can say nothing about proverbs, the Delaware version of profanity is related to the domain of anatomy.

A Delaware named Charlie Webber wrote to Frank Speck (APS: 1178) that profanity was an ancient practice for the Delaware among people who had not [p152] been properly raised. Mrs Dean also said that a woman should not use profanity while her father was alive out of respect for him. This helps to explain why the old women were especially noted for their frequent use of profanity or obscenities. Nevertheless, the constant use of profanity was said to cause a disease called məli• hukwɛni (a ring of pus around the neck). Unlike other American Indian languages, such as Nootkan and Kwakiutl of the Wakashan stock, which derive their terms of insult and profanity from besmirching someone's pedigree or from wishing them dead in creative ways, Delaware insult by using anatomical terms. As with English, Delaware pejoratives are explicitly genital and, thus, are better described as obscenities rather than profanities. Many are sex specific:

> čitkɔle <u>shut up testicles</u> said by one male to another male
> čitkoxa <u>shut up vulva</u> by female to female
> čitkwəšetia <u>shut your anus</u> by either sex to either sex.

Other obscenities were supplied to Speck (APS: 1178) by Webber. These were reviewed and transcribed with the help of Mrs Dean. She felt that some of them may have been Munsi and not Unami forms.

> mwialahkay <u>excrement penis</u>, said by male to male
> sputalʌkai <u>anus be damned</u>, said by female to female
> sput•ax <u>anus vulva</u>, usually female to female, but sometimes by either sex to either sex
> ma1ʌštiye <u>sticky anus</u>, <u>syrupy buttocks</u>, a general purpose exclamation.

Mrs Dean also supplied other exclamations:

> wah expresses surprise
> kɛsa exclaimed at hearing or seeing something nasty
> puxɔ• for an obnoxious smell
> pʰwit conveys a strong sense of disbelief, a stronger form of 'hogwash'
> awɛ• expresses pain or being tired

Positive expressions include

> pɩsi <u>yes, certainly</u>
> ɛ̃ɛ̃• <u>yes</u>
> xɩta <u>it must be</u>

Negative expressions include

ku <u>no</u>
mata <u>no</u>, <u>not</u>
ku tha <u>no</u>
ku nɔlɛ• <u>not true</u>
mata nɔlɛ• <u>not so</u>

In all then, while Lenape have many exclamations which convey a range of meanings, the most concrete and specific choices available are those which are anatomical and specifically genital.

While Lenape speakers of the present generation lack an integrated system of folk physiognomy, certain features of anatomy are singled out for personality and character assessment. These are most important in the selection of marriage partners. [p153] A Delaware intent on marrying a full blood Indian woman was cautioned to inspect her as circumspectly as possible for the following features:

eyelids − the more epicanthic fold, the more Indian.
ear size − if she has small ears, she is stingy.
wrist − examining the wrist will show whether she is a virgin.
neck length − the more Indian, the shorter the neck.
underarms − a full blood will have no underarm hair.
waist − a full blood will have no distinct waist.
rump size − the more Indian, the straighter the line of the back.
second toe − if this is the longest toe (a Morton' s toe), she can't be dominated.
body hair − the less, the more Indian.
general appearance − she should be seen before she has had time to fix herself
up, 'before breakfast'.

A Delaware intent on a full blood husband should check

eyelids − for epicanthic fold
ear size − for stinginess
musculature − the more smooth and slight, the more Indian
body hair − the less, the more full blood
ability − especially hunting ability depending on keen sight, hearing, and stealth

In addition, older Delaware remember expressions which equate characteristics of a person's mouth and voice with his or her genitals. For example, a woman with a high, squeaky voice is said to have a mattery genitalia.

Further, there is a general belief that a high forehead betokens considerable intelligence. This belief was taken seriously enough that formerly when tribal chiefs and elders met in council, each would shave his hairline back a few inches.

In the realm of traditional Delaware medicine, we can see the applied as well as the classificatory functions of Delaware folk science, especially as it relates to anatomy. Health and disease are relative concepts, very much depending on cultural considerations. Anthropologists and Delaware are well aware of this fact and so divide traditional Delaware medical practice and hygiene beliefs from those of Whites. White or Western medicine is only now beginning to generally realize this relativity.

An English physician has written "We utilize the concept of disease as if this notion has substance. However, in the final analysis disease has no existence outside the bodies of those that suffer from it, and the primary obligation of medical practitioners is to ameliorate the patients' illness, combating the disease being only a second-order function" (Wood 1970: 23). More philosophically, Kleinman (1974: 212) has said "Since Plato, there has been a persistent and more or less unspecified ideal in the West of an anthropological medicine, a kind of medical science and practice that would be concerned unashamedly with such problems as human nature and other Critical aspects of philosophical anthropology, a medical science conceived [p154] in radically human terms, just as medical systems have traditionally been structured, and taking its place as an essential part of the human sciences."

Delaware perceptions of Western medicine have changed over time. Most Delaware I talked with said that White doctors were initially called kɛhkitənikɛs <u>someone who hurts you</u> (in diagnosis). Later they were called wɛlamʌlsuhalwɛs <u>someone who makes people feel well</u>, although this term was not limited to White practitioners. When most Delaware had learned to speak English, the term daktəl was substituted. Since the Lenape language has no /r/ sound, daktəl is an approximation of the English word 'doctor'. Even now, traditional Delaware will still use the term daktəl with a blend of nostalgia and jest. Those who still remember the old Oklahoma daktəls have remarked to me that while White medicine has increasingly refined its chemical and cosmetic techniques, it has also decreased its psychologically comforting abilities. Older Delaware particularly object to the vagueness and seeming indecision with which modern daktəls deliver their diagnosis; a vagueness which seems to be necessitated by the increase in malpractice suits. Even so, Delaware have told me that adequate White medical care requires that the daktəl be a personal friend or be personally interested in the case. (I originally assumed that this opinion was linked to indigent considerations and the ministrations of the Indian Health Service. However, it seems to be a more generally American phenomenon in that most of my younger, and some of my older university colleagues hold the same opinion.)[7]

The Delaware recognize a category of diseases (šəwanʌkwi lʌŋələwakʌn) introduced by Whites and as such best treated by a *daktəl*. These include contagious or epidemic diseases:

---

[7] From one perspective, this statement hints that physicians can cure anyone if they really want to; but from another, it assumes that patients need the help of a concerned healer before they can begin their own recovery. It has been said that "any medical practice that is not actually harmful will relieve symptoms a good deal of the time, [making] it possible to avoid a fruitless discussion of whether singing and hallucinating are a more or less effective curing method than a belief in the Virgin of Lourdes or in little white pills" (Siskind 1973: 209, note 5). According to Weil (1972) the real culprit is not White medicine per se, but rather allopathic medicine because it is specifically concerned with the treatment of disease symptoms and not of individuals, with externals and not essences. Weil's cogent plea for a nonallopathic medicine seeking the etiology of disease and illness in mental states seems very compatible with the concerns of traditional Delaware medicine.

šəwanʌhkwi lʌŋələwakʌn White person disease

    təspehɪleɔkʌn small pox

    maxkpehlɪleɔkʌn measles

    apčihɪleokʌn whooping cough

    ɔxukɔŋəl ənwakʌn tuberculosis

    mahčʌŋələwakʌn venereal disease

In addition, the Delaware recognize other diseases, such as poison ivy, which occur among Whites hut not among Indians.

Except for herbal lore, the traditional Delaware medical system has almost fully lapsed at present. Hence, Delaware suffering from the more severe traditional diseases, such as witchcraft, must seek cures from specialists in other tribes. Creek and Cherokee doctors are said to be especially effective. Creek patients, however, seem to prefer Shawnee doctors. The surviving Delaware herbal lore has been discussed by Tantaquidgeon (1972), Hill (1971), and Weslager (1973). Most of the older Delaware still remember parts of the traditional medical system. Mrs Dean has the most complete memory of the system I have found.

Delaware traditional medicine had a religious justification, expressed as the power of animals and plants to cure or to harm people. The powers of these creatures derive directly from the various deities (*manituwʌk*) and ultimately all power derives from the Creator, 'The One Who Created Us By His Thoughts'. Various substances, especially menstrual blood and human [p155] hair, can also be put to evil purposes.

Paralleling this hierarchy of access to supernatural power are levels of medical specialization. Every Delaware had some hereditary herbal or curative knowledge of the sort that Americans call 'home remedies'. These are usually some sort of laxative (ɛhɛšikakwən). Higher levels of specialization require 'being gifted' by a guardian spirit or partner. There were three grades of specialization. The first was the herbalist: wathakɛs(ʌk) <u>someone who understands plants</u> (and their uses). The second was the <u>sweat doctor</u> nɛntpikɛs(ʌk), who cured a patient by using a sweat lodge (pimǝwakʌn) and various liquids, especially məlʌnčpe, a mixture of herbs that induces vomiting. At the highest level is the <u>Indian doctor</u> mǝteɪnu(wak) or mǝtexkwe(yok), from mǝtakʌn <u>hex, spell, curse</u> plus lɪnu <u>man</u> or xkwe <u>woman</u>. This was the real specialist, deriving his or her power and cures only from guardian spirits. Formerly, some training by a skillful and experienced predecessor may have been involved.

While the <u>power</u> (lantuwakʌn) itself is neutral, the Indian doctor could use it for both good or evil purposes. In addition to these specialists, and in contrast to those people who were <u>empty</u> (alʌxsu), there were Delaware who were gifted by a <u>guardian spirit vision</u> (lingwehəleokʌn) at puberty and who then concentrated this acquired power into a <u>medicine bundle</u> (*bisuni wiɔhšun*), consisting of metonymic items representative of the partner and its power, such as hides, pelts, claws, paws, beads, and plants. Some people also made <u>love bundles</u> (*ehɔltuwi wiɔhšun*) to influence the affections of others. Still others sought to benefit themselves with <u>witch bundles</u> (*nučihwei wiɔhšun*). There was also a very special class of visionaries who were gifted with the ability to cure without any aids at all (*ahasuma*). Sarah (Sally) Wilson Thompson, Mrs Dean's mother, had this ability. What distinguishes most of these specialists, as a group, is their ability to <u>cause a cure</u> (*gikɛyʌwakʌn*(a), *kikeha* <u>you cure him</u>).

Delaware recognize several types of illnesses:

1ʌŋgələwakʌn(a) <u>disease of any severity</u>

palsuwakʌn(a) <u>physical illness</u> or <u>sickness</u>

    pal̓suhal̓kʷən(a) <u>debilitating illness</u>, 'it makes one real sick'

    məšihəweɔkʌn(a) <u>contagious disease</u>

sakomalsəwakʌn(a) <u>being in discomfort</u>

      pasahtayɛ• <u>someone with gas</u>

mahtapasikʌn(a) <u>bad medicine</u>

alawatəmweɔkʌn(a) <u>mental illness, loss of mental faculties</u>

nučihəweokʌn(a) <u>witchcraft</u>

    mətakʌn(a) a <u>hex</u>

Witchcraft is held responsible for any unusual or chronic disease. Witches are called either nutčihweyok <u>pesterers</u> or nɛthənipapwisʌk <u>night travelers</u>. They were the owners of the witch bundles, among whose ingredients was a <u>bad thing</u> (mahči kɛko) which caused harm to people. The witch was motivated to cause this harm out of anger, jealousy, envy, hatred, or general nastiness. Witch bundles were passed down after the original visionary composed them according to the instructions of a guardian spirit. [p156] Vital ingredients always include wampum, human hair, and the bones of a fresh victim. The tuition for learning witchcraft was always the death of a loved one. Instruction ran in family lines, but anyone could request to receive instruction provided they were willing to pay the fee of a human life. Sometimes, a witch would ask someone if they would like to learn witchcraft in order to get wealthy and provide another's life in payment.

Each of the vital ingredients has a justification. The wampum beads and strings convey a sense of the wealth and ill-gotten gains attributed to witches. The human bones, fresh and otherwise, convey a sense of the powers and successes of the witch. The human hair is related to the universal symbolism of body dirt outlined by Edmund Leach (1967: 1, 7, 103) in his seminal essay Magical Hair: Everyone takes it for granted that verbal expletives in almost any language derive their magical potency from association either with sexual or excretory function or with God. The theory propounded in this essay is that the magical power of 'body dirt' (including head hair) is of precisely the same kind…. Finally I have made the point that hair, as a separable part of the body, is not only a symbol of aggression but a 'thing in itself', a material piece of aggression." The hair in a Delaware witch bundle is of the same piece. It is a representation of the aggressive hostility of witches, complete with sexual overtones. Similar sexual overtones lie behind the reasoning that witchcraft was ineffective on Whites because they ate too much salt, which is also a slang term for penis.

Less chronic, but nevertheless fatal, diseases are caused by improper conduct. Proper conduct exemplifies the ideal Delaware life (pilawsəwakʌn) <u>a clean, holy, chaste life</u>; in contrast to niskawsəwakʌn: <u>a bad, evil, promiscuous life</u>. Dangers to the clean life include becoming physically or spiritually dirty through sexual relations and contact with <u>menstrual blood</u> (niskənəman), mistreating animals, and eating food which has been eaten or touched by animals. Cats are especially dangerous because they are said to have <u>bad mouths</u> (*mahčətuna*). Mistreated cats and other animals will sometimes cause boils filled with hair. Improper conduct at rituals or failure to perform them causes insanity and congenital malformations. "The cause of insanity is attributed to the failure of a family to perform certain inherited ceremonials" (Tantaquidgeon 1972: 7). Paralysis can result from encountering a ghost. A permanently <u>twisted mouth</u> (pimtun) results from tampering with a <u>grave</u> (*təmaksuwakʌnike* the <u>place of the pitiful people</u>) or eating in the dark.

Delaware recognize several diseases related to spiritual and moral pollution:

mutələwakʌn <u>defilement</u>

niskiha• <u>to spiritually dirty someone</u>

matapaməweokʌn <u>causing a relapse or worsening by looking at someone after</u>
      <u>having sex or seeing a corpse</u>

šikɔndamən <u>someone tasted or wanted the food so much that the nourishment</u>
      <u>was taken out of it</u>

mikolahɛ <u>a mother who makes a baby sick</u> by not following the
      post-partem correction or restrictions [p157]

Before discussing specific diseases of the body, it is important to note that a healthy Delaware individual has six senses localized in six organs:

pənaylʊndaməweokʌn <u>thinking</u>, in the heart

pəndaməweokʌn <u>hearing</u>, in the ears

nɛməweɔkʌn <u>seeing</u>, in the eyes

məlaməweokʌn <u>smelling</u>, in the nose

wtəndamaweɔkʌn <u>tasting</u>, in the mouth

aməndaməweɔkʌn <u>touching</u>, on the skin

Specific diseases or illnesses of the body include the following:

<u>body</u> hɔkay(a)

    šiomʌndəməweokʌn <u>general numbness, paralysis</u>

    šipənəsəwakʌn <u>numbness</u>

    mačihəleokʌn <u>relapse</u>

    mahkʷisəweokʌn <u>swelling</u>

    maingalukʷ <u>gravitation, referred pain</u>

    kšɛlɛxeokʌn <u>fever, hot all over</u> (kšəlɛxin <u>someone has a fever</u>)

    nɛhənupəneɔkʌn <u>chills</u>

    winamʌndəmweokʌn <u>soreness, aching</u>

    kikitsuwakʌn <u>soreness</u>

    ahɛlindəmawakʌn <u>intense pain</u>

    wisʌhkamalsəwakʌn <u>extreme stinging pain</u>

    ɔhčipisuweokʌn <u>convulsions, epilepsy</u>

    nʌŋihaleokʌn <u>palsy, trembling disease</u>

    kiwsuwakʌn <u>drunkenness</u>

šiomalsəwakʌn weakness
hilusəwʌŋɛl rheumatism, literally, old man' s disease
mɛtatʌməweɔkʌn dying of old age
ʌŋəlawakʌn death

head wil
wilinɛɔkʌn head ache
sapʌleʌntpeokʌn baldness
kionʌskweokʌn dizziness

face, eye wəškiŋ^w

mʌmkihtəliŋweɔkʌn acne, literally, sore face
kəkhakihəleokʌn chappedness, literally, cracked face
sukšeŋwɛ someone has a blackened eye
ahpimškiŋweɔkʌn cross-eyedness
pimɛliŋwe someone has an eye that looks to one side
ahkɛpiŋweɔkʌn blindness
tuhənəšeŋ^w a sty
hmuk̓^wšeŋ^we someone has bloodshot eyes

nose hwikiyɔn
hmukwitʌm nosebleed
sanik̓^wineɔkʌn head cold, literally, snot aching
g^wəsk̓^wine I sneeze

ear hwɪtawk
ahkɛxeɔkʌn deafness

mouth tun [p158]
pisəlixsuwakʌn hoarseness, literally, wrinkled voice
nɛnahka1it someone who stutters
aluhu someone who is choked
lɛxɛwsu someone who pants
alətən halitosis, literally, rotten mouth
xuk̓^winakʌn spit heavy with mucus, mucoid sputum
məlʌndʌmweɔkʌn vomit
daluhwi I choke
dɛčkakoli I have something caught between my teeth
wipitinɛɔkʌn toothache
k̓^wəndakʌninɛɔkʌn throat ache
dukpɛkilahtʌ I swallowed something liquid and it went down too slowly and painfully

bičilahta I swallowed something and it went down the wrong throat, aspiration of food
or liquid
xukwineɔkʌn cold, literally, coughing disease

trunk tuhwɛpi
tulhayinɛɔkʌn chest aching
kolalhwɛ• gurgling in the chest
ɔwikʌnineokʌn shoulder aching
upxkɔnineɔkʌn back aching
sukʌnineokʌn an ache in the small of the back
puhɔkɛ• someone is humpbacked
ɔhtneɔkʌn stomach ache, with diarrhea
mutɛneɔkʌn stomach ache
xkukčaktʌn(a) stomach worms, literally, stomach snakes
nalʌihəle mutay settle the stomach
pk{{w}}utčɛ someone who is ruptured, hernia
ahoxahkəsʌwakʌn over-sexiness
pasahtayɛ• someone with gas
pasu someone is bloated
šapwihəleɔkʌn diarrhea, dysentery
piməwalehəle diarrhea from eating green or unripe fruit or a particular food,
literally, someone who is tilted
pɔsktəweokʌn constipation, literally, stopped up
bənčtiɛpala I gave someone an enema
ktanehəmalke something (a food or medicine) caused intermenstrual bleeding, a
resumption of menstruation between periods, literally, it threw you out
kukhusəwakʌn onset of menstruation, derived from the word for owl (*kukhus*)

leg hwikat
hwɪkatinɛɔkʌn leg ache, caused by 'growing pains' and cured by putting an
old woman's garter on the youth s leg, also any general leg ache
puk•atexin someone broke their own leg
kekʷ əluk•wihəleɔkʌn lameness [p159]
ɔkʷ čəsitat club foot, someone with a crooked foot
čilihəlɛ• someone has a sprain
aləsiteokʌn athlete's feet, literally, rotten feet
mahkʷisu someone is swollen, as in the leg, or area of injury, edema

heart tɛh
wəlamʌlsəwakʌn feeling well
wəteləndʌmawakʌn happiness, satisfaction
aholtəwakʌn love, strong affection
čipɛləndəmawakʌn feeling strange or astonishment

    aləwatəmweɔkʌn <u>loss of mental faculties</u>
    nəwiʌkskamʌlsi <u>I have mixed feelings</u>
    nəwiʌkskeləndʌm <u>I have mixed emotions</u>
    sʌkwelındʌməwakʌn <u>worrying</u>
    šiɛləndʌmʌweokʌn <u>depression</u>, <u>sadness</u>
    ǩʷilaleləndʌməwakʌn <u>being in a deep quandry</u>
    pahseɔtəmawakʌn <u>half-wittedness</u>
    mimãsʌweɔtʌmawakʌn <u>child-mindedness</u>

    kpʌteɔŋələwakʌn <u>insanity</u>

    ɔxpahəlɛ <u>someone regains consciousness or returns to a normal mental state</u>
        <u>after a bout with alcoholism or insanity</u>
    manuŋsəwakʌn <u>anger</u>

    šiŋgaltawakʌn <u>hatred</u>

    kʌŋwiltəwakʌn <u>jealousy</u>
    ǩʷitəmawakʌn <u>fear</u>, <u>awe</u>

<u>skin</u> xɛs
    maxkaləl <u>chafed </u>or <u>galled</u>, literally, <u>someone who turns red</u>
    zəkhɪksi <u>sunburn</u>, literally, <u>I am blackened by solar heat</u>
    sʌnʌǩʷtis <u>wart</u>, <u>mole</u>
    lusəwakʌn(a) burn
    wisɛ <u>sore</u>, <u>scrape</u>
    məki <u>scab</u>
    ɛhɛndawisɛk <u>scar</u>

5. ~   When the Delaware body system (partonomy) and its applications are compared to other anatomical systems, some interesting differences and underlying similarities emerge. Among those which I will consider are the cultural emphasis given to anatomical knowledge, different sequences of topographical ordering of items (parta), and the role of the specialist as sage and curer.

    According to the paleo-pathologist EH Ackerknecht (1943), much of what we now call 'folk science' is extremely scanty on physiological function. As examples, he cited cultural beliefs that deny any link between sexual intercourse and pregnancy or that place the vital principal in the stomach, kidney fat, larynx, pelvis, or big toe. He argued that the butchering of game or the practice of cannibalism did not contribute to the store of anatomical information because people were intent on things other than gaining knowledge. He strengthened his position with reference to the autopsies typically [p160] performed in Samoa and in parts of Siberia and Africa to determine the cause of death, especially from sorcery, where specific organs are unknown and anatomical details invented. I would prefer to modify this position, however, as we have seen, the Delaware did correctly observe that the deer has no gall bladder and attribute behavioral consequence to this, albeit the wrong one. Further, I was told that 'old time' Delaware were able to check a person's body temperature by taking their pulse. Nevertheless, Ackerkneckt (1943: 338) rightly concludes that 'only in the context of a culture pattern oriented towards a kind of 'science', do dissections furnish anatomical knowledge'. A superb example of this is provided by the Aleutian Islanders.

Anatomical knowledge is a strong cultural focus for the Aleuts. Marsh and Laughlin (1956) were able to list 19 pages of anatomical terminology, which they say was derived from five sources: (1) their extreme pragmatic orientation to the environment and skill at concentrated observation brought to bear on the butchering of fowl, fish, and mammal carcasses; (2) a well developed belief in the value of empiricism and experimentation; (3) the practice of human autopsies by native medical specialists and the observations of native midwives; (4) an interest in comparative anatomy per se, using sea otter and seal carcasses because of their clear morphological resemblance to humans; and (5) the practice of dry mummification of the dead. Laughlin (1972: 141) provides examples of Aleut pragmatic experimentation: two villages agreed to raise the boating team of each on either steamed or boiled food, later the teams raced to see which food gave better wind and endurance; also, two children were raised by different methods to see which gave the better resulting child.

The key to the Aleut cultural emphasis on anatomy seems to be the class of medical specialists, who doctored with a form of acupuncture, which unlike the Chinese system of 365 vital points, required a special prognosis for each patient. The anthropologists found the native doctors and midwives most adept at anatomical knowledge, with hunters less so. Limited surgery was done, sutured with sinew. There were important sex differences in treatment. Massage was mostly used by women as part of the treatment for pregnancy and childbirth. Native physicians would let blood only from men, because the blood of a woman was unclean to a man. Aleuts know enough human physiology to understand morphological development and use pressure points. Many Aleut men had some knowledge of human anatomy because Aleut warriors would dismember enemies, owls, and hawks to prevent their souls from avenging their deaths. In contrast, Aleut mummified their own dead in order that the soul or spirit remain with the body to help the descendants.

Aleut also metaphorically name islands, throwing boards, kayaks, and fish weirs in whole or in part with anatomical terms. As the Aleut language has singular, dual, and plural number, they quite explicitly designate the jaw as dual, both for animal jaws which separate at the symphysis and for the fused human mandible. Marsh and Laughlin (1956: 67, note 35) decided not to include Aleut slang and obscene usages, although they report that these exist. Laughlin (1968) reports that Aleut use their anatomical knowledge in [p161] training exercises for children, especially for hunting from a kayak, and in the observation of pet wild animal young. Such observation and learning was vital: "An Eskimo may wound a bear and then drive him down to a stream where he can be killed and boated home, thus eliminating backpacking some 1, 200 pounds through difficult country" (1968: 309).

While the Delaware clearly place less cultural emphasis on anatomy than the Aleut, when there was a more viable Delaware society in the past, physicians and hunters could have provided a fuller account than I was able to record.[8] Some variability in the exact peripheries of these *parta* would have also been present, although the reoccurrence of the same *parton* or *taxon*

---

[8] Further comparison indicates that two terminological styles are not represented in the Delaware partonomy: (1) the application of lexical suffixes in Halkomelem in order to create neat etymological systems such as that described for the Bella Coola (Saunders and Davis 1974) and (2) the reoccurrence of parallel formations such as that of the Upper Stalo where palms and soles are respectively the face of the hand and the face of the foot (Galloway 1976: 45). Both of these are Salishan languages.

at different levels (such as Delaware <u>face</u>) is a regular feature of folk classification (Brown and others 1976: 83) and thus does not represent a break-down of an earlier Delaware system. Landar and Gasagrande (1962) have noted the sort of periphery variability I have suggested for Delaware of past generations among present day Navaho. The Delaware may have also practiced some comparative anatomy since early sources indicate that they were well aware of the morphological and behavioral closeness between humans and bears (Miller 1982).

Actually, it is not that Delaware anatomical knowledge has been preserved into the present, but rather that one of its lower level specialists is alive and using the system. Other native speakers of Delaware exist, but their anatomical knowledge is far less systematic and useful. Another significant aspect of this system is that its presentation represents one of the few times in the literature when a full set of anatomical terms was transmitted across the sexes. Landar and Casagrande (1962: 371) and Marsh and Laughlin (1956: 42) remark that modesty often keeps anatomical knowledge within the same sex, much as Delaware obscenities are used.

Because the Delaware topographic sequence duplicates that of the White folk system, the possibility of other sequences might go unrecognized. Delaware and White American topography runs from top to bottom. Other logical systems are possible: bottom to top, and circular. These are reported in the literature. Among the Navaho of Arizona (Werner and Begishe 1966: 247, note 2), whose Genesis has humans emerging from the ground like plants, "the proper order of the creation of the human body by the Holy People is: Foot, Leg, Hip, Trunk, Shoulder, Arm, Hand, Neck, and Head. " A Tlingit of Yakutat, Alaska named the 'eight bones or joints' of the body as: left elbow, left shoulder, right shoulder, right elbow, right hip, right knee, left knee, and left hip (de Laguna 1972: 761). Some indeterminacy in the Tlingit terms can be expected as in this language nouns have no plurals.

In addition to such linear and circular sequences, auxiliary sequences are also possible, especially those involving distinctions between right / left and center / periphery. The almost universal priority of right to left suggests that most sequences will emphasize the right side. The Tlingit sequence noted above is distinctive because other evidence indicates that the Tlingit otherwise give priority to the right. Rare priority of the left has been reported for the Keres Pueblos and the Delaware (Miller 1972). The priority of the center to the periphery also seems to be pan-human. This may also [p162] explain the physiological and the intellectual importance that the Delaware attribute to the heart. But this is not unique, given the importance of the heart in early India, Greece, China, Egypt, and Mexico (Danek 1975: 68). The hearts of Renaissance French and English kings were even buried separately from the body and received special veneration (Giesey 1960: 20). In Western medicine, autopsies proceed from center to periphery (from proximal to distal in the argot) and top to bottom. 'Some etymologists assume that words denoting 'centrality', 'belief', and even 'firmness' might be derived, in some Indo-European languages at least, from the same root as 'heart' (1975: 68).

Lastly, we come to a consideration of the specialist in anatomical knowledge as a sage and curer. The Delaware system has, of course, atrophied. Nevertheless, the fullest partonomy was provided by a practicing herbalist. In a functioning traditional system, the importance of the specialist is even clearer. Among the Desana of Colombia (Reichel-Dolmatoff 1971: 175ff), the highest ranking members of each village are the priest and the shaman. These men are almost alone in having a complete cultural knowledge of the Desana world such that they believe the world to be based on male / female biocosmic energy flow. They also are able to act on this belief. For the Desana, diseases are caused by natural sources, by contact with agents such as pubic hair, and by 'wrappings'. In the latter case, the patient is enveloped in mystical bindings or wrappings caused by mythic creatures or enemy intent. These diseases are psychosomatic with hysterical overtones which are clearly related to the various strong cultural mechanisms repressing human sexuality, with the intention of promoting animal sexuality and multiplication so vital to these hunting people. After the disease has been diagnosed by a specialist, the cure is performed as a complex but explicit evocation of coitus and rebirth, executed through phallic personifications and gesturings from the center to the extremities of the patient (Reichel-Dolmatoff 1971: 185, 181). The effectiveness of the cure depends on the shared beliefs of patient and curer, and the confidence of the former in the special mystical, cognitive, and systematic abilities of the latter.

The crux of each domain of knowledge seems to be its specialists, who regularize and routinize the system for themselves and, by extension, for the other members of their community. In fact, native conferences on nomenclature are not unknown (Miller 1975a).
These specialists give order and meaning to their domain − if not to the whole world – and confidence to others. This psychological effect is a consequence of their intellectual and behavioral functions. Any skepticism, especially from White specialists, is unwarranted. It is not that an old woman' s garter cures <u>leg ache</u> for the Delaware, but rather that it renders concrete and objective the mystical and practical powers of the specialist curer, the concern of the larger social network, and the resolve of the patient. As Kleinman (1974: 208) has said "the acts of ordering, naming, interpreting, and offering therapy for illness are aspects of symbolic reality common to both the sick individual, the healer, and their society. Anthropological studies have continuously [p163] reiterated the ability of native specialists working in social and cultural contexts to treat, to kill, and to cure their patients." In his now classic study, Cannon (1942) showed that social pressure can be finely applied to over-stress an individual into a 'voodoo death'. Jelik (1974: 28) has also stressed the 'lethal outcome of severe anxiety states'. Conversely, Levi- Strauss (1967) has suggested that skillful psychology and social structure can permit a Panaman Cuna shaman to produce a successful childbirth by a chanted poem, or a priesthood in the Pueblo of Zuni, New Mexico to produce a recognized witch from a rejected suitor.

In all then, an important feature of human knowledge, whether technical or folk, and its cultural emphasis and utility, is that each domain has its specialists recruited on the basis of natural propensities and trained through a process of rigorous apprenticeship and self-motivated curiosity to become a focus of public service and manipulation, a nexus of social supports and pressures, and a source for individual catharsis.

anatomy

Endnote Thanks

*For a paper devoted to categorization, it seems only appropriate for me to differentiate my debts of gratitude to Delaware, physicians, and others.

Delawares: special appreciation must go to my Lenape friends and relatives, but most especially to Nora Thompson Dean, Lucy Parks Blalock, Leonard Thompson, and Jim Rememter.

Physicians: my interest and understanding of the medical aspects of the partonomy has been fostered by references from the late Robert G. Bull, by the assistance of the University of Washington Pathology Department chaired by Earl Benditt and especially the help of Tom Norris and his young, able staff, by the careful reading of Thaworn Hangledarom, and by the karma of Doug Allderdice. Assistance and terminology was provided by George R Kennedy and William J Russum of Bartlesville, Oklahoma.

Others: as always, my severest critics and loyalest supporters have been selected colleagues in Anthropology, at Monday Nite, and under sail or paddle. Particular thanks must go to the intellectual elite of Saratoga, Wyoming.

Originally published
Anthropological Linguistics Vol 19 (4): 144-166

Summary

Orafices		Products	
skin	xɛs		
ears	hwɪtawk(a)		
eyes	wəškiŋ^w	səpiŋ^w(o)	tear(s)
nose	hwikiyɔn(a)	hmukwitʌm	nosebleed
nostrils		sʌnik^w	snot, nasal mucus
mouth	tun(a)	sukwinakʌn(a)	spit, mehʌmičŋi food
breasts	nunakʌn(a)	nunakʌn	milk, nipples
navel	wilhwi		
penis	škiyɔn(ak)	ških, spəlaš	urine, semen
vulva	maax(ak)	^hmuk	blood
anus	sputi	mwičti	feces

A Struckon Model of Delaware Culture
and the Positioning of Mediators

Abstract

Astruckon (structural configuration) model of Delaware culture is presented, subdivided into sensory, interpersonal, and cosmic emanations of an apical opposition called a paideuma. Then consideration is given to the origin and position of mediators within this cultural tradition in order to specify the process called "intrusion" whereby mediators enter contrast sets within the generalstruckon model.

The purpose of this article is to explore astructural-configuration (hereafter:struck*on*) model of the culture of the Delaware ~ Lenape Nation of Native Americans and to suggest a source and process relating to some of the important mediators in this cultural tradition.[9]1 vUnless otherwise cited, the ethnographic data have been drawn from my own fieldwork among Delaware currently residing in Oklahoma, who trace their ancestry to the Unami (Winami) or southern division, which was resident along the lower Delaware River drainage when the nation aboriginally resided on the mid-Atlantic slope of the eastern United States.

Struckon Model

Thestruckon model is intended to provide a consistent, integrated description of the configuration of a culture. The accompanying diagram (Figure 1) outlines a model for the description of a structural configuration (astruckon) that fulfills requirements basic to any scientific endeavor: holism, parsimony, and coherence. The model itself is a unique blend that has been inspired by the German configurationalism of Leo Frobenius (Honigmann 1976:178), the French structuralism of Claude Levi-Strauss (Rossi 1974), and the theory of "marking" of the Prague Linguistic Circle as interpreted by Joseph Greenberg (1966). The model owes to Frobenius the recognition of the integrated coherence of a culture as derived from a shared,

---

[9] This essay was written as the second part of a trilogy articulating the strucon (pronounced "struck un") model. The first, A New Approach to Configurations of Culture in North America, examines the inclusive / exclusive in regard to the ethnography of five American Indian language isolates: Yuchi, Keres, Kootenay, Yuki, and Quileute. The third, The Keres Pueblos: A Diachronic Study of a Struckon Model in Southwestern Prehistory, considers the Keres struckon through five thousand years of archaeological data. If these others ever see the light of print, the trilogy should be read in the order just given.

Continuing reflection on the struckon has raised two points:

1. More empirical colleagues might want to subdivide cosmic emanations into "natural" and "supernatural" components so that biota and other "scientific" data might be separated from less tangible myth figures and philosophical assumptions, and

2. A heuristic scheme for organizing sensory emanations in an etic fashion might be that of Watson and Nelson (1967).

Both of these provide accommodations to the practicalities of ethnography and the diversity among anthropologists, but nonetheless preserve the general integrity of the strucon model. The binary character of emanations and the paideuma relates to the simultaneous expression of similarity and difference, the minimal expression of a relationship from which greater complexities can be generated.

pervasive property called a "paideuma" (Greek: "that which is instilled"). By adopting this term from Frobenius, I also intend to separate my configurational model from the more diffuse, personality-based configurationalism of Ruth Benedict (1960) and Alfred Kroeber (Honigmann 1976:201-204). However, like Benedict, Frobenius overdrew his concept by trying to divide all of Africa into only two areal paideuma and by regarding the paideuma as a unitary, static concept. Drawing upon structuralism, I have redefined the paideuma as binary. In keeping with a general structuralist orientation, the focus of the struckon model is upon relationships rather than objects. In terms of marking, the model recognizes the dyadic and inherently triadic relationships that are universal in human conceptualization. To better express these relationships, more strictly linguistic [792] phenomena of marking are distinguished below from the cultural ones by introducing the terms "inclusive / exclusive" to apply to cultural categories.

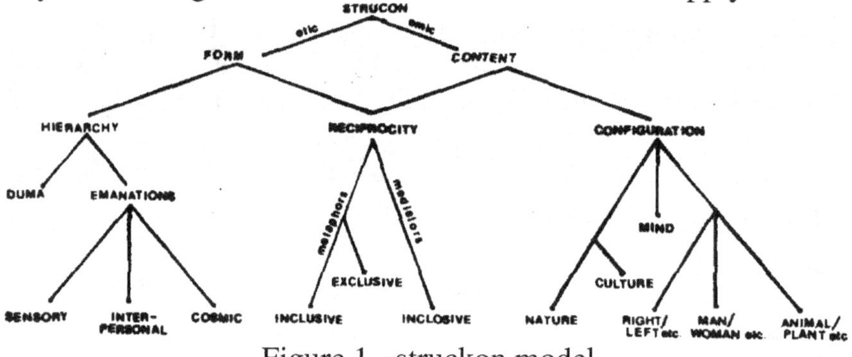

Figure 1 ~struckon model

Throughout the discussion, "culture" is used to refer to an integrated conceptual system for bringing order and meaning to the world. "Society" refers to the behaviors and institutions that result from the dialectical interplay between culture and environment. A "strucon" is defined as an integrated system of relationships among concrete expressions (signs or objectivized ideas), which I have called "emanations," subsumed by an apical, all-pervasive, logical opposition (the paideuma).

The model has two aspects: a universal etic one and a culture-specificone. The etic aspect relates to the form of the relationships, whereas the emic one depends upon the content of relationships specific to a culture and its interplay with an environment by means of a society. The etic relationships of form will be considered first, although this is strictly for purposes of exposition, because the form and the content of any struckon are always dialectically related through reciprocity.

The struckon aspect of form is derived from the recognition of two basic types of relationships: hierarchy and reciprocity among binary contrasts (Levi-Strauss 1944). The backbone of the model consists of a graded hierarchical sequence articulated by reference to the paideuma at its apex. The hierarchy itself is composed of paired metaphors, which I call "emanations." Integrating these emanations at various levels are mediators, which serve to bridge some or all of the distinctions between the members of an emanation pair, in addition to having properties unique to themselves as mediators. The exact qualities of these mediators will be more fully discussed after the term "inclosive" has been introduced to clarify the inherently triadic properties of various relationships.

Following Levi-Strauss, in terms of the emic content, the panhuman struckon for all cultures is the paideuma of Nature / Culture mediated by Mind. In particular, this recognition of Mind (Intellect) as the ultimate apical mediator also establishes a fixed point of reference for a universal form hierarchy. Such a hierarchy serves to set the emic parameters of an "etic grid" from which the various alternative "emic" cultures are derived through a process of transforming or rearranging the emanations within the overall hierarchical and reciprocal relationships. In this way, from this invariant form of etic hierarchy, it is possible to derive variable contents for specific cultures with different paideuma. The etic hierarchy can be usefully viewed as a sequence of three types of emanations.

With the Mind as point of reference and proximity as our criterion, these three types are hierarchically arranged in terms of what I have called sensory, interpersonal, and cosmic emanations. Sensory emanations are paired sets nearest to the apex because they relate to the mind of an individual culture bearer, specifically, to the sensory aspects of a person. Interpersonal metaphors are intermediate in the hierarchy to refer to the collective interactions of society members within the contexts of various social institutions. Furthest [793] removed from the apex are those emanations concerned with interplay of humans and their cosmos.

Each of these emanation types has some typical representations that can be usefully listed to further clarify our recognition of them. Sensory emanations, because they relate to mind-body interactions, include colors, sights, sounds, silences, smells, styles of cooking, foods, tastes, hand (laterality) priority (and by extension tactile expressions in shapes, textures, and manufactures), physiological states, and even pattern numbers because they are often used to bring order to sensory experiences. Interpersonal emanations, because they represent the collective interaction of individuals, include various institutional contexts such as economy, polity, descent, life cycle, religion, and language. Cosmic emanations, as expressions of the relations among humans and their total environment, include symbolically charged aspects of biota, terrain, geography, meteorological phenomena, celestial bodies, myth characters, temporal progressions, philosophical conclusions, and abstract or other-worldly dimensions.

In addition to its relationships within the hierarchy, each of the emanation pairs is also characterized by a relationship of reciprocity. This reciprocity is defined in terms of the attribute of "inclusivity," which is related to the notion of marking used for linguistic phenomenon. Because of the position of reciprocity within the struckon model, the aptness of the terms inclusive / exclusive for this reciprocal relationship, and the ability to pun with the terms "inclusive" and "inclosive," I prefer to use these terms to reserve "marking" solely for reference to linguistic usages. Linguists already familiar with the use of the inclusive / exclusive for first-person plural pronouns (Haas 1969) might be initially confused by my terms, but the reasons given above serve to justify my choice. Of the eight criteria for distinguishing marked from unmarked forms (Greenberg 1966), the primary one is a much greater frequency of use for the unmarked. Similarly, a primary criterion for recognizing the inclusive from the exclusive relates to a greater frequency of occurrence for the former. This higher frequency seems to derive from an ambiguity inherent in the inclusive attribute.

In each reciprocal relationship, the exclusive member of a pair specifically asserts the presence of a certain property (X), but the inclusive ambiguously asserts either the absence of that property (not-X) in some contexts or the presence of both properties (X and not-X) in these and other contexts.

This relationship was captured nicely in the translation by JNB Hewitt (1928) of the terms for the Iroquois Great Beings as "Man-Beings" (males) and "Woman-Man Beings" (females). In this example, Man is exclusive and Woman is inclusive. Before considering other Native American data, I give some comparative examples, one from China and one from Western biology, to illustrate the universality of inclusive / exclusive aspects of the human metaphor. In Chinese, the important opposition between yang / yin is also associated with light / dark and male / female. Closer investigation shows that whereas yang equates with high, bright, male, sun, and the male sex organ; yin equates with dark, shadow, moon, female, and both the male and the female sex organs. Culturally, a Chinese man must guard constantly against any loss of his yang, but yin is considered to be boundless. In other words, the Chinese yang is exclusive and yin is inclusive. Similarly, a Western biologist describes the chromosomes of the female as XX and of the male as XY. Whatever the physiological basis for this statement, it is nevertheless clear that conceptually the female is exclusive and the male is inclusive. These examples also illustrate an inversion in the relationships of inclusive / exclusive attributes. In the Iroquois and Chinese examples, Man is exclusive but Woman is inclusive, whereas Western biology reverses these associations, indicating the flexibility permitted in such reciprocal attributes. The exclusive is always highly specific whereas the inclusive remains ambiguous. Foreknowledge of these features permits one to arrange the various signs and metaphors in emanation pairs into one or the [794] other category. Such a sorting enables the logical consistency of a struckon to emerge with a meaningful clarity that goes beyond the confusing surface, the dazzle of data of ethnography. For, in the words of Levi-Strauss, "if social phenomena are first objectivized systems of ideas, to explain them is to rethink them in their logical order" (quoted in Rossi 1974: 79).

By way of summarizing the etic aspect of form within thestruckon, we can again note the salience of an etic hierarchy composed of sensory, interpersonal, and cosmic emanations depending upon a paideuma of Nature / Culture mediated by Mind: Nature is inclusive because it both includes Culture, the adaptation of the human animal, and is opposed to it as accident or chaos is opposed to order. Culture is exclusive, therefore, and uniquely human (Figure 2).

By and large, however, anthropologists have no familiarity with this etic grid ofstruckon form. Each professional has his or her own familiarities, but they relate to content and not to form. In terms of thestruckon model, therefore, I must now shift to discussing the content aspect of thestruckon in order to provide a procedure for sorting out the relative merits of emanations and paideuma for a particular culture. Which of the emanations of the potential etic form apply to a particular culture and how can we determine their relative rankings in order to establish the paideuma and the overall relationships of that particularstruckon?

In initial stages, a struckon analysis duplicates the four steps of a structuralist analysis (Rossi 1974):

1. Immersion in the data

2. Analysis of the data into abstract categories and relationships expressed as several alternative models

3. Mental experimentation and manipulation of these alternatives in order to reject the weaker models that account for fewer of these data

4. Assertion of the Structure as that model which best includes all available data and re-combines all the relationships into a meaningful whole.

Like a Structure, a struckon must be characterized by holism, coherence, parsimony, and exhaustiveness. In addition, a struckonal analysis includes two steps that distinguish the particular emic content of a culture from the etic form:

5. Determination of the relevant emanations of a society in terms of their content, and their inclusivity [795]

6. Recognition of the pervasive redundancy of the paideuma as that emanation pair that apically subsumes the others for that culture.

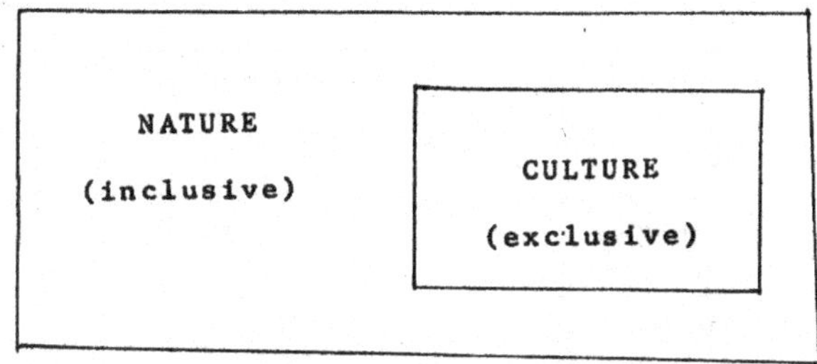

Figure 2. Nature : Culture :: Inclusive : Exclusive.

Although eachstruckon has to be explored, analyzed, and understood in its own terms, enough research has already been carried out to suggest three content pairs that are crucial for substantiating a paideuma. In terms of analytical efficiency, the most informative sensory emanation is right / left (Needham 1973); that for the interpersonal is men / women (Douglas 1970); and the cosmic pair is animal / plant (Fernandez 1974). While part of every etic form, these emanations are also sensitive indicators of the manipulations of hierarchy and reciprocity that are so important for understanding the content of a particular struckon.

To date, I have found nine pairs of categories that can function as an "etic grid" for an intensely emic paideuma (see Table 1). It is my impression that, given the invariant, crosscultural hierarchy of emanations listed above, the distinctiveness of astruckon should be related to the movement of a metaphor pair into the apical position; equally fascinating is the way in which the same paideuma can be expressed in different emanations depending on such factors as local ecology, historical precedent, and deliberate reversals to distinguish one culture from another. Miller (1974a) calls attention to several such reversals in Native North America.

As should be obvious, thestruckon model is synchronic. It represents a configuration, which is defined as the combination of emanations congruent with the paideuma for a particular time and space in the life of a culture. However, once the paideuma is recognized and the struckon worked out in detail, it is possible to use the emic aspect in a diachronic study. At present, archaeological and historical (written) data are not sufficient in and of themselves to articulate a struckon model because so much of the relevant emic data cannot be recovered from these selective sources: "history does not reveal causes; it presents only a blank succession of unexplained events" (Berlin 1953: 13). In other words, the true reality is the least obvious and often missed, although it should be even more readily apparent to anthropologists "in the care which it takes to evade our attention" (Levi-Strauss in Rossi 1974: 64). In sum, a properstruckonal analysis requires the collection of data either from voluminous published ethnography or, best of all, from a planned program of concerted fieldwork always mindful of the dialectic between form and content, such as my experience with the Delaware summarized below.

Because the true reality is meta-empirical, all social phenomena can only be understood through the use of models at various levels of removal from actual description. In the words of Mary Haas (1965:1558), the best solution for attaining reality and for narrowing the gap between own-culture and other-culture "is the use of models − not empirical models ... but formal models, the more formal the better." However, purely formal models are also flawed because they are too static. They do not allow for the dialectic, [796] which not only captures the order and meaning of cultural worlds but also allows for the manipulation of relevant relationships for specific emic purposes.

Table 1. Categories composing an etic grid

Paideuma	Society	Emanation Type
Right/left	Purum, Kansa (?)	Sensory
Red/white	Creek	
Man/woman	Delaware, Keres	Interpersonal
War/peace	Cherokee	
Summer/winter	Tewa Pueblos	Cosmic
Sky/earth	Winnebago	
Male/female	Desana ~Tukano	
Pure/impure	Hindu India	
Outside/inside	Akwe-Shavante	

The advantage of thestruckon model is that it more adequately accounts for more cultural data than previous attempts because it both provides for the etic aspects of form, hierarchy / reciprocity, and inclusive / exclusive, while at the same time it recognizes the dialectical flexibility between these relationships and the emic content of particular paideuma / emanations.

Delaware Struckon

In the interests of condensing the discussion, I will first diagram a partial Delaware structural-configuration (struckon) before proceeding to an examination of the ethnographic support for it (see Table 2). Afterwards, I will specifically examine the functioning of mediators within the theoretical model

Unfortunately, an exhaustive treatment of the struckon will require a monograph-length discussion so I can focus only on the more important emanations as provided in Table 2.

Table 2. Partial Delaware Struckon

Paideuma	Man	Mind	Woman
Attributes	(Inclusive)	(Mediators)	(Exclusive)
Emanations			
Sensory	black, white, yellow, red		red
	meat foods		plant foods
	left	heart	right
	linear shapes	semicircle	circular shapes
	two	three	one
Interpersonal	hunting	fishing	farming
	Canine matriclan	Turtle matriclan	Fowl matriclan
	ritual cycle		life cycle

struckon

	Doll Dance	Otter Rite	Bear Rite
Cosmic	forest	stockade	town
	animals	water creatures	plants
	north, east, west	center	south
	air	waters	land
	Cosmic Tree	Cosmic Turtle	Mother Earth
	Sky Keepers (Masing)	Creator	Maize Mother

sensory emanations According to my data, Delaware men were not specifically limited to any color face paint. Men applied lines behind their eyes in black and red with highlights in white or yellow. Women, however, used only red face paint applied as dime-sized circles on their cheeks. In other words, men were not limited to any single color, whereas women were restricted to red. Men were expected to supply the meat foods and women the plant ones, especially maize. Further, once the meat had been brought home it "belonged" to the women and, in the same way, stored maize "belonged" to the men. Thus far, all food appears to be inclusive; however, the critical case occurred when women secluded themselves during menstruation or labor and meat was taboo to them. At this time, they exclusively relied on plant food. Among the Delaware and many other tribes, the seat of intelligence and emotions was the heart. Because it was said to be closer to the heart, the left hand had priority over the right (Miller 1972). When men recited their guardian-spirit vision experiences on each night of the twelve-day long Big House Rite, last held in 1924, people [797] raised their left hands. When the few female visionaries recited on the last day, people raised their right hands, but when one contemporary woman visionary makes offering to a sacred fire, she uses her left hand. In general, as with the face paintings, linear shapes were associated with men and circular shapes with women. The mediation of these forms was the semicircle or horizontal D-shape best represented by the sky dome arching over the earth disk. Delaware mythology abounds in references to pattern numbers of 3, 4, 7, 9, and 12. I had originally established these as logically related to permutations of 3 and 4: 7 (3 + 4), 9 (3 x 3), 12 (3 X 4). However, the exclusivity of these numbers remained problematical until I realized the salience of the number 1, especially with regard to the isolation of women during menstruation and labor. The number 2 thereby represents the inclusive, but the number 3 is the smallest of the recognized pattern numbers. The reason for this is that throughout the Delaware cultural system 3 represents closure, the joining of 1 and 2. For example, the Delaware had three matriclans and may have formerly consisted of three tribes. From the preceding we can begin to formulate an understanding of mediators as members of the inclusive category, without the ability to oppose par excellence the exclusive, but rather only to represent the entire pair. However, this understanding fails to approach the most salient characteristic of mediators, which will appear in a later section.

interpersonal emanations In the traditional economy, men usually hunted in small groups except when large communal parties went hunting in the spring and fall. Women went to work in the fields and occasionally organized to gather berries, shoots, and other wild vegetables. Fishing was predominantly a male activity but the women had the responsibility for cleaning, preparing, and storing the catch. Whereas the proper offering for animals was maize, and the proper offering to maize was deer or bear flesh, the proper offering to fish was cornbread shaped like fishes (Zeisberger 1910:139). Notice the closure of this threesome: meat and maize were reciprocal, but fish was given maize in the guise of flesh, simultaneously maize and meat, indicating that fish was a mediator. The Delaware had / have three matriclans, sometimes called phratries, known by generic terms as Canine, Turtle, and Fowl or by specific terms as Wolf, Turtle, and Turkey. Each of these terms has complex associations. All available data indicate to me that Canine (Wolf) was directly opposed to Fowl (Turkey) with Turtle providing the mediating closure. For example, the Canine matriclan has associations with haired, roaming, land, carnivorous, viviparous, tailed quadrupeds; Fowl was associated with feathered, air, stationary, herbivorous, egg-laying bipeds; and Turtles were considered shelled, beaked, amphibious, omnivorous, egg-laying, tailed quadrupeds. Of these, the Fowl is the most exclusive, being represented by birds with limited flying capacities (turkeys). Both men and women participated in the ritual cycle as performers, cooks, or audience, but the life cycle for the Delaware was an exclusively female domain. In terms of the major life-cycle events; birth, puberty, marriage, and death were all associated with women, usually in seclusion. Especially telling is the report that previously a death was announced to the community by a woman and that women dug and filled in the graves. In addition to the Big House Rite, the three most important rites were celebrated for male and female wooden dolls, for the Otter spirit, and for the Bear spirits. Once again there is closure for the threesome, because the Doll Dance was inclusive, the Otter Rite mediated because of its amphibious or water association, and the Bear Rite was exclusive both in terms of its performance within an enclosed space and the exclusive attributes attached to the hibernation of bears.

cosmic emanations Although not reported in the archaeological literature, my Delaware sources insist that their protohistoric towns were surrounded by pole stockades. In this way, the matrilocal, matrilineal towns where women were permanently resident were [798] divided off from the forest where men hunted, traded, and traveled. This use of timber poles as mediators is significant within the broader context of the use of sticks as mediators. Women in seclusion, boys on guardian-spirit quests, selected members of the Big House audience, and warriors were given sticks to use as implements, which served as mediators between themselves and their food or various spirits. Of related interest is a myth about a cannibal giant who was killed by being rectally impaled on a sharpened pole, reversing the normal process of ingestion and elimination and mediating between life and death. I will more fully consider the role of sticks as mediators below For reasons related to the Delaware technoeconomy, animals were associated with men and plants with women, although all animals species had male and female (literally "man" and "woman" in the Delaware language) members. The mediating category was water creatures, specifically distinguished in the Delaware language by the /bi-/ prefix. Turtles and otters provide two examples of this mediation. The Delaware call "grandfather" the directions north, east, and west, whereas south is called "grandmother" and treated as an exclusive category. The Delaware marked the center of their word with an *axis mundi*, which was the center post in the Big House. The air is the abode of several male supernaturals, including the Creator ("The One Who Created Us By His Thoughts"), but the land is designated Mother Earth. The Waters provide a complex mediation that took me some time to decipher Delaware address as "mother" water in wells, springs, and containers but address as "grandfather" water in large bodies or currents (Miller 1975). In other words, when water is excluded or bounded it is treated as womanly, but when inclusive or unbounded it is manly.

According to the Delaware account of creation, in the beginning only the Creator and the primal water existed. An enormous turtle rose from the water and the Creator placed Mother Earth on its back. At the very center of the earth, a tree grew and from the tree came two shoots. The shoot growing up produced the first man and the shoot growing downward produced the first woman. From this first couple, other life was created. Above the earth disk were twelve levels, each inhabited by a Sky Keeper who passed the prayers and supplications of people progressively upward until they reached the Creator sitting in the highest level. A special representative of these Sky Keepers, probably one of them, was a being called Masing, who was patron of game and plants and who was sometimes impersonated by a Delaware man wearing a tailored bearskin suit and a carved wooden mask. As Masing was patron of both game and plants, so Maize Mother was exclusively patron of maize, cautiously treated by everyone because of reputed oversensitivity and jealousy. Mediating these and everything else in the Delaware cosmos was the Creator, the ultimate personification of Mind eternally creating by his very thoughts. Having attained this identity of Mind with the Creator, we can conclude the treatment of the Delawarestruckon and now specifically focus on mediators.

Source and Role of Mediators

Like other aspects of thestruckon model, my early thinking with regard to mediators was strongly influenced by the discussion of "marking" by Greenberg (1966). Several times in his discussion, Greenberg mentions three-way contrasts and explains them in terms of differential degrees of marking. His examples include unaspirated, aspirated, and glottalized consonants in Chiricahua Apache (1966: 17) and singular, plural, and dual number in Sanskrit (1966: 29). I initially hoped for a clarification of the positioning of mediators from his discussion of pronoun systems, "these considerations would lead one to posit, tentatively at least, a hierarchy in which the third person was the least marked, and the second person [799] the most marked, with the first person intermediate" (Greenberg 1966: 45). However, it has not been possible to generalize from this example of linguistic marking to cultural data on exclusivity in large part because mediators must be phrased in terms of complete inclusivity as discussed above for the pattern number 3. In the three-way contrast for pronouns given by Greenberg, the first person is intermediate but in no sense a mediator between the third and second person By analogy with Delaware ethnography, the third person unmarked would be most analogous to a mediator, at least structurally in terms of the other two members of the series. However, it is not a mediator and here the linguistic analogy fails us.

Yet if we turn to the dialectic, we can see that the thesis is the exclusive term, the antithesis is the inclusive term when mutually exclusive of the thesis, and the synthesis is both the inclusive as an expression of the complete pair and the mediator between them. The difficulty with this formulation is that mediators are usually tangible properties intermediate between highly abstract categories: for example, the stockade that stood between a settlement and the forest. A related factor is that whereas the three-way contrasts discussed by Creenberg have an inherent relationship to each other, mediators are usually more inherently related to each other than they are to what they are individually mediating.

For these reasons, I have been drawn to characterize the source and positioning of mediators within thestruckon model as a process of "intrusion" into the emanation pair. In keeping with the logic of the Delaware struckon, relationships can be diagramed among the inclusive, exclusive, and mediator in terms of rectangle, circle, and D-shape (see Figure 3).

The position of the mediator seems to be best regarded as analogous to a "blank space" into which mediators from other emanation categories might intrude. The salient characteristic of these mediators is their origin in emanations of extensive pervasiveness in the emic system, most particularly as primordial features in the Origin Myth. In the case of the Delaware, these are specifically the Primal Water and the Cosmic Tree.

The Primal Water has the ubiquity of the cosmos before anything else was created. This was the "grandfather water," which continues to occupy large bodies and flowing currents. With the appearance of the Cosmic Turtle and the creation of the world some of this water became excluded in springs and seeps. Still later with the creation of humans some of this "mother water" became confined in wells and containers. Because of its fluidity water serves as an apt metaphor for full inclusion among the Delaware. From these waters are derived other mediators such as amphibious turtles, otters, and water creatures. These aquatic creatures by their very "nature" serve to mediate the contrast between "grandfather" and "mother" waters along the horizontal axis of the Delaware cosmos (Miller 1974b).

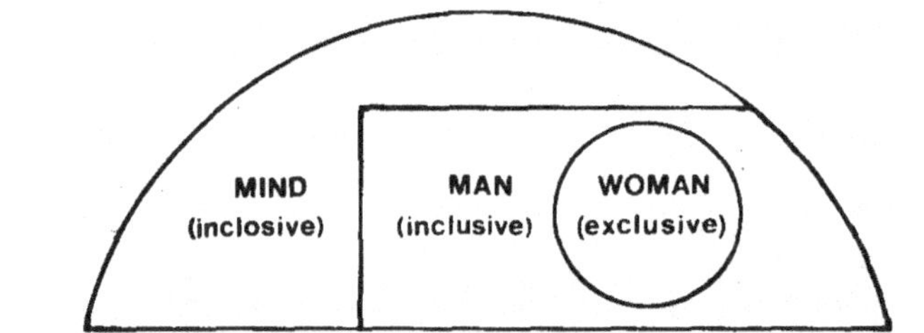

Figure 3 ~ Interrelationships of the Delaware paideuma.

The source for mediators along the vertical axis of the Delaware cosmos was the Cosmic Tree, which grew from the back of the Cosmic Turtle. Important mediators in Delaware [800] culture such as sticks and poles seem to be metonyms of this Tree. As the building used for the Big House Rite was a metaphor for the Cosmos, so the carved center post was a metaphor for the Cosmic Tree as *axis mundi*. The Cosmic Tree grew at the exact center of the world and the center post recreates its formal position as the center for the Delaware cultural world. In the same way, the center of the world is paralleled by the belief that the heart is the center of the person. The center post is the nexus of the macrocosm as the heart is the nexus of the personal microcosm. As the center of individual thought and emotions, the heart is also the locus of Mind and as such an evocation of the Creator, providing closure to this set of logical relations among these mediators.

Greenberg did not provide a distinctive term for the marked form when it encompassed both the marked and the unmarked, providing closure, but the character of mediators requires that such a term be provided to distinguish the inclusive from the "blank space" filled by mediators. For obvious reasons, I have chosen the term "inclosive" because it indicates its close relationship to the inclusive and its independent existence: the inclusive and the inclosive have different formal properties. The inclusive / exclusive is a dyadic relationship, whereas the inclusive (inclosive) exclusive is a triadic one that admits the possibility of a mediator in the inclosive position. Because the Mind is the ultimate inclosive mediator in human cultures, it is referentially involved in the various tangible mediators selected by different cultures and our own (Miller n.d.). In this regard, all mediators appear to share a certain commonality or dominant characteristic.

I interpret the predominant characteristic of these mediators as the ability to represent a "permeating nexus," as though Mind were conceived as a central point from which some sort of tendrils emanated to permeate and engulf everything else in the cultural realm. Such permeation is ambiguous, ubiquitous, and sometimes subtle enough to appear amorphous. Indeed, classic examples of such permeating nexi include references to spiders as important culture heroes, to a cross as defining the four cardinal directions, to a pole as *axis mundi*, to a shape like that of the six-pointed toy used in the game of jacks that conjoins the cross and pole, to a cube as delimiting the three dimensions of volume, and to water, the most ubiquitous permeator on a planet largely covered by this element. The significance of water is further indicated by references to amphibians and reptiles as important mediators. The World Turtle of the Delaware is but one of many examples that could be cited. Another recurrent mediator is the D-shape, a roughly triangular shape that also serves to conjoin linear and circular expressions, while providing closure. One example is the frequent description of the universe as a sky dome over on earth disk (a horizontal "D": 0). Because these mediators can be related to the pervasiveness of mind, they all share a metonymical relationship that serves to keep them distinct from the particular emanation pair mediated by each of them.

On the other hand, the metaphorical emanations are related to each other by their shared inclusivity or exclusivity, their reciprocity, and their position within the hierarchy. Whereas mediators have interrelationships of contiguity and sequence (the syntagmatic), metaphors are related by reciprocity and substitution (the paradigmatic).

Conclusion

Thestruckon model is a hybrid with a vigor of its own. Its advantages include a comprehensive model for providing an integrated, consistent description of a culture − a description bridging the etic / emic distinction that so divides the anthropological community; a means to transcend the structuralist interest in the structures of a myth, a ritual, a meal, and so forth, and to move to the totality of a culture in terms of its configuration; a [801] way to move beyond or behind the dazzle of detail to achieve a meaningful, insightful understanding of a conceptual system that is analogous to a grammar ~ ethnography; and, most importantly, a practical technique for focusing on the phenomenon of culture, the sine qua non of anthropology.

Overall, the analysis must conform to four criteria that are sufficient to establish the verification of the paideuma. These are deduction, commutability, elegance, and intersubjectivity. The analysis proceeds by means of deduction (movement from the known to the unknown by logical steps) in quest of relations that are commutable (producing the same results by variable sequences: 3+1= 4, or 2x2= 4) and leads to a struckonal paideuma that is scientifically elegant (parsimonious, exhaustive, and coherent) and confirmable intersubjectively (by like-minded researchers).

Astruckonal analysis should not be an end in itself necessarily because each and every aspect of a human community deserves specialized treatment. The role of the analysis of astruckon, rather, is to establish the particular relationships and emanations that characterize the hierarchy of that culture as articulated in terms of its paideuma. In the process, we all will benefit from the reminder that there are human possibilities, that they are somehow limited, and that they form part of a conceptual whole called a culture, the investigation of which remains the intellectual inheritance of the anthropological community, despite changing fads, fancies, and far-gone fascinations.

struckon

Thanks

Like the Meso-American cyclicity of creation and destruction, thestruckon model has periodically died and been resurrected phoenix-like in my consciousness. Throughout, the cycles have been influenced by colleagues and informants of whom only the most creative need mentioning: Robin Fox, Alfonso Ortiz, Marilyn Richen, Gerald Eck, David Spain, Libby Prussin, Nora Dean, John Dunn, Elizabeth Brandt, and Esther Goldfrank.

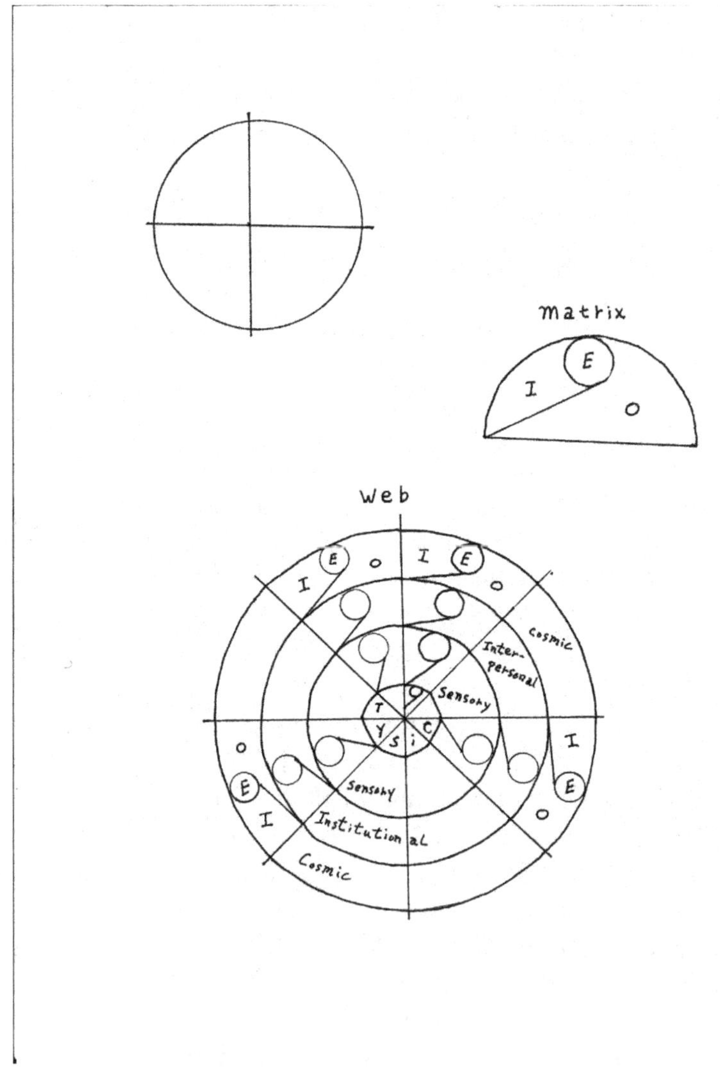

Date of Submission: November 29, 1978
Date of Acceptance: March 24, 1979
American Ethnologist, Volume 6, Number 4,
November 1979: 791-802

Delaware Masking

Abstract

Recent considerations of masking in the Northeast have been strong on Iroquois traditions but weak on others such as those of the Delawares. Far from being moribund, masking beliefs and practices persist among surviving Delawares and shed light on comparable phenomena in other societies.

Comparative treatments of the aboriginal Northeast often have a curiously disjointed quality because the Iroquois, many of whom remained in the region and continue to provide outspoken commentary and criticism, are presented in terms of both past and contemporary perspectives. In contrast, most of the other communities of the Northeast, particularly the Delawares, are represented only by previously published materials.

In the interest of balance, Krusche's (1986) recent treatment of masking will serve as a foil to review and amplify one such example. Although most Delawares are far removed from their homeland, contemporary data from Oklahoma Delawares can contribute to ongoing comparative scholarship.

Frank Speck (1931, 1937), Rolf Krusche (1986), and William Fenton (1987) agree that the Iroquois and Delawares represent the core of the masking tradition in the Northeast, although the comparison has been uneven. While Iroquois practices are well reported, those of the Delaware (Lenape) are not, with the implication that Delaware masking is extinct. Krusche (1986: 2) says that "memory of the mask rites of the Lenape was lost forever." Fenton (1987: 461) says that "to our regret, Delaware masking has not survived with comparable vigor; we know it from Harrington and Speck's salvage of the now-extinct Big House Ceremony and from eighteenth-century missionary accounts." Although masks are no longer made or used in public by Delawares, the reports of their demise have nevertheless been exaggerated. Memories and beliefs persist, even though their physical representations do not.

Among the Iroquois, masking was and is elaborate because the use of masks has been encouraged by the longhouse religion and the market for tribal arts. It is the Delaware tradition, however, that has sometimes been judged to be more important for understanding the regional system, because it had the appearance of great age and simplicity. "Although the Delaware and Iroquois share certain traits of masking, it would appear that the Delaware kept the mask tradition of the Eastern Woodlands in a relatively archaic form" (Krusche 1986: 36). The greater elaboration of Iroquois masks may be [106] rooted in their historic practice of adoption. "Just as the Iroquois have adopted whole peoples, they accepted and reinterpreted customs of neighboring peoples and then elaborated them" (Fenton 1987: 486). Thus, it is possible to find comparable features and parallels in Iroquois usages because they represent an amalgam of Northeastern patterns. In this the Iroquois are like the Hopi, who also borrowed masks and rituals from other Pueblos and so display a masking complexity that was also accessible to outsiders. It has consequently been widely referred to in the scholarly literature.

Throughout the East, masking involved an interrelated opposition between wooden and cornhusk masks, the former carved by men and the latter woven by women (Fenton 1987: 489). The wooden false faces symbolize the forest and game animals, with the braided husks representing the fields and crops. Among the Cherokee, the comparable units were, and are, masks made from wood and from gourds (Fogelson and Bell 1983: 54).

Among the Unami, descendants of the southern Delaware, a single wooden mask, held steady with a hand, was worn over the face by a man impersonating a deity. The deity was known as Masing[W], who had complex associations with nature, particularly deer, forests, mountains, sky, and vegetation. While a deity known as Mother Corn had direct control of crops, wild and domesticated, Masing[W] had more general stewardship of all life, particularly the sustaining foods gathered from nature. He occupied the lowest of twelve levels between earth and heaven. The Creator sat in heaven, lost in thought for all eternity. At each of the levels there was a sky keeper much like Masing[W], although it seems that the more ancient ones, their visages marked with heavy brow wrinkles, were at the higher tiers. Masing[W] was honored in a spring rite (Speck 1937: 49-56), when those attending were fed hominy, but he also played a prominent role during the twelve days of the Gamwing (Big House rite) in October.

Although Krusche (1986: 29) says that Masing[W] was "finally, limited to a more or less brief episode during one of the ceremonial days," recent Delaware elders agreed that while the [b] costume was in use in Oklahoma, it hung just outside the camping area throughout the rite. There, any young man of ability could don it and act the part of Masing[W], visiting the camps to receive gifts of tobacco from frightened children. In addition, *Masinghawlikun* (the fully costumed figure) visited the Big House during practice sessions and during the three days that the hunters were out (Figure 1). Although the Delawares regarded *Masinghawlikun* as a more recent addition to the rite than Masing[W], he was well integrated into its social aspects. Speck's (1931) description, Krusche's principal source, is flawed in this and other particulars because Charlie Webber, his Delaware informant, attended the rite infrequently (Miller 1976).

In all, *Masinghawlikun* is a cosmic mediator who bridges sky and earth, plant and animal, and land and water. This is done through associations with the wooden mask, sapling staff, tobacco pouch, bearskin, and snapping turtle rattle (Miller 1979). His mask was painted half black and half red, symbolic of his mediating quality between night and day, death and life, and men and women. The costume was once kept by a matrilineage responsible for an annual feast in honor of Masing[W]. This was much like the family feasts held for the dolls, otters, and bears that were kept as pets by children (often girls) and their families in legend. The Masing[W] Dance was more elaborate, however, and interlinked with the Football and Green Corn dances that were held to celebrate intervals in the farming year from planting to harvest (Miller 1990).

In counterpoint to the single wooden mask, two husk masks were worn by each of the two men who went around to announce the date for the Green Corn (Maize) rite in the fall. This occurred while the corn was in the milk stage, prior to maturation and harvest. These men were called "excrement daubers" because they smeared a feces decoction upon anyone they met who was not quick to give them a gift. Their errand marked the end of the agricultural cycle and the passage from the old year into the new one. Such times were associated with chaos, which is often symbolized by feces in cultures around the world. A further transition from summer harvest to fall hunting was marked by [108] the celebration of the Gamwing, where female crops and male venison, "both branches of the economy" (Krusche 1986: 8), were exchanged.

Other signals for holding the ceremony in the fall were the appearance of the Pleiades in the night sky and changes in leaf colors. In legend, the seven Pleiades had been Delawares before they rose up into the sky. Thus, Trowbridge's reference to seven *Masinghawlikun* (Krusche 1986: 20) probably involves these stars rather than any of the twelve sky keepers.

Masing[W] was much in evidence in the Big House when the three-day hunt was held during the middle of the Gamwing. But in a sense, he also was managing the bounty of nature brought forth during the entire two weeks of the rite. Delaware elders still acknowledge this, even though the Masing[W] costume and these ceremonies have lapsed for much of this century.

The Masing[W] mask, bearskin costume, and snapping turtle rattle were sold during the first decade of the 1900s (Speck 1931: 14, 43) to the Museum of the American Indian. The other ceremonies lapsed a few decades later, but present Delaware retain knowledge of Masing[W], and some of the elders profess a continued belief in him. While the masks are gone, the meaning remains. The masks, after all, were intended to represent the deity and, regardless of the disappearance of artifactual trappings, the being continues to exist in memory.

Present-day Delawares also have other tangible reminders of their masking traditions. Contrary to the claim that Harrington and Speck "found the last testimony of this old icon cult among the Delaware in Oklahoma and Ontario" (Krusche 1986: 14), a Big House center post with carved faces is located at the Philbrook Museum in Tulsa, only an hour away from where it originally stood. It is also illustrated on the dust jacket of Weslager's (1972) The Delaware Indians, a book owned by many Delawares. Even more to the point, an Anadarko physician, half Delaware and half Kiowa, carved a Masing[W] into a tree stump when he was younger. This image is on display at the Anadarko Delaware tribal museum, where it has helps to keep Masing[W] fresh in Delaware minds, even though this group has replaced Delaware traditions with Caddo ones.

At least one Delaware family among the traditionalists around Dewey, Oklahoma, preserves a support post with a carved face from a prior Big House. These faces are referred to as "other Masing[W]" and they are addressed in prayers as "Grandfather," thus perhaps contradicting the arguments of Speck (1931: 39) and Krusche (1986: 18-20) that Masing[W] and the Grandfathers were separate beings.

The carved faces on door posts represented Sky Keepers, Masing[W]-like intermediaries between people and Creator. Such images presumably had a long antiquity, although the best early account refers to Newcomer's Town in Ohio, in 1766, as described by Rev Charles Beatty: "On each door-post was cut out the face of a grave old man, an emblem I suppose of that gravity and wisdom that every senator there ought to be possessed of (Weslager 1972: 293).

As Oklahoma Unami preserve traditions, so too do the Canadian Munsee, where at least one mask is still in native hands. A few others are held in Canadian museums. Because so few Delaware masks exist in collections (Krusche 1986: 2, 37), mention should be made of the white mask sold by Speck to the Reading (Pennsylvania) Public Museum (#41-284-1). His correspondence files provide background. It is a copy of the one that hung over the west door of the Canadian Munsee-Delaware Big House made by J Henry in 1936. It was pronounced a faithful rendition by Nicodemus Peters (*Nekatcit*).

The white / red masks of the Munsee represent a distinctive color symbolism that contrasted with the black / red colors favored by Unami. Frank Speck apparently owned one of the Munsee masks. However, in a letter of July 1, 1941, Speck wrote "I had the misfortune to lose the red mask (or it may have been stolen from my office)."

In addition to his public role in ritual and ideology, Masing[W] could also appear to singular individuals, such as Reuben Wilson, one of the last visionaries among the Dewey-Copan Unami. Wilson was a carver who produced many images [109] of Masing[W]. His existence challenges the statement that "as a rule the False Faces are more frequently created according to individual dream experiences, an impossibility for the Delaware masks" (Krusche 1986: 35). Indeed, a distinctive house post mask (illustrated in Ewing 1982: 116-117 #62) seems to have been the work of Wilson. When shown pictures of various masks, Delaware elders were quite accepting of such efforts because Wilson had proper supernatural sanction to make them. They are less kind about the masks made by Joe Washington (cf Speck 1937: 82), who was motivated by a need for money and produced things for sale that the elders felt had no Delaware cultural validity. Interestingly, Krusche (1986: 2) reports that Washington's masks are now lost.

Discussion

With these clarifications, Delaware masking can be placed within a wider context. Its origins are both distinctively human and culturally specific. While Iroquois masks are explained in terms of encounters with *Hadu'i*, a supernatural, Delaware masks refer to the beginnings of the world and the axiomatic tensions inherent in its organization.

The face has played a crucial role in the individualization of human beings throughout the evolution of our species. Hence, the creation of masks and facial coverings is probably a universal of the species. Not all societies use masks as such, although all make some use of facial paint and coverings. Facial icons are ancient in North America, as illustrated by many petroglyph sites, finely carved Olmec heads, more recent miniatures from the Lenape homeland, and many other specific finds. Together, these suggest a continental spread and long chronology for stone heads and faces (Wormington 1964: 154-155).

As background of Delaware and Northeastern masking, Krusche (1986: 4) reviewed linguistic and archaeological evidence for Algonquian origins, except for Walker (1975). As a hypothetical schematic, Krusche has argued for a single source for Northeastern masking, rather than the result of an interaction of Iroquoian and Delawarean traditions. "The typical carved [b] wooden masks originated from faces on trees or posts, and that mobility was achieved first by carrying posts in processions, later by detaching the faces, and finally by hollowing them and making eye openings" (Krusche 1986: 1). This association of trees and masks makes good sense in terms of Delaware cosmology, since the progenitor of humanity was a tree, a red cedar, placed by the Creator at the center of the back of a World Turtle. This cedar then reached up to sire the first man and touched the earth to make the first woman. Thus, for Delawares, the trinity consists of three elements. First, there is the Creator, deified Thought, who gave their world coherence. Second, there is Turtle (land / water), the Earth Bearer. Third, there is the cedar tree (earth / sky), deified as Masing^{w}, the bearlike spirit with turtle shell rattle and wooden face who summarizes the cosmos.

Furthermore, as Tooker (1968: 1173-1174) has argued, Delaware clanship may also be involved. She argues that it "may be that there is something in the structure of matrilineal societies that predisposes its members to use masks" and that this "suggests that there may well be basic differences in structure, system of authority, relationship to the supernatural, and world view in general in matrilineal societies as contrasted with certain other types" (Tooker 1968: 1173-1174). Among the Delaware, men are closer to the supernatural than are women. Traditionally, many more men were visionaries than were women. Therefore, it was men who hosted and managed the rituals owned by the matriclans. Appropriately, it was men, interlopers in a matrilineal society, who acted on behalf of the larger community as masked supernaturals.

In the Delaware taxonomy of "living things," deities are characterized as immortals with souls that can speak, alter events and things by thought, and confer power on humans (Miller 1975: 436). As immortals, they function without the extremes of emotion and expression characteristic of mortals. It is therefore appropriate that Masing^{w} and the husk faces were rigid visages, devoid of apparent emotionality.

The link between such fixed-feature coverings and the deities is well illustrated by an [110] incident reported by Juliette Kinzie. "To guard against the burning effect of the sun and the prairie winds upon our faces, I had, during some of the last days of my visit, prepared for each of us a mask of brown linen, with the eyes, nose, and mouth fitted to our features; and, to enhance their hideousness, I had worked eyebrows, eyelashes, and a circle around the opening for the mouth, in black silk" (Kinzie 1901: 236-237). After starting out, they stopped briefly at a homestead outside Chicago, where some natives, probably of Algonquian-speaking tribes were also visiting. "Two Indians were seated on the floor, smoking. They raised their eyes as we appeared, and never shall I forget the expression of wonder and horror depicted on the countenances of both. Their lips relaxed until the pipe of one fell upon the floor. Their eyes seemed starting from their heads, and raising their outspread hands, as if to wave us from them, they slowly ejaculated, '*Manitou*!' (a spirit)" (Kinzie 1901: 236-237).

The seemingly whimsical anecdote from pioneer Chicago suggests that the very nature of the link between masks and the *Manituwak* is their common lack of expression. In the case of fixed demeanors, the intent, therefore, seems to be descriptive of spiritual qualities rather than emotional states. Thus a fixed expression appears to have been an attribute of divinities because it represented eternity. It was a characteristic of masking throughout the Americas, save for the distinctive transformation masks of the Northwest Coast tribes, who nevertheless relied on the expectation of fixity to heighten dramatic impact. There, too, matrilineal societies relied on male maskers, expressive of the link between men and spirits, fathers and children, similarly pervasive throughout the Northeast.

Figure 1. This, the only known photograph of a *Masinghawlikun*, is from the Richard C 67apers in the Kansas Collection, University of Kansas Libraries. Perhaps intended to illustrate his account of the Delaware in the 1890 Census Report, it was never published. Though faded, it portrays the mask, bearskin suit, and snapping turtle rattle used by a Məsing[w] impersonator. (This photo was found by Rodney Staub and called to my attention by James Rementer.)

Delaware Personhood

Abstract

Delaware conception of the "person" (*awεn*) has remained viable among older speakers of this language, both living or recently deceased in Oklahoma, and can be projected into the past using ethnohistoric and ethnographic sources. Delaware personhood is summarized using a generalized life cycle as an outline, allowing for particular variations derived from age and gender. In contrast to previous treatments, which dealt with sociological aspects, symbolic dimensions are especially emphasized and Delaware soul beliefs are clarified. Gender asymmetry is such that man is the generic, inclusive, and unmarked category, while woman is the specific, exclusive, and marked one.

Delaware Personhood:
Oklahoma and Before

Centuries after their contact with Europeans in their Atlantic homelands and despite repeated dislocations, Delawares living in Oklahoma and fluent in their language (Lenape) have retained views of the self or person that are uniquely grounded in their ancestral traditions. Relying on a variety of sources and the insightful reflections of the late Nora Thompson Dean, Lenape elder extraordinaire, this article summarizes data from the Oklahoma Delawares, together with supportive information from earlier times and places. During her lifetime, Nora believed and practiced the tenets of Delaware culture, upholding a tradition exemplified in the data of CC Trowbridge (nd), Truman Michelson (nd), and MR Harrington (nd) but at variance with that reported in the early Delaware research of Frank [18] Speck with Charlie Webber. As such, Nora provided a check and a corrective for much of the classic ethnography.

While Unami or southern Delawares are now largely living in Oklahoma, Munsi or northern Delawares are mostly in Ontario. After dislocation from their coastal and Delaware River locations, most Delawares moved westward into Pennsylvania and Ohio. Munsis branched off from there after the American Revolution. Unamis went on to the regions of modem Indiana, Missouri, Kansas (where many became Christians), Texas, and finally, Oklahoma, where they have been living since the 1860s.

Mary Black (1969) claimed that among Algonquian-speaking cultures the Ojibwa lacked a clear concept of the person. However, Straus (1975, 1976) described Northern Cheyenne notions of the person in terms of a complex dynamic between human and animal components, or reasoned and crazy tendencies. [18] Delawares provide another case example like that of the Cheyenne.

The Delaware Person

Delawares regarded the person (*awεn*) as a blending of various degrees of personal autonomy, respect for others, clan membership, selfless motivation, pleasant attitude, proper upbringing, and subsequent training for productive adulthood. Yet all of these together merely constitute someone defined as "empty." He or she could become full, complete, and socially prominent only with the addition of an immortal ally, a *manitu* ~ supernatural that was friend, protector, guardian, and motivator.

Among both empty and *manitu*-gifted Delawares, two genders were recognized: man and woman. Man was the unmarked, inclusive category, acting like a container; woman was marked, exclusive, and contained. For example, traditional Delaware land use involved concentric rings of activities ranging from women-dominated households and fields to male-frequented forests and trails. During various rituals women formed an inside ring and men the outside one. Only in the Big House, the major religious domain, did women encircle the men as a deliberate reversal to concentrate powerful forces inside the building.

Mediating junctures where men and women shared across their domains involved the (1) heart, the symbolic center of a person; (2) the hearth, where food contributed by men and by women was cooked and eaten together; and (3) the all-powerful Creator, who provided life forms with mind, rational thought based in memory.

A few Delawares believed that the same advice could only be given to a person four times, either volunteered or on request. If an opinion was asked for directly, then it could be given outright. Among other tribes, advice could only be given while someone was being fed, so he or she would swallow the good words and food together. After it was repeated four times, it was assumed the person knew better but chose to do otherwise. [b]

Children, especially those of the distinguished or better families, were raised to manifest responsibility, respect, courtesy, self-discipline, generosity, and social graces. In fact, the children of the most traditional families of the Oklahoma Delawares and related tribes were raised with great strictness, exercising the discipline lacking in lesser families. One man, a Shawnee married to a Delaware, was brought up on a country homestead. Even as a teenager, he had to ask permission from his parents to cross the desolate road in front of their farm. One Delaware woman grew up without ever learning that there were vulgarities in Lenape, because her family shielded her from them and made sure that she was never left alone with playmates known to have foul mouths. Generally, children were closely watched by the elders, and their actions were evaluated in terms of how they reflected individual ability and family pride (or, in some cases, pretense).

The concept and place of the person among the Delawares can best be presented in terms of a standardized life cycle, from conception to death and beyond.

Gestation

Delawares were aware of the connection between coitus and pregnancy, holding life so sacred that sex was only permitted for purposes of procreation. It was never treated, according to Nora Dean, as "a fun thing." Once a child was conceived, the couple practiced continence or sexual abstinence, although this did not apply to relations between a husband and another wife, or, according to Newcomb (1956a: 31), a mistress. Even so, a husband was expected to be solicitous of a pregnant wife and to join with her in the many ritual injunctions she was obligated to follow, especially for a first child. She could never touch meat with her bare hands, eating it instead from a stick. She had to refrain from certain foods, particularly fresh bird and animal flesh, to avoid a bloody delivery. Throughout pregnancy and delivery, she had to monitor her behavior closely. For example, if she looked at a rabbit, the baby might have a hare lip; if she [19] paused in a doorway, she might block the birth passage.

In the aboriginal past, Delawares probably believed that conception began when the mother contributed the blood, the father the bone, and the Creator the spark of life instilling the mind. The Munsi believed that the father was accompanied everywhere by the spirit of his unborn child, whose invisible playfulness frightened away the game. To keep the spirit close and quiet, the father attached a toy to his garments, a miniature bow and arrow for a boy or a tiny mortar and pestle for a girl. He first made and attached one of these, but if his hunting luck did not improve, then he knew the child was of the opposite sex and wore the other toy.

Delivery

In the past, a mother tied a rattlesnake skin around her waist to lessen the pain during labor. Birth took place in a secluded hut, built in anticipation of the birth. Sometimes, a menstrual hut was cleaned and used for birthing. A midwife assisted, or a close female relative with a large and healthy family of her own. Since this woman had produced many healthy children, they provided apt testimonial to her talents, bringing good luck to the delivery. In particular, women who had twins were considered blessed by the Creator and much admired, making them ideal midwives. Delivery was women's business, but exceptions were sometimes made in special cases. Thus, Nora Dean's father was present at her birth, but the actual delivery was handled by a white midwife. Sarah Wilson Thompson, her mother, gave birth to Nora while kneeling, straining against a rope fastened at one end.

After being washed, the baby was usually kept bound on a cradleboard. Old women came to visit every newborn, looking carefully to determine if he or she were a reincarnation. They judged this by whether the baby looked or acted like someone deceased, or carried scars or the marks of ornaments, such as an indentation in the earlobe where an earring had been worn. Sometimes, these visits also served clerical needs. According to Isaac Secondine (nd: 9: 194), "At the time a child was born and [b] we wanted to get them on the Pay Roll [tribal membership roll], there had to be as many as three old Indian men go to the home and certify the child's birth. Then every so often there would be a man come around and register the new born children." However, this federal agent could only register a child if the parents consented. While the Delawares always consented, members of other tribes sometimes rejected enrollment to assert tribal sovereignty and avoid governmental impositions.

Each newborn was given a puppy or other young pet to act as his or her surrogate, taking upon itself any illness, misfortune, or disease destined for the child. Nora was able to name both dogs and cats who had given their lives to keep her healthy.

The afterbirth (Newcomb 1956a: 32 says the umbilical cord) was treated with considerable care because the life of the child was influenced by the manner in which it was deposited. For example, Nora's afterbirth was placed inside a split tree, and, in consequence, she grew up to be straight and dignified. That of one of her brothers was buried in a field, and he became a good farmer. That of another was buried in the forest, so he became an excellent hunter, fisher, and woodsman.

To fool those spirits of the dead intent on luring a newborn away, babies were disguised in adult clothes, and their moccasins had holes in the soles so they could tell the spirits they could not travel far. Strings of deerskin or cornhusks were tied around their wrists "to bind them to the earth." The same type of wristlets were tied on the immediate kin after the death of a relative, providing the person wearing them with a closed, protective ring of safety.

Naming

A child inherited clan membership from the mother. While there were ancient subgroups, apparently based in various locales, three distinct matriclans predominated in

Delaware society. These were associated with air, water, and land. The Fowl was depicted as a bird foot or turkey. The Indented Heel or Turtle was represented as a top-view outline. The Round Foot or Canine [20] was associated with a paw or Wolf. Modern Delawares insist that their ancient villages were each owned by one of these clans, or a named segment. Special bundles and rituals were inherited through these segments and clans, attributing social rank to the family or mainline having responsibilities to conduct such rites and influencing the life course of each new generation.

An infant was called by an age-sex and birth-order term, or by a nickname, until it was reasonably certain that the child would remain with the living. In the past, the child was publicly given a personal name when about five, during a Big House rite or some other ritual with a large audience. A wide range of naming practices has been summarized by Newcomb (1956a: 33), but the principal means rely on conditions of gender.

David Zeisberger, lifelong Moravian missionary among the Delawares, said that the mother might name a child after a physical feature, but this practice was really more appropriate for a nickname (Weslager 1971: 271 #11). Alternatively, the father might dream a name. Old people might be specifically asked to dream a name, receiving wampum as a gift afterward, because their proven longevity was expected to "rub off on the baby, conferring a long life.

Names were never permanent, changing after each momentous or successful event. Harrington (nd) reported that some people took the name of an ancestor late in life, which sounds like an elite practice to honor and glorify their predecessors. While everyone had a name, it was never used in public because it was too closely bound up with personal existence and vulnerability. The only time it was used in public was at a Summoning during the Big House rite, the only sanctuary powerful enough to provide protection. The primary function of a name, unique for each individual, was to permit identification by the Creator.

Around Dewey, Oklahoma, during the 1970s, Nora Dean was the only name giver qualified by the ancient rules. By virtue of her visionary gifts, she would not refuse anyone who requested a name from her, otherwise her power would have become offended and would have left her. Once the request was made, however, she had to wait until a name came to her. In the case of those [b] not entitled or deserving, a name never came. The name had to be received as in a vision, never planned or arranged, and it had to be consistent both with the powers of the giver and with the personality, physique, and talents of the recipient. Sarah Wilson Thompson, gifted by trees, bestowed names that made reference to them. Hence she named her daughter Nora 'Tips of Leaves Rustling As They Touch Each Other + Woman', freely translated as 'Touching Leaves Woman'.

Traditionally, every name had to be unique, allowing for such a vision and idiosyncratic cross-referencing, because it set that person apart within the purview of the Creator. Recently, several younger Delawares out of touch with their traditions have assumed names taken from older tribal roles. Elders have been shocked and worried by this. They said this was asking for trouble by calling the names of the dead and creating confusion among the *manituwak*.

At a traditional name giving, the name received was never spoken out loud until that moment in the ceremony when it was announced to the Creator. He already knew the name, of course, but this served as a reminder of the uniqueness of that particular individual at a special moment in time. The announcement opened a channel between person and Creator, initially following that of the visionary name giver.

Important features of the modern naming ceremony were the presence of daylight, a sacred fire (kindled with flint and steel) for smudging cedar and tobacco, and the repeated invocation of the new name. Earlier, namings differed by gender. The late Tom Wilson, when he was over 80, said that he and his brothers were named by an old man, while his sisters were named by an old woman.

In all, Delaware names indicated the singularity of each individual, special recognition by the Creator, and distinctions of gender. Not only were boys named by males and girls by females, but the names themselves were sex-specific, either by inference or overt markers. Some, but not all, names had endings meaning 'man' (*-lənu*) or 'woman' (*-xk^we*), as Nora's did. Names also imply gender by referring to a male activity or to female associations with plants, flowers, or [21] beauty. Further, each name had to be appropriate for the personality and gender of both the named and the namer.

Childhood

Childhood was a time for focused attention, growth, and training. Children were rarely punished physically. Rather they were trained by being scolded, ridiculed, or embarrassed by their elders if their conduct was unbecoming. Sometimes, they were threatened by mention of "bogeymen," such as Məsing or the Naked Bear. Learning consisted of watching and imitating. Girls played at domestic tasks and helped with farming, while boys played at the chase, marriage, and careers. Crafts were learned by practice. During long winter evenings, tribal lore, family history, and mythology were transmitted as part of the entertainment.

When the first tooth fell out, it was blackened with charcoal and thrown toward the east, accompanied by the Lenape prayer, "Come back soon, I will feed you some white beans," presumably because these were shiny, white, and evenly shaped.

Puberty

At puberty, a girl was secluded in a menstrual hut under the care of an older woman. She was expected to work hard during this time, avoid touching herself with bare hands, and only eat food with a stick. The girl was called "like an owl" because she was secluded in dimness or darkness like this nocturnal bird. At the end of her seclusion, a girl was dressed as a woman and her toys and dolls were taken away. When Nora entered womanhood, she was secluded for several days in a darkened room of the family farmhouse. Afterward, she was brushed with smoke from a red cedar smudge and dressed as a woman. In kindness, her mother let her keep her dolls. During such a period, a girl was likely to receive a vision, but she was not expected to seek one out as deliberately as boys were.

The signal that a boy was entering puberty was an unsteady voice. At that time, he was deliberately ignored, abused, or made to feel [b] unwelcome by his parents. He had seen others receive the same treatment and knew it was time for him to fast and pray for a vision, far away from the community. His training prepared him for this, but the community sometimes took the initiative to force him to leave. His face was blackened by the family so everyone would know not to feed him or offer him hospitality. People had his best interests at heart, although such ostracism made the boy feel badly enough to wander off alone in genuine sorrow. Eventually, a deity (*manitu*) took pity on him with the gift of a vision, song, and career. While away, he might build a conical mat shelter, but otherwise he made himself as "exposed" as possible. Although he was made to feel totally abandoned, an old man (a relative or trainer) surreptitiously watched out for his safety. After several days of hardship, the boy went home to be washed, fed, and indirectly scrutinized. On his return, he might drop a hint to indicate that his quest was successful, or even discuss generalities of his vision with a revered elder, but he was never explicit about his ally because that left him vulnerable to sorcery or spirit theft by a more powerful and selfish person.

Nothing was overtly done or said about any of this, but people closely watched how the child performed any undertakings from then on. Continuous success indicated that he was indeed a visionary. An inept, failing, or lackluster performance could mean either the boy was empty, his ally was determined not to reveal "itself for a time, or, if he had shown pretensions, that the vision was false. A confirmed visionary demonstrated repeated success and lived a moral life free from taint of gossip. If he or she did all of this, eventually they would be asked by a Big House messenger to recite with other gifted young men and selected women at the end of the twelve-day service. Otherwise, people waited patiently for the promised potential to be fulfilled.

The first public acknowledgment of a proven vision came when someone recited at one of the public rituals. Then the general context of the vision was broadly outlined and the general class of deities hinted, but nothing more was specified. Before the Big House reforms of Beata in [22] Indiana (Miller 1989a), portrayals of the encounter were much more mimetic and dramatic. In most cases, it was more likely for a woman who was a good wife and mother to recite at an earlier age than was the case for a man, however moral and respected. Maturity seems to have had more to do with character and responsibilities than with actual age.

Marriage

A successful hunter of old, or a steady and reliable worker of today, was the preferred husband. The most desirable wife was hard working, provident, nurturing, and sensible. In the past, women married around thirteen years of age and men about eighteen, with the elite careful to have their children marry prestigious mates. A spouse could never be a blood relative of any degree, nor a member of the same matriclan. Proper marriages were arranged by both sets of parents, with those of the elite enlisting a go-between to conduct the actual negotiations. Sometimes, a young man was married for the First time to an ancient spouse, because of the care, wisdom, and stability she provided.

Marriage was a secular event, specifically expressed as an exchange of food. The mother of the groom, representing her son, brought meat to the family of the bride. If this was accepted, the mother of the bride, representing her daughter, reciprocated with a gift of corn bread and vegetable products. These exchanges continued between in-laws for the duration of the marriage, strengthening the affinal relationship. A young couple "needed time to get to know each other" so there was a lull between the betrothal and the consummation, sometimes with the couple going off by themselves on what has been called an expedition, vacation, or honeymoon. The traditional chief officiated at elite marriages in Oklahoma, giving a moral lecture to the couple and the guests on the duties and conduct of proper spouses. Nora recalled that the last chief married a couple at the home of the bride, placing a white wampum string around their shoulders to bind them together. Increasingly, however, Delaware couples have married in churches.

Elite men were expected to support more than one wife, an indication of their wealth, prestige, and generosity. Marriages between the young were especially brittle, usually ending in divorce or separation, but this was not always mutual. Colonial records mention Delawares who committed suicide as revenge against adulterous or abandoning spouses. Most often, these were women who ate mayapple roots to make everyone sorry.

As Nora often said, in any successful marriage, binding love was based on many little gestures of mutual caring, respect, and support. In any human society, marriage was a requirement for full adulthood, confirmed by the birth of many healthy children who later took up productive careers. In the event of a barren marriage, children were adopted without stigma, being offered to the couple by relatives or others with numerous offspring. There was a strong belief that children were a special gift from the Creator, cherished and shared by all as a communal joy and responsibility. As they learned the Lenape language and assumed more and more responsibility, they were regarded as increasingly more human.

Adulthood

Adulthood was concerned with the complementary roles of men and women in all tasks, activities, and contexts. Women filled the roles of wife, mother, homemaker, and member of a church or civic club. Many worked in the health and clerical professions to augment the family income, but their strongest sense of personal worth continued to come from the home and family. Delaware men preferred to work outdoors at physically challenging jobs in road crews, the local cement plant, farms, and ranches. Many now hold blue- and white-collar jobs indoors, usually with small businesses or oil corporations based in Oklahoma.

In the past, adults were separated by gender. Women were closely associated with the home, town, and fields, while men were linked to the forests and chase. Once the game was in the home, however, it "belonged" to the woman, while harvested crops "belonged" to the man. [23] Newcomb (1956a:21) observed that women worked communally, but men frequently worked alone. John Heckewelder, Moravian missionary and author, made the acute observation that men worked constantly and women worked intermittently. Their hard and difficult employments are periodical and of short duration, while their husband's labours are constant and severe in the extreme" (Heckewelder 1876:154). Given the sporadic demands of child care, female co-operation, and plant cycles, women had the more varied labors. Men and women also had different styles of clothing and hairdressing, depending on age, status, and event. In the case of murder, the wergild for a woman was twice the wampum paid for a man, ostensibly because she could bear children and, thus, provide community continuity.

Men and women constituted separate political caucuses, although decisions of the women or a woman were announced in public by a man selected to do so. Delawares explain this practice in terms of female modesty and greater concern for family than public policy. When gifted women recited at the end of the Big House ceremony, each was accompanied by a gifted man, probably a clansman. Certainly, both public and domestic space were equally valued and lacked the unequal statuses sometimes attributed to these arenas because of a shared reliance on matrilineality to determine roles and activities (Albers 1989; Mukhopadhyay and Higgins 1988).

Maturity

The old were respected and heeded, largely by virtue of their seniority, tempered by an evaluation of their competence or senility. They were especially regarded if they had grey or white hair (Zeisberger 1910: 76). Many Delawares had black hair all their lives, so grey hair was regarded as an indication of great wisdom. The young were expected to give occasional gifts of wampum, tobacco, and game to the elders, receiving in return their attention, prayers, and knowledge. Because of their great age and continued health, the old had access to the greatest power, which they could use to help or hinder anyone. Zeisberger (1910: 91) illustrated the [b] great significance that age once had for the Delawares in his remark that, during a hunt, the oldest man was automatically the leader and if a dispute arose as to which of several hunters had killed a deer, it was immediately given to the oldest man present.

Among the elders, the most independent grouping was that of "the old ladies," who had full license to drink alcohol, use profanity, and smoke tobacco in a clay pipe with a reed stem. This freedom was their reward for a life of modesty and devotion to husband and family. Like a saint who earned the right "to muck about" with the mundane world after a life of discipline and penance, to "Love God and sin mightily" according to Saint Augustine, so the old ladies were famous for their fun-loving behavior, often lewd and ribald, but nevertheless tinged with authority. For example, if a teenager took to sleeping late in the morning, an old person of the opposite sex would come into the room early and threaten, "Better get up soon, or I'll get in bed with you." This was usually sufficient to produce a more disciplined life.

Death

Eventually, Delawares, as everyone else, came to terms with death. There was no hard and fast line between the living and the dead, no crisp division, so people never lost contact with their ancestors. When a close relative died, the immediate kin put on buckskin wristlets "to bind them to the earth," more accurately, to put them in a safe, enclosed space from which the spirits of the dead would have a difficult time luring them away. When these thongs fell off, each was put on the ground to decompose and return to nature, presumably because they had bound up power during use and this had to be released. Mourners blackened their faces to indicate to others that they were internalizing their remorse.

According to Newcomb (1956a: 39), in the past, a death was announced to the community by a woman hired to do this. The family selected four aides or undertakers, two men and two women, who were not relatives. These washed and dressed the corpse, leaving the hair ungreased, because in life the hair was always [24] lustrous with bear grease. As death was not always final, there was a wake of several days (three days in summer or seven in winter) in the hope the person might revive. People stayed with the body all day and all night to offer support to the family and to prevent any attempted sorcery. During the wake, men played the moccasin guessing game to keep them alert and awake. Finally, the body was taken to the cemetery and displayed beside the grave for several hours before it was lowered into the grave and buried (Newcomb 1956a: 40). In the past, Loskiel (1794: 119) reported that old women dug the grave and Heckewelder (1876: 273) said that women filled it in. A fire was built at the head of the grave for four nights, "to guide the soul on its path," and a small fence was set up around each grave.

Today the Delawares have typical Christian funerals like those of white Americans, but sometimes a family also decides on a traditional one, usually consulting with the Dean family for the proper procedures. The last funerals done completely in this fashion were that of James Thompson, Nora's father, conducted in 1964 after his Catholic service, and that of Nora herself in 1984.

Traditionally, the corpse was dressed in everyday clothes, visited all night during the wake, and buried before noon (when spirits of the dead start to become active). At midnight, guns, formerly arrows, were shot eastward, and at dawn or daylight, they were shot westward to speed the ghost and souls on their way. A person of the same gender, younger than the deceased and not a relative, was selected to stay up all night with the body. Meanwhile, the four undertakers made the funeral arrangements and packed up all of the deceased's clothes into two bundles. These were placed upon a piece of cloth, 2 x 4 ft wide, near the coffin, with tobacco offerings placed on top of each one. After the funeral, the clothes and cloth were given to the two helpers of the same gender. If the deceased were a man, his clothes went to the two men, if a woman to the females.

At a modern Delaware funeral, the coffin is usually opened a last time at the graveside for everyone to file by and say quiet farewells. After [b] the grave is filled in by the mourners, people stand or sit around to visit, avoiding any appearance of haste so as not to offend the dead.

During the last century, Delawares went to Coffeyville, Kansas (where their friends the Dalton brothers were killed), to buy wooden coffins. The helpers either dug the grave themselves or arranged to have it dug. One of them made or arranged for the grave marker. That for a man was a milled 2 x 4 in., six feet long, with a diamond-shaped cut out at the top. That for a woman was a 2 x 4 in. cross, with diamonds cut out at the three upper ends. During the wake, this marker was placed under the coffin braces. Before burial, a small bole was made in the end of the coffin nearest the head and greased with red paint to smooth visits by a soul. Newcomb (1956a: 4) reported that this paint was made from bloodroot. When the coffin was put into the grave, the wooden marker was put against this hole and the grave was filled in. The marker was painted in red with double zigzag lines, forming diamonds, so a soul would have a path to follow when visiting the body. In the past, markers indicated career as well as gender. That of a shaman was hung with his turtle shell rattle, and that of a chief or warrior had painted designs depicting his honors.

Incongruously, Harrington (nd) said that a warrior killed in battle was leaned against a tree and left without formalities, much as Adams (1906: 53) mentioned a boy "treated as one who was killed-simply thrown away." Watomika, a self-identified Delaware who became a Jesuit in the latter 1800s, reported the same in his short autobiography (Miller 1989b). Such hasty disposal may relate to fear of an angry or vengeful ghost, or was intended to deflect its anger toward the enemy.

The Delawares maintain several cemeteries in the Dewey-Copan area, differentiated by kindreds. The one called the Delaware Cemetery includes many of the traditionalists, including the last traditionalist chief, Charlie Elkhair. Rites held in this cemetery tend to be more conservative. There, a body is buried with the head to east, facing up.[10]1 A hole is filed into the head end of a coffin and coated with bloodroot paint (Newcomb 1956a :4). Against it is placed the [25] marker, painted with red Xs in a zigzag pattern, a path used by the souls to and from the body, as illustrated by Weslager (1972: 442).

When Lewis Henry Morgan visited the Delawares in Kansas in 1859, he was told by William Adams, who later became a Baptist minister, that "Last year he made a coffin for an Indian, and his friends made him bore a hole in the head of the coffin, the object being to allow the spirit free egress and regress to and from the body" (Morgan 1959: 56). While coffins are known archaeologically for colonial era Delawares who lived along the Atlantic, the antiquity of the filed bole is not known. Perhaps it perpetuated the open tube sometimes made at the head of prehistoric graves by extracting a pole.

Formerly the chief, now the best friend of the deceased, talked (properly in Lenape) to

---

[10] Other rules applied for other burials. Dogs were buried with heads to the north, facing east.

the body at the graveside, bid it farewell, and told it not to return to trouble the living. The surviving spouse was led around the grave and expected to mourn for a year until the former afflnes either arranged another marriage with a member of their family, through the levirate or sororate, or released him or her from further alliance by providing a complete set of new clothes.

Through much of this century in Oklahoma, a feast was held at the graveside after interment. Large tarps were spread out at the head of the grave and six tubs of food were arranged on them. Everyone was welcome to eat, but the youngster selected to spend the night at the wake was fed as a surrogate of the deceased. After the feast, the clothes and cloth were given to the helpers. Then, everyone drifted away leisurely.

Fred Falleaf (nd) said that people should never return to visit the graves of relatives because the corpse was only a suitcase for the soul, requiring no further attention. When I mentioned this to other Delawares, they strongly disagreed. While visiting cemeteries with the Delawares, it has been only too obvious to me that they have strong emotional attachments to the graves of relatives and friends. This is an important aspect of their bond with the land, called the bosom of Mother Earth. During these visits, I was cautioned to go only in the morning, before noon, when the spirits of the dead were [b] weaker. I was also supposed to feel weak and sluggish afterward, because the dead were so glad to have a visitor that they huddled dose and sapped vitality. Forewarned, I did have such a reaction after my visit to the grave of Colonel Jackson, a famous but dangerous leader and shaman. On occasion, during interviews, when a grave could not be located or a name not recalled, it was assumed that the deceased did not want to be identified, so we left that subject, hoping for a change of heart by the ghost to jog the memory. As protection against too close contact with the dead, mourners and others "washed" themselves in cedar smoke, paying particular attention to the eyes, as these had fixed on the corpse and could transfer mortality to the old, weak, or infirm.

A fire was built east of the head of the grave for four nights to light the path to the afterworld. Later, from time to time, offerings of food were sometimes left on this spot. The belief is that one of the souls does not fully depart the body until the eleventh day after death, joining the Creator in the twelfth level on the twelfth day. Meanwhile, it rests in the body, hovers about the grave, or visits its former kin, homes, and favorite places.

A commemorative feast was held for the dead four days after burial if the deceased were Unami, or twelve days if Munsi. While there were no "full-blood" Munsi in Oklahoma, certain families with Munsi ancestry chose to hold twelfth-day feasts. There was also one family of Winetkok origin, usually simply referred to as Nanticoke, who kept the memory of a third type of burial, although they never exhumed the bones of their dead to celebrate a Skeleton dance. While this bundle reburial rite was never held in Oklahoma, it nonetheless played a significant role in community belief. The Unami and Munsi memorial feasts are still held by certain families, with the favorite foods of the deceased specially prepared and served.

At a Shawnee memorial feast I attended with Delaware friends, food was put on the table steaming hot, but no one ate until it had cooled. This steam was the "essence" of the food and was "eaten" by the dead. By the time family and friends were ready to eat, therefore, the [26] nutrients and "heaviness' of the food had been consumed by the honored dead. As a result, this food never seemed particularly filling. During the meal, everyone had a taste of everything else the dead enjoyed, such as particular brands of gum, chewing tobacco, cigarettes, drinks, and candy. Although this was a Shawnee memorial, Delawares told me it was identical to their own. In addition, a Peyote meeting is now usually held shortly after a funeral, consoling the bereaved by helping them "not to think a lot" about the dead. Otherwise, mourners were likely to be drawn off by the dead (Newcomb 1955, 1956b).

Souls

Previous publications indicate that the Delawares recognized two souls. Nora Dean and Lucy Blalock, however, indicated a third one formed from the blood (Miller 1977). In sum, accordingly, there was (1) a "body soul" localized in the heart, seen by shamans as a tiny person or a spark; (2) a "blood soul," coalescing after death into a sphere that lurked on the earth; and (3) a "ghost," looking like a transparent skeleton and potentially dangerous.

The body soul returned to the Creator, who had provided it in the first place, on the twelfth day, after spending the intervening time visiting favorite locales and people. Some souls also had to spend time gathering up any hair and nail clippings that had not previously been placed in a fire. The blood soul was bound to the earth, hiding as a bloody blob in dark places, often under logs, during the day and wandering about at night. If someone met one of these, death was instantaneous unless they were very powerful. A famous Oklahoma shaman survived such an encounter, but he was left with purple splotches like birthmarks on his legs. I have deliberately refrained from publishing the Lenape word for ghost out of respect for Delaware belief. The word should never be mentioned, but it was given to me for purposes of scholarship during the early hours of daylight when the dead were weakest. Hearing the word "makes the dead cry," and has the possibility of causing disaster if one of them decides to return to chastise the living.

These three souls comprised a related set, those of blood and ghost forming an opposition, mediated by that of the body. The sphere and skeleton were confined to the earth for an uncertain period, eventually decomposing after many years. As the Delawares may have formerly believed blood came from the mother, bone from the father, and thought from the Creator, the blood soul is spherical, womanly, and exclusive, while the ghost is lineal, manly, and inclusive. As the body soul comes from the Creator (in the form of a homunculus ~ spark) and returns to Him, it is inclusive. The combination of all three helped create a living person, albeit an empty one. Becoming a Christian seems to have added another soul to the person, but did not convert or remove other souls. Moravians used the Lenape word for "mirror" to refer to this Christian soul, which traditional Delawares recognize but fmd confusing. Such usage, however, may explain why some Delaware families cover all mirrors in their homes during mourning periods.

Summary

A typical life cycle began and ended among women much as clanship and matrilocal residence defined the major outlines of social identity during life. In the past, a woman assisted the mother in childbirth, represented her children during marital exchanges, announced a death, dug graves, and, foremost, transmitted descent, inheritance, and authority. As women managed the secular, mundane, and biological, so men dealt with the sacred, religious, and transcendent. Women gave and sustained life; men protected and empowered it.

The life of a Delaware person was essentially additive and integrative. Beginning with the combination of blood, bone, and mind, a person was molded by expected roles as a female or male, accumulating appropriate training, experience, and good works. Women led more restricted lives than men, but achieved their own satisfactions in hearth, home, clan, and community. Inherently empty, a person became gifted or whole with the completion of a successful [27] quest and the acquisition of a *manitu* ally. More recently, however, Delawares have acquired a Christian soul to compensate for their basic emptiness.

After a lifetime of further additions, both physical and mental, death came not as an end, but rather as a reversal of the constructive process. Souls and ghosts separated, blood congealed, and bones began the long process of decomposition. Similarly, the artifacts of that life began to scatter and fade from usage, much as the grave posts disintegrated and the grave became overgrown and lost from sight. All that remained was the memory of that person, with associated names and past events, a possibility of reincarnation, and an eternal soul dwelling with the Creator, "the one who created us via thought." At base, then, the essence of a person was thought, fusing with a body at the beginning of life and returning to the Creator at the end, infused with human experiences and benefitting from the aid of supernatural allies. Far from being simply an onionlike construction, the Delaware person was made from the center outwards by the addition of successive ingredients to a forgelike heart, a centering of the person and the locus of thought, emotions, and self both in the past and in the present.

Doll Dance

During recent fieldwork in northeastern Oklahoma, I was given an account of the Delaware Doll Dance by Mrs Nora Thompson Dean, a committed traditionalist and fluent speaker of her native language. Since her account differs from those of Harrington (1921:162-171) and Speck (1937:61-66), I think it important to present it here and to compare it with the published accounts.

There may have been as many as 7 dolls owned by Delaware families in the early part of this century, but at present only 2 are known to exist. Most of the others were buried with their last owners. Of the 2 remaining, 1 was sold to a private collector and another hidden away. Pictures of the doll that was sold show it was female with wooden head and body and a complete woman's wardrobe. I would like to publicly thank James Rementer for showing me the pictures. Even now the dolls are regarded with mixed fear and respect. Mrs Anna Brown Parks told me a terrifying story in which her father witnessed his mother's doll leaving its trunk, walking out of the house and returning before dawn. Mrs Dean mentioned that when dolls were taken from their trunks to prepare them for the annual ceremony, their moccasins were found to be worn and the hems frayed from their nocturnal journeys. The dolls were considered to be alive, with a will of their own. Female dolls were addressed as grandmother and male dolls as grandfather. What follows is Mrs Dean's description of the ceremony.

<u>Origin</u>: The Doll Dance began because Delaware parents went to a Stomp dance and left their children together in one house under someone's supervision. The children decided to have their own Stomp dance with dolls made out of sticks. Later, one of the little girls got sick and the doll dance was started to cure her, and was continued until about 1933. Each of the dolls required the Doll Dance annually. The purpose of the dance was to placate the doll from sending further illness among the Delaware and their children.

<u>Preparations</u>: The Doll Dance was held in the spring after planting, when leaves budded on the trees. Mrs Dean mentioned that one Doll Dance was held in late April or early May, because she spent the day of the dance harvesting onions, an activity specific to that season. Several days before the dance, the doll and its owner visited a well respected woman of the tribe. The doll was left with this woman to be cared for and made a complete wardrobe of doll clothes for the next year. Mrs Dean's mother, Sarah Wilson Thompson, was given this [81] honor twice. About a week before the dance, the doll owner also selected the leading man and woman dancers and someone to eat for the doll at the feast after the 12 dances. Just before the dance, an area was cleared, a fire made, a canvas tent erected and 2 forked poles with a cross beam set up near the fire (see diagram).

<u>The Dance</u>: The dance began just before dusky dark when the speaker, usually Charles Elkhair, the last traditionalist chief, stood in front of the tent entrance, facing east, and addressed the people. He explained the origin of the Doll Dance and exhorted the people to live well and to be friendly to each other. His talk lasted about half an hour. As he spoke, he turned slowly to the north and south taking in his audience, who sat on half log seats arranged in an oblong. At a later time, board benches were substituted. When the speaker finished, the two drummers began the Doll Dance songs.

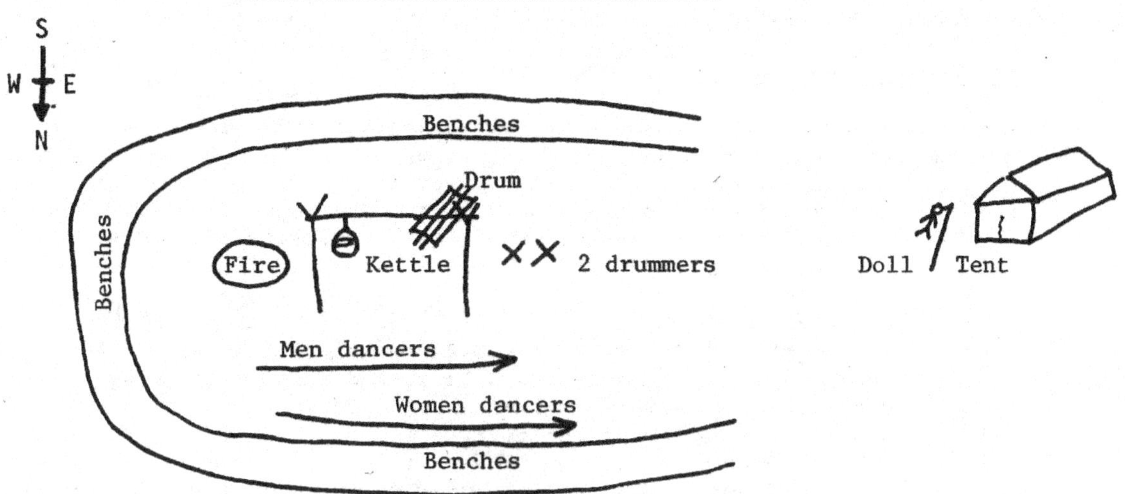

(After a sketch by Nora Thompson Dean. Not to scale)

The drum used was a folded deer skin with the hair inside and two slats tied to the top and two tied across the bottom. The drum sticks were flat and plain. The drum and sticks were exactly like those used for the first eight days of the annual Big House Rite, pictured in Speck (1931: 71, figure 19; figure 22). The drum was rested on the west end of the cross beam, and a pot of food hung on the east end.

Before the dance the doll, or dolls were suspended from five foot sticks stuck in the ground before the tent entrance. When the drumming began, the leading man and woman dancers took up the sticks with the dolls attached. Only men carried the male dolls and only women the woman dolls The face of each doll was painted, red lines for the males and a dot on each cheek for the females. None of the humans wore face paint. Mrs Dean does not remember any doll dances held only for male dolls. Rather she remembers dances for a female doll or for both a male and a female doll. Analogously, she remembers [82] that the required twelve dances alternated between those with only women dancers and those with both sexes dancing. The men formed an inside circle and the women an outside one. During each dance the doll owner stood before the tent. Each Doll Dance song had several pauses during which the doll was passed backwards to the next dancer in line. When the dance ended, the stick holding the doll was returned to the spot beside the tent where it was retrieved when the next dance began. After the twelve dances a feast was held at about midnight.

<u>Feast and Bread Throw</u>: Before people were served, the speaker prayed. Then everyone who could brought up bowls and were served corn gruel from the kettle by the leading woman dancer. The aged and sick were served. As everyone ate, the person designated previously ate for the doll. At the end of the feast, the singers were given wampum for their help. A yard of wampum was the ideal but sometimes there was not enough wampum for this. Then the speaker announced that the rest of the night was devoted to social dances. These dances stopped at daylight before the sun appeared. Some men scattered leaves on the western edge of the dance area. The doll owner and family stood before the tent with a bushel filled with tiny loaves of corn bread about six or eight inches long. Mrs Dean described them as oversize biscuits. These loaves were made from the fine meal sifted from the corn pounded in a mortar for the feast gruel. The loaves were apportioned between the family members, who placed them in aprons or

squares of white cloth. The family then cried *wee'hee'* twelve times and threw all of the loaves on to the leaf covering. People scrambled to get as many loaves as possible. The most fortunate person got the loaf called the Bear. The Bear was larger than the others and was modeled as a bear effigy. It had a string of wampum about its neck and other beads baked inside. Because of this bread throwing, the Doll Dance was also known as *ahpona aspanihin* = "to throw up the bread." When all of the loaves were claimed the dance was over and everyone went home.

Comparisons

Since this account is more complete than either Harrington or Speck, comparison with these is instructive. The comparison will follow the subheadings used in the description of the Doll Dance.

Origin. Harrington refers to stick dolls as does Mrs Dean. Speck, however, mentions corn husk dolls and associates the dance with placating the offended Corn Mother. Harrington and Mrs Dean say that it was a spring dance. Speck calls it a fall dance, which is the case for the Monsi Delaware Doll Dance.

Preparations. Mrs Dean indicated that there were several Doll Dance grounds, with seats arranged in an oblong. Harrington refers only to a square dance ground. Speck does not specify the dance area. Harrington says that the dance required two men workers, a speaker, dance leaders, a hunter, and two singers. Speck lists a man and a woman lead dancer, a fire keeper, and two singers. Speck also makes reference to new clothes made for the doll. Mrs Dean lists a doll dresser, lead man and woman dancers, a speaker who is chief, an eater for the doll, and two singers. All three sources confirm the positions of speaker, dancers, and singers. I would [83] add the doll dresser and doll eater as necessary to the dance. The other positions were probably filled by men who volunteered their services for the task at hand but probably not the dance itself.

The Dance. For Harrington the dance began in the midafternoon and for Speck sometime in the evening. Mrs Dean specified dusky dark. All three agree that the drum was a folded deer hide and the drum sticks were plain, that the men danced as an inside circle and the women as an outside one, and that the doll was carried on a stick for twelve dances. However, Speck has men and women dancing in alternation, each taking the doll for six dances. Harrington has the men and women dancing with the doll. Since both anthropologists ignore the consequences of male and female dolls being danced, I would believe Mrs Dean that only men carried the grandfather doll and only women carried the grandmother doll. Harrington and Mrs Dean mention that the doll was passed back during a dance.

Feast and Bread Throw. Harrington ends the dance after the feast and mentions neither the social dances nor the bread throw. Speck includes both. However, in addition to the Bear he includes a large load representing a male corn spirit. Since corn is always called Mother this is rather startling. Further, Speck has the bread eaten there, which Mrs Dean found humorous since the loaves were so hard they had to be soaked before being eaten or alternatively steamed and fried.

Conclusion

Mrs Dean's account is by far the most complete and personal. It has the detail and directness of the participant that she was. Despite its incompleteness, the Harrington account is closer to hers than that of Speck. I had an opportunity to specifically check the Speck account with Mrs Dean after she had given me her own. She specifically denied ever having seen or heard of turtle shell rattles, six men and six women leaders, a tarpaulin, or a male corn spirit effigy ever being used in a Doll Dance.

In seeking the source of the Speck discrepancies, I focused on Mr Charles Webber, Speck's Delaware collaborator. I single out Webber rather than Speck because Webber sought out Speck in Philadelphia and thus initiated and focused the research. There are two factors that seem to have influenced the Webber account. First, while he grew up in northeastern Oklahoma among Unami Delaware speakers, his family background was Monsi Delaware. He shows this background in his fall placement of the Doll Dance, rather than in the spring when it occurred among the Unami. Second, none of the four surviving traditionalist Delaware over sixty-five can remember Webber regularly attending ceremonies. One 84-year-old man, in explaining lapses in his memory of the Big House Rite, volunteered that he and his friend Charley Webber only went a few times to look on. While Webber was not a committed traditionalist, several members of his family were and it was presumably from them and others that he got his information secondhand. It is also important to point out that Webber is recalled with considerable fondness by many Delaware. He was well liked personally, but traditionalists deny that he had any authority to speak about Delaware religion. [84]

For these reasons, I regard the account by Mrs Dean as the most accurate and reliable. It is possible that slight variations occurred in the Doll Dance, since it was essentially a family rather than tribal rite. However, the consistent use of Charles Elkhair or previous traditional chiefs must have standardized it. In short, the account given by Mrs Dean represents a significant contribution to Delaware research.

A Last Delaware Doll Dance:
An Eye-Witness Account by Vincenzo Petrullo
Jay Miller, ed

Background: This account is based on a typescript of this ritual drafted in two versions by Dr. Petrullo and edited with commentary by Dr Miller. Dr Petrullo (2 January 1906 - 23 February 1991) is well-known in the Delaware literature for his published dissertation, *The Diabolic Root* (1934), a study of peyotism among the Delaware. While he was engaged in that fieldwork, he was privileged to contribute ($5, $7) to and witness the last Doll Dance on 29 August 1930. During his stay, he lived in the Washington household and so was familiar with Joe Washington, the master of ceremonies at this rite, whose son Fred was about his age. Further, Charlie Elkhair, the last traditionalist leader, who died in 1935, was still involved.

After his Delaware research, Petrullo undertook research in Brazil and Venezuela representing the University of Pennsylvania Museum. Later, he supervised WPA archaeology programs during the Depression, and began a career in international relations at Colgate University. A sturdy Sicilian, he began to take his leave of anthropology after attending Margaret Mead's "Italian Character" seminar, which lie found disagreeable. As Jane Howard (1984: 268) wrote "All Mead's life she had had a weakness for one-line generalizations about nationalities, as about practically everything. Foreign-bom, Petrullo's career was harmed during the McCarthy era. He later worked as a consultant to industry. This article and (the set of photographs he took at the time) testify that he has sustained an interest in Delaware research into his eightieth year.

Doll Dance
Vincenzo Petrullo, Lansdowne, Pa, 11 Jan 1937

In late August of 1930 the Delawares around Dewey, Oklahoma were deeply concerned over the prolonged period of drought that had destroyed their meager crops and was destroying [2] their few cattle. In characteristic Delaware fashion, they held themselves partly responsible for this phenomenon of nature. They believed that the lack of rain was a natural consequence of their failure to hold their traditional yearly ceremonies. This reasoning was in conformity with their belief in the obligatory nature of ceremonial observance. They hold that the Creator established a world pattern which prescribes for every form of life a mode living and behavior. For instance, each variety of bird was given a song. If they were to neglect singing it, the pattern would be disrupted with regretful consequences for the entire world. Likewise, each people were enjoined to perform certain ceremonies; their failure to do so will bring calamity not only on themselves, but upon all people. In this case, since Delaware had been remiss in holding their rites, the land was visited by a drought affecting everybody. Their poverty and tribal disorganization would seem ample excuse for this condition of affairs, but not to the Delaware. Accordingly, hearing that the Doll Dance would bring rain, I made available a small sum of money for the purchase of meat and maize and to pay the singer. It is of some worth to note that three days after the ceremony, it rained gently.

There existed four dolls at Dewey. Three of them were owned by Mrs Beaver of the Turtle "clan" and the other one by Mrs Falleaf of the Wolf "clan". Two dolls had been passed down through her family to Mrs Beaver, but the third was a "stranger" doll, no one knowing its origin. All of them were about 8 inches tall, dressed and painted in the Delaware ceremonial style. They wore silk shirts, skirts, and ornaments. The male doll wore trousers. Decorations included silver wire earrings, broaches, wampum necklaces, and braid ties. They were painted red, including the hair, with the exception of the male doll which had the right side of his face painted black on the right half of the face and red on the other half as well as the head. The male owned by Mrs Falleaf was more elaborately painted and had legs, lacking on the other three, dressed in moccasins.

Both owners kept their respective dolls carefully packed away in box trunks, and only [3] handled them with intense veneration. Each expressed a desire to have them preserved from falling into profane hands. The only solution current among them was to have the dolls buried with them.

The dance was held under direct family sponsorship with the active participation of the "clan" to which the owner belongs. In this case, it was decided to have Mrs. Beaver, the possessor of three dolls, hold the dance. Accordingly, the Turtle "clan" rallied around her. However, the other ceremonial groups may help if they care to, although they are excluded from the dance itself. The present day disorganization of the tribe and the loss of culture forced two concessions to be made by the Turtle clan. Elkhair, a Wolf clansman, was the only individual credited with knowing how to conduct the rite from beginning to end, and his nephew, Joe Washington, was the only one thought capable of preparing the paraphernalia and acting as master of ceremonies.

The actual ceremonial day was 24 hours, from sunrise to sunset, but preparations for the event occupied the previous day. Formerly, a hunter was sent out for deer, but since it became impossible to find game, beef has been substituted, cattle falling within the Delaware concept of "clean" animals. The burden of this work fell upon the master of ceremonies. He busied himself clearing the dance ground, a circular space with logs arranged around it for visitors to sit on.

He prepared the paraphernalia: the drum, drumsticks, firesticks, dollsticks, and the game pole on which the meat was to be hung. The drum consisted of a dry deerhide folded on itself two or three times, tied with deerskin thongs under which were inserted several sticks. The drumsticks were flat, slightly curved. The upper surface of each bore a face carved in high relief. The stick with the face painted entirely red was considered female, and the other bearing the face painted right-half red and left-half black was regarded as male. These drumsticks were like those used for the Big House Ceremony. The firesticks and dollsticks were merely sharpened and cleaned. The former were pokers; the latter were about three feet long and used for holding up [4] the dolls tied to the top. The game pole was a sapling stripped of bark with several branch stumps left on. Since only "pure" food could be eaten, only maize loafs, in addition to the beef, were served.

The master of ceremonies had other duties, besides preparing the dance ground and objects. During the dance, he walked about with a staff keeping order and, at times, acting like a cheerleader. He also tended the fire. The only other official was the singer, who received an obligatory ceremonial payment of $1. Formerly, he would have received one yard of wampum. In this case, the singer was John Longbone, who requested that Elkhair assist <u>him</u> with the songs, claiming that he might forget some of them otherwise.

At sunrise, the fire was lighted from a flint-steel spark. The Delawares insisted that everything connected with the rite has to be "pure". Fire produced from matches is an European product and so is "impure". Matches could not even be used to light individual's cigarettes during the rite. Formerly, a fire drill would have been used. The game pole was erected at the east end of the clearing, while at the west end where three tents arranged side by side. The middle one housed the dolls, who were tied to sticks stuck into the ground in front of the doorway. The tent to the north served as night-before sleeping quarters for the women sponsoring the dance. The southern tent provided quarters for clansmen. Only social activities occupied the day. Visitors began to arrive, including Delawares, Cherokees, Creeks, Quapaws, and even Osages from a hundred miles away. The Delawares have the reputation for possessing "powerful" ceremonies and being wiser in a more deeply religious way. When allowed, other tribes like to attend them. During the night, whites from Bartlesville also came to watch, showing respect for the ceremony.

In the late afternoon, the meat, after being allowed to hang on the game pole for a short time, was put into pots to be cooked over the sacred fire. The women had been busy since before sunrise pounding kernels of maize into flour. At noon, they made this into maize cakes. [5]

There was no ceremonial feast in the evening, but lots of time was spent talking and visiting.

At sundown, the fire was enlarged and the dolls planted in front of the tent, with the male on the north side and the female "stranger" on the south side. The other female, the proper mate to the male, was in the center. Elkhair made a speech in which he described the purpose of the ceremony and warned us not to participate in the dance until the Turtles had fmished their Itwo prescribed sets. The singer than took his place at the east end of the fire, in front of the drum resting on a waist-high platform. With one of the drumsticks, he accompanied himself on the drum. Elkhair joined in, the two singing in unison as each used a drumstick to keep time on the drum. The participants formed two lines, an inner one of men and an outer of women, each headed by a member of Mrs. Beaver's family. She herself led the line of women. Mrs. Beaver and the woman behind her each picked up a female doll and the leader of the men picked up the male. They danced around the fire, shuffling counter-clockwise.

At the end of the song, the singers moved the drum to a platform on the west side of the fire and they sang again to resume the dance. The drum alternatively occupied the east and west sides during four songs, which composed a set and allowed a rest period. During this interval, the dolls were placed at the west end of the fire, facing east. At the start of the second set, they were carried around in the same fashion as previously, but now the members of each line took turns carrying the dolls. Altogether four sets were sung and danced, carrying the ceremony well beyond midnight.

Then the master of ceremonies announced that the sacred dance was over and the social dancing was to begin. Anyone wanting to join in was welcome. The dolls were again stuck in the earth in front of the tents, the paraphernalia was stored inside, and the visitors entered the grounds. Several men, among them a Quapaw noted for his singing voice, immediately began singing and beating on the drums they had brought along with them. Many of the visitors accepted the invitation and urging from the master of ceremonies.

At sunrise, Elkhair made another speech. At its conclusion, Mrs Beaver tossed handfuls of maize cakes into the air for everyone to pick up. One of the cakes was supposed to contain a bead of wampum and whoever found it was supposed to be especially blessed by the dolls. The meat was then passed around in the cooking kettles, and everyone was asked to take a piece with his-her bare hands. No knife or fork was permitted to be used. This feast marked the end of the ceremony.

This account shows discrepancies with the published material on the Doll Dance and other Delaware ceremonies. The right has not been analyzed critically, rather the aim has been to provide a record of the actual manner in which one such dance was performed. Some discrepancies must be due to the erosion of the ancient form and lapses in memory among the participants. This version was not that of one of the usual annual performances. It was instead a specific request for rain. For such a plea, it would be natural for Delaware to combine several ceremonies and even to include foreign elements. Being engaged in researches on Peyotism at the time of the performance, it seemed best not to distract my friends by asking them too many questions about another set of beliefs.

Discussion

By comparison with Miller (1976) on the Doll Dance from elder Nora Thompson Dean, Petrullo's account agrees with those of MR Harrington and Nora Thompson Dean, both of whom challenge the correctness of the classic account published by Frank Speck from information supplied by Charles Webber (Miller 1979). My earlier report that the last dance was held in 1933 obviously stands corrected to 1930.

Of particular note is the continuing regard for the culturally "pure" quality of meat, maize, and fire. Delaware cosmology set the orientations. The three dolls were arranged, in front of the middle one of three tents, with the male on the north and the females on the south.

Women are associated with South, the direction addressed in prayers as "Grandmother". At this dance, however, the women used the north tent, the dolls the middle one, and the men the south one. This arrangement of tents parallels that of the "ushers" at the Delaware Big House Rite (Gamwing). At the Big House, the three tents of the men ushers were on the south side and the three of the women on the north. Importantly, their duties were exactly reversed inside the building, men for the north and women for the south, because it was a microcosm of the universe. Uniquely detailed by Petrullo is the alternating placement of the folded drum on braces, platforms, or scaffolds on either side of the fire during each song series.

Petrullo is particularly good on the description of the face painting of the dolls, shifting of the drum, and the "clan" basis of the rite, especially for the first set of 12 dances. His account is closest to that of Nora Dean, a traditionalist who probably participated in the rite described herein. Together, their accounts tell us much about the persistence of Delaware beliefs into this century.

Women's Dance: Origins and Expressions

Abstract

The Women's Dance stands out among the other Woodlands "social dances" because only women crowd before the singers and occupy the line moving around the central fire in the hallowed square ground. For the other dances, the names and actions appropriate to each of these festive night events clearly indicate that each is dedicated to another fellow being (by species or tribe) in their cultural universe. The origin saga for the Women's Dance, reported here for the first time on the basis of two versions provided by a Caddo-Delaware elder, shows a link to the Orpheus motif as a failed plea to return a mother from the dead. Richly meaningful to the communities that maintain the dance, these women's dance traditions also say much about the solidarity of women throughout Native North America.

Today, about 4000 Caddo have their tribal headquarters near Binger, north of Anadarko, Oklahoma, where they have lived since fleeing Texas in 1859. Among the few elders still speaking Caddo (as well as Delaware and other native languages) in the 1980s, the daughters of the late Chief Enoch Hoag, Lillie Hoag Whitehorn and Esther Hoag Homovich, were particularly helpful in providing continuity with the Caddo (and Delaware) past (Miller 1996). That one family, albeit a chiefly one, could represent so well two such diverse traditions bespeaks the catastrophes of European land hunger and violence.

The Delaware (Lenape) homeland was the namesake river of the Northeast. They were divided, at least, into the Monsey to the north and the Unami to the south. A distinct coastal division quickly succumbed to diseases. Three matriclans were and are known as Wolf, Turkey, and Turtle, but these are likely the surviving triple phratries of many named clans. Driven successively westward from New Jersey to Ohio, Indiana, Ontario, Missouri, Kansas, Texas, and Oklahoma, Delaware communities still live in Wisconsin, Ontario, and Oklahoma. In Oklahoma live both the main body of Unami (Eastern Delawares) and a second group of Unami (Western Delawares) who had allied in Texas with the Caddos.

The prehistoric Caddos were the westernmost of the Mississippian mound builders, with an array of priests, mounds, and ranked towns. Once the aboriginal occupants of major tributaries, Caddos suffered greatly from European-derived epidemics, which took a heavy toll. Survivors relocated to form confederacies such as the Cadohadacho at the great bend of the Red River in the southwestern corner of Arkansas, the Natchitoches of Louisiana near Shreveport, and the Hasinai along the Neches drainages of East Texas. Neighbors included the Natchez and Tunica, other important mound temple using nations. Nearest Osage enemies, the Cahinnio Caddo along the upper Ouachita River concentrated into a single town of 100 cabins (near Camden, Arkansas) by 1687, but eventually joined the other confederacies.

Caddoans did not have clans, though their priests and doctors were organized into specialist guilds named for animals. Very numerous, communities included graded economic, social, and religious ranks. Kinship was bilateral, and residence matrilocal, with village endogamy. In keeping with this complexity, the Caddo language uses polite forms indicating rank and status that include the title of *sah*, translated as Ms or Mrs to indicate a woman, and *tsah* as Mr.

The importance of women is well illustrated by the epic about the creation of Moon

(Neesh), the Caddo culture hero. A mother and her two daughters were living together when the pregnant one was killed by a monster and a drop of her blood was nourished into the miraculous birth of Moon. In time this family went to live in the sky. As distinct from the usual practice, Caddos address Thunder as "grandmother" (below). They call the Earth "mother," but do so using a kin term borrowed from the Osage to mean "my own mother."

Grandmother Thunder was not alone. Both Thunder and Lightning were once linked with twin boys, the sons of the Creator, called the *kokonikis ~ koninisi* ("little ones"). They were believed to occupy a single or double building containing a central fire and two small storage trunks. The Spanish called the priestly leaders of the Hasinai Caddos the *shinesi*, probably derived from the title *Tsah Neesh* ("Mr Moon"). While other town priests had temple mounds, only the *grand shinesi* had this twin's shrine near his main temple. It was burned down among the Hasinai during an attack by Yowani Choctaw in 1714.

While Caddos today perform the Women Dance, its origins are set among the Delawares, for whom the Thunders are a group of young and old males.

Choreography

Woman's Dance is one of the named social dances, each with special song texts and movements. In the past, these were distinctive of community and tribe, but they are now being lost in favor of more generic Stomp Dances. As the name implies, they include all the community – women, men, and children. By general understanding, each of these dances honors and propitiates the named species or entity (e.g. Jackson and Levine 2002 for Garfish). Among the most specialized, only females participate in the Women's Dance. It occurs among Woodland tribes (Delaware, Shawnee, Kickapoo, Sauk, Seneca-Cayuga (Mingo)), as well as those like the Caddo who are influenced by participation in this network.

In their remarkable history of the Hasinai Caddoan Confederacy, Newkumet and Meredith (1988: 46-50) divide the topics among chapters that are named for illustrative social dances. Chapter VI is Women's Dance: Family Relationships. Two dozen songs occupy phases either of standing or shuffling near a drum or of double-stepping counterclockwise around a central fire. Women sing with a drummer as well as alone. At the very end, men join in, each facing a woman partner and dancing backwards until their positions reverse.

Donald Ahdunko (1926-), a Delaware-Caddo, has had 400 songs in his repertoire recorded for posterity by Tom Blanchard (http://members.tripod.com/~BlanchardT/, accessed by Dr Jason Jackson on 11/3/2003). His Woman Dance, done exclusively by women moving counterclockwise, has three distinct parts – "swing and sway," "back and forth" and "dancing." The women actively participate in the singing during the fires. Ahdunko vaguely recalled a fourth part that once allowed men to join in (above).

Shawnee call all of these "Nighttime dances" (Howard 1981: 309-312, photos Plates 39, 41, 44, 45). At the White Oak ground in 1970, Women's Dance began the all night festivities, lasting from 9pm to 8am. The Women's had three variants – straight, cluster, side. For straight, women are in single file, circling the fire counterclockwise, stepping toe-heel left, toe-heel right. For cluster, the women form rows facing a drummer seated in the middle of one side, singing along with him. For side, also called "dove" or shuffle, women in a ring face toward the central fire, balancing back on the heels and swinging the toes out at 45 degrees to the right, balancing again, swinging the heels out at 45 degrees to the right, and so on. Iroquois women are famous for their skill at this feat, known as *Enskanye*.

The Delaware versions have been called row, shuffle, and file dances (double tapping twice left then twice right (LLRR)), where "The head dancer may clowningly bob and pirouette" (Roark-Calnek 1977: 247). Texts "may combine vocables and words which often have the sense of courtship or sexual joking. Two old Absentee Shawnee songs went: "You fight with your woman, I wish it was me," and "I'm going with you wherever you go, even if it's looking for horses" (Roark-Calnek 1977: 247).

Literally called "the answer for the woman," this dance was described by Nora Dean, the consummate Unami Delaware elder, as having five phases accompanied by drum and rattle (Adams 1977: 111). These are straight ahead, twisting the torso from side to side; sideways shuffle; short steps in file; sideways steps; and cluster moving back and forth, singing "alewi kiluna" (We're the greatest). The actual sequencing may vary depending on the drummer and head dancer. Adams (1977: 131, 142-155) provides a summary analysis of Woman Dance Songs, as well as a transcriptions that include four by Lillie Whitehorn (Adams 1977: 143, 150, 154, 155).

In general, therefore, Women's Dance has three phases. The first has the women clustering around a water drum struck by a male singer. The second has the women shuffling back and forth. The third has the women dancing in file, led by elders that moved by double taps of each foot around the inner edge of the square lit by a central fire. Animated by a sense of fun and good cheer, these women lure the soul back among them. In an occasional fourth part, men and women face off and pivot in each other's directions, confirming the role of couples in the continuity of the group.

In all, the drum presumably evokes the sound of Thunder (below). The cluster summons the deceased mother, the shuffle anxiously awaits her arrival, and the line in file provides an opportunity to entice her to materialize among them and rejoin her family and abandoned baby. This was never to occur physically but instead only in spiritual terms.

Origin of the Women Dance:
Three Versions by Lillie Hoag Whitehorn

On two separate occasions, drawing on different sources, Lilly was taped by Jay Miller telling this epic in English. In 1979, she told it in Lenape, and a translation by Bruce Pearson and Jim Rementer was kindly provided by them. The first English version, attributed to Lillie's older sister, Josephine, identifies the killing force as Thunder and sets the pattern number at 3. The call of a turkey sets the action in motion. The later one by her mother, told properly in the Spring context of these events, identifies the force as Lightning and the pattern number as 4. This latter has more to recommend it as accounting for more of the features of this dance. The translation adds considerable detail about the type of hoe, the mother's constant supervision of her boy, the blackening effects of the blast on the woman's body, the use of a gourd rattle to hold her soul, and the formations of the dance by women in double line and in a circle to bring her back.

12 Dec 1986, Attributed to Josephine Hoag

One time, there was a couple. There was a couple. There was a young man and a young lady. They lived by themselves, kind of away from the folks. Just a little ways.

It was getting along about toward Spring. Maybe it was early Spring, when the corn was growing, just getting good. It rains all the time.

They had a little baby boy learning how to crawl. It was a boy. He could crawl and sit, but he could not walk yet.

Then, one time, this man, he heard a turkey. He heard a turkey, distant, you know.

He went and got his bow and arrow. He was going to get that turkey. He went out. At the same time, I guess, it was going to rain. He went out, anyway.

They were still in there. These two were still asleep. Finally, that lady, she got up. She thought to herself, she would go out to that patch while the baby was asleep. She could go out there and finish that hoeing. She had hoeing to do. That was early, early in the morning, before breakfast, while that man is gone out, but she would be back in time. She left the baby there and she went out. Her garden patch was just a little ways from there. She had squaw [field] corn there. They call it łənχaskʷim[11]. She went out there and got her hoe. (Well, them days, they didn't have no [iron] hoe. They used to use deer joint, jawbone of a deer. They used that for to scratch the ground with. They hoe with it.) She went over there.

Meanwhile, she seen there was a cloud coming, coming up. She thought she could beat it back before it got there. But that was too quick for her. But, anyways, she worked a little ways. When she worked a little ways, that cloud was over her already. (I've seen this done. Well, sometimes rain will, it'll come up so fast that you don't know [until it hits you].)

It stormed and it thundered. It thundered. Maybe so many times. One time there, that thunder hit her, killed her. She was hit back here on her neck, burned all over, on clear [down] to her back. She was laying there.

In the meantime, this man, he come back to their place. He seen that baby. He was crawling outside. He was crying. He was all wet. He [Father] picked it up, and he thought there was something wrong. He picked it up and he looked in there [inside the wikwam]. Nobody. Gone. He was wondering where she went to. She never did do anything like that. So, he gets the baby.

In the meantime, it was kind of sliding down, this rain [falling on a slant]. He went over there. He tracked it, and he couldn't see nothing. He went a little ways. Some places it showed where she went. Then he come up to her. She was lying there. She was dead. She was burnt. Lightning had struck her. He just cried.

He come back. He left from there and took the baby to the village, to his folks, and he told 'em what happened. And so they come. (Now, this is just a story.)

So, he come back. He got that baby over there, and he come back. And the others, they told 'em about it and they told those putchel [pučəl = attendants, ushers]. They got them to notify the people and notify the chief. They come and they got her and they took her to where they live. They brought her in. Then they all got together. They got all together with the chief and everybody in the village there. They were discussing about what happened.

This one man, he tells the chief, "I could, I could bring her back. (This was way back in ancient times.) I could bring her back. Only one thing. You all got to do like I tell you. If you do wrong, you'll be missing somewhere, and I can not do it no more. That's going to end it all. Just that one time." They talked about it. He said, "I have a gourd, a little bitty gourd. I keep that." (I don't know, maybe that's what Delawares call it. Maybe so. It means a certain thing. But always, maybe, for instance, you could say *mikušiken*. It's something that old people keep. A [sacred] bundle.) He said, "I got that."

---

[11] The prefix *len-* is the same as that of the tribal name and means "standard, usual, common, real" while the rest of the word is the name for corn (maize) itself.

They told him all right. Try it. He's going to try it. He said, "I'm going to be gone 4 days. I'm going to the East. Nobody follow me. I'm going East. I'm going to be gone 4 days. Then I'll come back and I'll have her with me, stored in there, in that gourd. Her soul in that little gourd."

Anyway, he come back. He come back and then the chief called up a council. Everybody got together. They set a certain date. When he brought her back, they talk it over. Everybody was waiting.

He said, "We going to have a dance. Dance 4 nights. 4 nights. The third one [in line], it'll be her. These 2 leaders, they go [ahead], one by one, and she'll be the third one, then another one." Then he told that man [husband], "You stand on the side with that baby. You going to be standing there and holding that baby. She's going to come and when she sees you (She won't see you the first time, but the second round), then she'll come up to you. She's going to try to get that baby from you. Don't you give it to her." He said, "If you give it to her, you'll never get it back. She's going to take it with her. You'll never get it back. Don't you turn it loose. No matter how much she beg."

So (I guess), he told 'em to line up. They all dance the Women Dance. Them women, they all dress up. They had certain women to be leaders. They start off them songs. They didn't see her till third time. Afterwards (you know). When they sang that song, sure enough, it was her. She was there. He said, when he was talking that time, "When you all see her, meet up with her, don't any of you go up to her and cry to her. Don't cry to her. You just hold yourself back. Don't do that. If you do that, you'll spoil the whole thing." So they didn't. Nobody.

Anyway, this man [husband], he goes and she comes out, and tries to take that baby from him. But he won't turn it loose. She told him, "Let it go. I want to hold it. Hold it a little." He said, "No." He just held on to it. Then, while she was doing that, while they were at it like that, there was another old man that lived way out to himself. He was never among that clan, always way out to himself. And he come up. He cry. He goes right up to her and he cries to her. He told her, "My little granddaughter, I'm so happy to see that you come back."

He started crying and telling her he's glad to see her. And that minute, she was gone. That killed the whole thing. That's what he [the shaman] meant.

Five months later, in the midst of Spring itself, Lily returned to the epic again, but this time used the version told by her mother. It is important to know that it was triggered by a discussion of the clans. Specifically, she recalled what her mother had said about boys having their matriclan emblem tattooed on their chest so they could be readily identified among the huge population. Daughters, of course, carried their clan inherently. The prelude to Nellie's version was the following.

Tattoos

They say. It could be Delawares, cause there's a Delaware story to that. It is not at all Kickapoo. My mother said there used to be three clans of Delawares. They were in the villages. There was tuk^wsit, pukuongu, and pəlay. [Wolf, Turtle, and Turkey by emblem.] There was. And she told me. Pukuongu, them boys, they were all tattooed, right here on the chest. So I guess there used to be a lot of Delawares. So if a Delaware child got lost, they can't find his folks, they take him to the village were the Pukuongu live. They turn him loose there and he find his folks. They find out that way where he belongs. That's what my mother used to say. She tell me most about. Then them pəlay, she didn't much say much about pəley, and them tuk^wsit.

She said, tukʷsit is like dog-foot clan or coyot. Pəlay is Fowl clan that flies up in the air. My grandmother belonged to that. She belonged to the Fowl. But our grandpa, *Kasiya*, he belonged to the tukʷsit – so that's what we are. She didn't tell me that, whether this woman was tukʷsit or what. But anyway, she said that, Years ago …

27 April 1987 Attributed to Nellie Thomas Hoag

Long years ago, they were all in villages, each one of a certain group. But this here couple, they kind of live away from these people.

One time now, they say, this young man, he heard a turkey [gobble]. He heard a turkey out there. He went after it. He made up his mind, he'd go to get it. So he gets to go after it while she was still [asleep]. I guess, she knew that he got up and went after it.

And they had a little baby boy that could kind of crawl, and, you know, sit up.

But she went. When this man went, she gets up too. That baby was still asleep, and she left there. She thought she had so much to hoe yet. She could hoe that out right quick before he gets back. And so, she goes out there. (They say, they used to have a hoe made out of the jawbone of a deer. They used that for hoe.) She went to her corn patch and she had a little more [to do]. When she look back that way, here, that rain was coming. It didn't look bad. It was coming, so she got over there. She started hoeing. All at once, it come so quick, so fast. (I guess this lightning didn't give her no chance.) When it lightninged, it hit her. It killed her right out there, and it start sprinkling. Started sprinkling. She was already dead. She was hit from the back. She was dead.

Finally, that man, he come home. (They didn't say whether he had turkey or not.) Anyway, he come home. He come home. He seen that baby. He seen that baby. It was crawling out, crawling outdoors from that wikwam, or whatever it was. Looking for his mother. He was crying. He was all wet. He was crying. This man, he goes over there and picks it up. He wondered. There's something wrong here. So, he (meantime, this rain it kind of stopped. It was going that way. It stopped) he took the baby, and he looked around, and he didn't see nobody. He had that baby.

He was thinking, "I wonder what could [have] happen to her." So he went around there, and then he thought, then he got to thinking, and he kept tracking. It showed one place there where she stepped. Her track. He went on a little while and he seen another track. Then he knew something was wrong, but he didn't see nothing yet. Then he went on. When he got there, there she was. She was lying there. She was dead. That lightning killed her.

Oh, he felt bad. He come back. He went to his folks, her people. Told 'em about it. They all come in and they brought her home to where they live. They don't know what they're going to do. Talking about it. They said, Well, the best thing would be to notify the head chiefs, to let them know, to tell them what happened. Course, they never did have that to happen like that.

So, anyway, he told 'em about it. Then they sent a word to one man. He was kind of a prophet like (you could say). He come. They hold councils and they talk about it. He said, he said, "I could try. I could try it. I could give it a try." And then he start telling what they must do. He said, "Let there be a dance. Women Dance. There must be, he named a certain woman that's going to be the leader, that's got to take lead in that dance." So, so, they said, all right. There was 2, 4 of these women, and this woman was the leader, and then the next ones. He said, "When I get her," he said, "she'll be the fourth one." When he bring her back. Course, they talked it over and this man, that was going to try it, why, he said, "If everything goes well, it'll be all right. If something goes wrong, then I can not do that no more. I lost that way." And he said, "Let there be 4 nights dance, and you all get singers to sing that song. They told him, "All right."

Then he told this man [the husband], "You be there with the baby. She's going to come to you while you're standing there. When she sees you, don't you give her that child. If you give it to her, she's going to take it with her. You can't get it back. (That means it's going to die.) You keep it. You hold it tight, don't you turn it loose."

So they got ready. They said, "All right." This man, he went. He took his gourd and he went East. He was gone for so many days, and when he came back, they were ready to have that dance.

The first two nights, nothing happened. Then the third night. Then the fourth night. Here she was, she was dancing with them women. She was the fourth lady from that first. That man, he was standing there looking on with that child. They danced several times.

Here that old man that lived way out to himself, he come and he seen her. He grab her while she was talking to that man (you know), her husband, trying to get that baby from him. He grab her and he told her, "Oh, little grand daughter, I'm glad to see you. You come back." That minute, she was gone. That ended the whole thing. But she didn't get the baby. They said that's the way that dance was. That's why some of those dance songs, they kind of sound sad. Some of them. That's the way that went.

Translated from Lenape, 1979, attributed to Nellie Thomas Hoag

This is a story that was told to me about when they sing exclusively for the women when they dance. My late mother told us this a great while ago about the origin of the singing for the women when they dance.

Long ago, the Delawares lived in three parts, the Turkey clan, the Wolf clan, and then the Turtle clan. The Turtle clanspeople are my clan. Then, it was said, they lived together, but by themselves. There was a man and a woman who lived by themselves a short distance away, and they had a little son who was just then beginning to crawl. Then one day the man told his wife, "I want to go hunting, I want to go hunting, I am going to look for a turkey." The woman said, "That's good."

The man left, and the woman stayed home with her little son. The boy was just now beginning to crawl, and he could stand occasionally, but he couldn't walk yet. Then it began to look like rain, and was getting cloudy. Then the woman went outdoors, or rather, she went out. Then she got her hoe and went to the garden. It was the old type of hoe like the Delawares used before they had iron as it was made out of a deer's jaw. That was what they used to use when they made a garden. She went to the garden to hoe her corn which hadn't yet started to tassel. Then the woman thought, "I could cut down or pull up some of the grass [weeds] in the garden." Then the woman went there. It was just a short distance to where their garden was, and she began to work.

Then it was just about to rain, and all at once it thundered. Then that woman was struck by the thunders. It then began slowly to rain. Before long, it rained hard, and it thundered repeatedly.

That child must have been asleep over there in the house. Then he awoke and began to look for his mother. When he couldn't find her, he crawled outside. Then he began to cry.

About that time, the man returned home. Suddenly he saw his little son crawling toward him, so he picked him up. He thought, "Whatever is wrong with him?" Something was wrong because the woman never left her son.

So he picked him up and carried him inside, he was really wet. Then it slowly began to stop raining. He went outside, carrying his son, and he began to hunt for his wife. Then he remembered that she liked to go to the garden. Then they went there, and then they got there they found the woman. She was lying there dead, as it was there that the thunders struck her. She was really burned and she looked very black. Then the man went and got his little son and carried him. They left to go to where his relatives lived, and he went to tell them. They then all notified each other at that place. The chief was notified and all the people. Then they held a council. They went after the deceased woman and brought her. The deceased one was really burned when she was struck by the thunders. Then they had a council.

They were surprised because she was struck by those thunders. One man said, "I could bring her back." The man said, "I know what I could do to bring her back." Then he said, "That's it!" Then he said, "But for four days I will be gone," he said, "I will be gone for four days. I will go to the east. I will hold this little gourd rattle. This is what I will hold," he said. "Then if that woman is to be brought back you will hold a dance, you will have a dance," he said. He said, "All the women will be two at a time behind each other. The old women will lead," he said. "Then it will seem like when the women are in fours we will see that woman on the fourth [day?]," he said, when he brings her back. "Then they will have a dance," he said, "the men will sing, and the women will dance in a circle," he said. Then when they have this dance for four times at night," he said, "she will be there, she will be there, that will be her. The man will carry his little son," he said. "Then when the woman steps aside she will tell her husband, 'Give me our little son.' Don't give him to her," he said, "because if he hands him to her she will never again return, and she will take him to where a person goes forever," he said. "Don't anyone cry," he said. "If anyone cries he will ruin it and I can never bring her back. He will ruin it for me, and in the future I cannot bring anyone back." Then he said, "You all have a dance!"

It really happened [the dance]. Then they had held a dance for four days. On the fourth day when it was night the woman returned and there with the people she danced, she danced with those women. Then she saw her husband, and she stepped to one side. She told him, "Give me our little son. I love him, my little son, I want to see him." The man tightly held onto his son. While they were doing that [dancing] an old man who lived separately came toward them. He was not often there among the people, he was always separate. He came there and he said, "Grandchild," he began to cry. He said, "Grandchild, you have truly come back. I am glad to see you." When he did that, when he told his granddaughter that then that deceased woman disappeared. She was not seen again, never was there again.

Now this is where it comes from when they have the Delaware Woman Dance. This then is the length of the story. This is what I heard from my late mother and grandmother when they told stories. My Delaware name is Wèndataèxkwe ~ "Where the Flowers Come From Woman". My grandmother named me that. I am half Caddo. My late father a chief was named was named Enoch Hoag, and he was the last chief of the Caddo. That is my tribe of the Caddo. I am half Caddo and half Delaware woman. My mother was a Delaware woman and her name was *Kweihtiti* in Delaware. In English her name was Nellie Thomas Hoag.

women dance

Motivations

By combining these three versions, a clearer context for the dance emerges. Her sister Josephine identified Thunder, the intensely burned body, and 3 as the pattern number. Her mother Nellie provided more plausible details, specifying Lightning as blackening the body and numberings by 4 behind paired women leaders.

Turkey

The turkey that lured the father away has military aspects since its waddle is said to be a scalp(s) lock taken in war (Hall 1997: 171). Among the Caddo, the Turkey Dance is the primary vehicle for expressing their history (Newkumet and Meredith 1988: 102-6; Sabo 2003). Though turkeys can not fly high into the sky (and contra the anglo-American image), their wisdom, valor, and gobble do link them with the Thunders in the sky for much of Native America.

Thunder

The source for a vindictive Thunder was the Southeast not the Woodlands, by comparison among Delawares, Caddos, and Natchez. In Delaware tradition, Thunders were seven beings with birdlike bodies and human heads. The deep, rumbling booms were made by the elderly and the quick, flashing cracks by youngsters. Boys and men have visited them, usually by riding up on a huge cloud of steam (Newcomb 1956: 73, Miller 1975). But women are never mentioned in connection with these very male beings.

In diametric contrast, the Caddo recognized Grandmother Thunder, as well as the *kokonikis* ("little ones") of Thunder and Lightning, who parallel the Pueblo war god twins of the Southwest. Their sky associations linked them with birds, and Lighting is said to have a long sharp nose. Such a nose-as-beak linkage recalls the "long nose face" that appears on paired shell ear pendants (Williams and Goggin 1956), and on the masks with two-foot noses reported hanging in a Calusa temple near the tip of Florida (Hann 1991: 195).

Of particular note, in a Natchez tale, after Thunder, who seems to be solitary, blasted a person with lightning, he hung body parts in his house. He was away so much that a big Frog kept his fire, which also smoked this drying meat. While waiting between tasks, Frog burrowed into the floor. Sometimes, however, this meat got angry and shouted back. Then Thunder had Frog bury it so "In that way he had made mounds of earth" containing human remains (Swanton 1929: 239-240).

Water

Returning to a consideration of the Women's Dance epic, we have to ask, Why would Thunder kill this woman? Among Delaware, it may have been enough that she was female and a mother to draw the ire of celibate Thunder. Moreover, despite constant attention, she neglected her son just this once to work in the field. Throughout the Americas, great antipathy existed between the Thunder of the sky and the Snakes of the water. Often these are cast as Thunderbirds and Underwater Panthers, who combine attributes of many species but were generally serpentine. If the woman was Turtle Clan, she might have been a hapless victim of this water association.

Moreover, in the most famous example of spiritual retribution, the origin epic of the Midewiwin, Wolf is killed by the Underwater Beings for hunting overzealously and killing more game than he or Hare (*Nanabush*) actually needed. Thus, it may be that the woman was keeping too big a garden, but this seems unlikely. Instead, she may have failed to watch the weather, a foremost consideration among all farmers, and thus suffered for her inattention by getting caught out in a thunderstorm. Therefore, the woman was partially to blame for her own death. That this is the most likely scenario is indicated by her second chance to come back.

It is expressly a time of Spring rains. Struck in the neck, her entire body is burned, much like the smoked meat hung in the house of the Natchez Thunder. After the shaman returns with her soul inside his special gourd rattle, she took the last (or fourth) place in the dance line, behind the senior women. Only women dance. She only became manifest at the ending rounds of the dance, with only a last (or fourth) one to go. Her husband holds their baby boy as a lure. He is not included in the dance. Everything is spoiled, however, when the old hermit enters the town. Either he weeps for the woman, and she vanishes; or he reminds her of her own death. In the sister's version, first, she is taken in the rain, and, second, in a flood of tears, both watery conditions hostile to Thunder. Both parents are punished, the wife by death and the husband by grief, though, in hope of the future, the baby lives.

Alabama Mama

It is suggestive to look at another story famous in the Southeast concerning an absent mother, that of the Alabama Sky Skiff (Swanton 1929: 138-139). Its outcome is more successful for on-going maternal relations.

In short form, sky people repeatedly come down to earth, singing and laughing in a canoe. They play stickball for hours. Then they went back up. A man watched their visits. He captured one of the woman when she chased an out-of-bounds ball. They married and had children. When they got older, their mother kept having them ask their father to hunt away from home. Meanwhile, the woman made a canoe and tried to take her family heavenward. The husband prevented her just in time. Next the woman made two canoes, put herself in the big one and her children in the little one. The husband rescued his children, but the wife escaped.

The children pleaded to visit their mother so the father took them aloft. An old woman told them that this woman was dancing. The family was fed from a dish of never-ending squash. An old corncob was broken up and the pieces were given to the children. When they saw their mother dance by, they threw these at her. The first few times they missed, but then they hit her. She recognized her own children and returned to earth with them. They lived together for a time, but then the mother and children returned to the sky. After an interval, the father followed but on his way up, he looked down and immediately fell to his death.

In northern latitudes, only the three circumpolar constellations appear to swing down to earth and rise into the sky (Williamson 1992). These are the Big Dipper (Ursa Major), Little Dipper (Ursa Minor), and Cassiopeia. Since the length of time on the ground was enough for a ballgame, which could last hours, only Ursa Major for Summer and Cassiopeia for early and late Spring would fit. The annual harvest Green Corn (Busk) and the ballgames, however, are Summer events so it has to be the Big Dipper. As confirmation, the Alabama native name for the bowl of this constellation is indeed "canoe, watercraft" or Boat Stars.

In late July, the Big Dipper in the Alabama homeland appears to set at 1am and rises just after dawn. On the autumnal equinox, the sun rises at 6am and sets at 6pm, with an hour and twenty minutes of twilight, when the Big Dipper begins to set. The small canoe holding the children is probably one of the three stars in the handle, all of them bright. And they do indeed follow along with the body of the dipper's bowl.

During the Busk, Alabamas (Swanton 1928b: 602) placed a taboo on the touching, eating, and using of corn. By fasting, praying, and purifying, people prepare to eat the new corn. Old pottery, clothes, and presumably stored food was discarded.

The Alabama Busk was held in June and until then "it was wrong to touch" the corn. Each family brought roasted ears to the square, where they were placed on a cane-covered scaffold four feet high.[12] Everyone danced until midnight, the women forming an inner ring near the fire and the men in an outer ring. Anyone who did not participate was ostracized. Some of the roasted ears were shelled, "and a few men took a handful [of kernels] apiece and threw it over the house. This was done four times." They ate what was left. A pot of medicine was brewed and heated. Then a man blew into it through a cane tube to make it bubble and receive special prayers. Men drank this medicine and then retired to purge.

The next dawn, a new fire was kindled in the woods and brought into the square. Women took embers from it to restart their kitchen fires. Each of the four nights of the Busk, roasted ears were brought to the scaffold, everyone danced until midnight when handfuls of kernels were thrown over the house.

Conclusions

Women Dance concerns the solidarity of women throughout Native North America. As only women give birth, so here only women dance. Throughout there is a strong sense of planning for the inevitable. In her own lead-in to her mother's versions, Lilly talked about matri-clans and their emblems tattooed onto boy members, marking there membership in dye as that of women is traced in blood. In the cited Alabama story, mother and children stay together in the sky, but this is not the case for this Delaware epic.

Similarly the social dances (named Garfish, Turkey, Tick, Bean, Bell, Duck, Alligator, Quail, Quapaw, Turtle, Morning, Snake, etc) are (or were) held to convey regard for the named species or quality. Their inherent qualities and differences are celebrated by humans enjoying themselves.

What is inevitable and distinct is honored. It is taken for granted by any audience of the Orpheus saga, with its ultimately failed plea for the return of a wife or mother from the dead. Since these souls nevertheless become ancestors, though maybe not direct ones, death itself becomes accepted as part of the fabric of the universe.

In all, these dances are distillations of tribal regard for otherness. Much as clans are pseudo-species, so too are differences among species themselves as well as beings of many forms and qualities. Women Dance is about womanhood. The best of mothers, nevertheless leaves her crawling child to hoe up her field before a rain. Food came before family.

Her fate rested on a conflict in alignments. Her husband, who was probably Turkey clan, was drawn off by his desires as a hunter, lured, falsely or not, by the call of a turkey. Such a gobble was also a war cry of humans and of Thunders on attack. The wife, probably of the Turtle clan, trusted in the Spring rains to nourish her crop. So, leaving her baby boy, she took up

---

[12] This placement of the corn atop a scaffold recalls the first stages in some Southeast burial ritual, where the body is left on a platform to decompose before the bones are prepared for the temple.

her jawbone hoe and stood in the open field to be charred by the fatal bolt.

Men play pivotal (if tragic) roles in the epic, but they orbit around the core of women. It is only the women who dance, the more surely to attract back the ghost mother. Men are away or apart. Before her own death, the husband had departed their home and she had left the boy behind. After her burial, the medicine man showed the ghost the way back, held within a gourd rattle. Ultimately, despite dire warnings, the old man frustrated all attempts to bring her back, except as an ancestor.

Yet even so, women stay together, helping each other and celebrating the Women Dance, in a world where males are both dangerous and fickle despite the best of intentions all around.

Delaware as Women:
a symbolic solution

Abstract

Previously several authors have discussed the circumstances whereby the entire Delaware nation became known as women and the Iroquois confederacy known as men. These authors have debated whether these designations were the result of military conquest or political agreement. My own view is that the Delaware became women and the Iroquois men as the result of what is known in structural analysis as a transformation. Three other examples of man / woman transformations are also suggested for Native America.

Included within the early historical records of the eastern woodlands are numerous references to the whole Delaware nation as women in contradistinction to the Iroquois nation as men. The meaning of the terms women and men in this context has been debated by many authors. The debate opposes those authors who believe that the Delaware became women as the result of conquest by the Iroquois and those authors who believe that the Delaware became women and the Iroquois became men by reciprocal agreement.

After the main arguments on each side of the debate are reviewed, I will present an argument derived from structuralism which accounts for these designations as a transformation. Other examples of man / woman transformations are also discussed to support the argument. Finally, the advantages of a symbolic or structural solution are discussed.

By Conquest

The minority position states that the Delaware became women as the result of being defeated by the Iroquois. The evidence for this position is drawn from historical documents where Iroquois chiefs are reported to have reminded the Delaware about such a defeat and their subjugation to the status of women. As women the Delaware could not fight, sell land, or sign treaties on their own. The historical records also refer to tribute wampum sent to the Iroquois by the Delaware and to a metaphorical skirt, earrings, and a corn pounder used by the Delaware.

Lewis Henry Morgan

Morgan (1972: 15, 338) clearly showed his Iroquois bias when he reported that the Iroquois made women of the Delaware by prohibiting them from going to war or having any civil powers. As a token of their subservience, the Delaware sent tribute wampum to the Iroquois. But then the Iroquois say that the Delaware attacked another Iroquois tributary nation. The Iroquois responded by "degrading" the Delaware to the status of women. Quoting a speech by the Iroquois chief Canassetego in 1742, [508] Morgan also specified that the Delaware were forbidden to sell their land without Iroquois consent.

Clinton Alfred Weslager

Weslager has discussed the Delaware as women three times (1944, 1947, 1972). In the first article, he surveyed most of the early historical documents and concluded that the Delaware were "degraded" to the status of women by being denied by the Iroquois any involvement in political or military matters. Although he reported the conflicting belief that the Delaware became women to act as peacemakers, he believes that the Delaware were duped, humiliated, and subjugated into the position of women. The Iroquois claim that the conflicting belief was a Delaware fabrication to win sympathy. In fact, the Iroquois say that they defeated the Delaware in battle. Weslager relied upon the Minutes of the Provincial Records of Pennsylvania to document Delaware political disintegration as a result of European intrigue in land sales and Iroquois pressure. In 1712 two Delaware chiefs showed the governor of Pennsylvania thirty-two wampum belts intended as tribute to the Iroquois. By 1755 the Delaware petitioned the Iroquois to recognize them as men so that they could defend themselves from the French and English. In 1756 the Delaware actually claimed the status of men and were able to do everything except declare their own wars. According to the colonial records, the Iroquois conveyed this masculine status in specifically anatomical terms. It was not until 1794 that Joseph Brant formally declared the Delawares to be fully men in the eyes of the Iroquois.

In the second article, Weslager defended his sources against criticism by noting that they were among the few available, they were based on translations made by reliable interpreters, and they capture many of the figurative and idiomatic expressions of the Indian languages. He provided fuller documentation on the thirty-two wampum belts intended for the Iroquois in 1712. Each of them was sent by a child or a woman seeking assurances of protection. These wampum belts seem primarily involved with protection but not explicitly with tribute. Weslager believed that Sir William Johnson arranged for the Iroquois to reinstate the Delaware as men in order to win them over to the English cause. Weslager argued that the Delaware felt ignominious as women and would have willingly supported any change in this status.

Recently, Weslager (1972: 181) has stated, "I still hold to the view I first expressed in a paper in 1944, which has been reinforced by subsequent study, that the Delaware had been subjugated, and the Iroquois reduced them to a subservient position." Still lacking any identifiable battle or incident to mark this change in status, Weslager refers to the assertion by Dr Paul Wallace that the defeat of the Delaware was in forest politics and not in actual battle. Wallace referred to forest politics as a cold war involving the judicious application of a little heat to certain spots.

By Agreement

The majority position states that the Delaware became women and the Iroquois became men by reciprocal political agreement. The evidence for this position is primarily ethnographic and historical. These sources indicate that the Delaware favored the designation of women and willingly refrained from manly activities. Any association of women with inferiority, ignominy, or subjugation seems to have been due to European influence. As women the Delaware refrained from overinvolvement with Europeans but the Iroquois did not. The end of English colonialism and the rise of the American [509] government changed the Iroquois position which in turn had repercussions for the Delaware as women.

David Zeisberger

Zeisberger was a Moravian missionary to the Delaware for over fifty years. His notes on the Delaware, Iroquois, and other tribes were written between 1779 and 1780 in Ohio and served as the basis of the later accounts of Loskiel (1794) and Heckewelder (1876). However, the notes were not translated from German and published until 1910. In his discussion of this topic, Zeisberger (1910: 34-36) mentioned the long antipathy between the Delaware and Iroquois, in which the former was always stronger. Therefore, the Iroquois plotted by wile what they could not achieve by force. The Iroquois preached that one nation should have the exalted status of women, of peacekeepers, of sanctuary. The Delaware assumed this status and became known as cousins (sister's children) to their Iroquois uncles (mother's brothers). The Delaware were figuratively attired in long dresses and earrings; they were given oil to open the ears of their hearers, medicines to anoint other nations, and a corn pounder and hoe to assure sustenance. They were entrusted with the belt of peace and the chain of friendship. The Delaware chose the status of women because it assured their safety while the Iroquois and others waged wars. They consistently refused all formal offers to support any side or nation. It was only after the Iroquois betrayed the covenant and fell upon the Delaware that the latter threw off their dress and revenged themselves. It is clear that the Delaware recognized themselves as a nation of *women*. Zeisberger (1910: 143) reported that the Delaware "call one another *Nitgochk* "my companion [feminine] in play' for the reason that the whole nation has become the women."

John Heckewelder

Heckewelder divided his life between work as a cooper and as a missionary. In his later years he was encouraged by the American Philosophical Society to record his knowledge of the Eastern Indians. His history was published in 1818 and reissued in 1876. Heckewelder has a lengthy discussion of the Delaware as women. He begins by mentioning the Iroquois claim to conquest of the Delaware but discusses the evidence to the contrary. The strength of the Delaware was always considerably more than that of the Iroquois because the Delaware were allied with many other Algonquian nations, all of whom addressed the Delaware as "Grandfather" in recognition of their seniority among the Algonquian speakers. Since the Iroquois were unable to deal with the Delaware, they enlisted the support of the Dutch. The Delaware and Iroquois reached their agreement under the watchful eyes of the Dutch on Nordman's Kill near Albany, New York. The Dutch had built a fort on this stream in 1617. Later, the English replaced the Dutch in this agreement. The Dutch became involved in this agreement in order to facilitate trade with both nations and their allies. The Iroquois were fighting both the Delaware and the French and hoped to be able to concentrate on only one front; the Delaware wanted the safety of being peacemakers. As the Iroquois rose in power as the middlemen of English colonial society, they could threaten the Delaware with combined Iroquois and English power. When Iroquois raids and pressure became intolerable, the Delaware threw off their skirts and took to the warpath. After the American Revolution, the Iroquois lost their power and, seeking allies, formally declared the Delaware to be men in 1 795 at the Treaty of Greenville, Ohio.

Frank Speck

In his article Speck (1946) countered the belief that the political emasculation of the Delaware was a result of their ignominious reduction to the status of [510] women. In reviewing aspects of his own vast knowledge of the Eastern woodlands, he called attention to the use of kinship terms among the Indian nations and Europeans. The kin terms were always those for males, indicating that the nations were masculine. Generally, equals called each other "brother," unequals used "uncle" and "nephew," and "grandfather" was used for the venerated or senior nations. The Delaware were called "grandfather" by the other Algonquians. However, the Iroquois have a tradition of denying that any nation is superior to them in any way. The Iroquois could not be expected to glorify the Delaware or anyone else. Yet among both the Delaware and the Iroquois, women were matrons with superior social and political powers with respect to making and keeping peace. The designation of the Delaware as women was therefore an important one. Among contemporary Canadian Delawares, Speck found that their position as peacemakers was uncompromisingly preserved. Speck concluded that the Delaware and Iroquois worked out an arrangement whereby the former became women with social supremacy but political impotency. Feminization was ignominious only in colonial eyes, and it was the English colonists who suffered when the Delawares cast off their skirts.

Anthony FC Wallace

Wallace (1947) added more ethnographic data gathered from the Canadian Delaware and Iroquois. The antipathy between these two nations is now expressed by a children's game in which the Delaware are analogous to "robbers" and the Iroquois to "cops." However, the Canadian Delaware were adopted by the Cayuga Iroquois in 1763 and as such are represented by the Cayuga in Iroquois councils. The adopted Delaware are Props, not Members, of the Iroquois confederacy. Props act as buffers, scouts, guards, and messengers for the Iroquois; only the six Iroquois nations are considered Members. It is extremely interesting that the Cayuga call the Delaware by the term, *gantowisas*, which means 'matron' or 'lady' rather than woman generally. *Gantowisas* is a cognate of the term, *tonwisus*, which is the title of the male assistants appointed to help cook at important Iroquois rituals. This position is a great honor and is usually filled by a chief or subchief. In a footnote, Wallace added that the Mohawk Iroquois refer to the Delaware as *gonongwe* because their cognate of the Cayuga term, *deyonatonwisa*, is not considered respectable enough for the Delaware. With this background, Wallace believed that the designation of the Delaware as women only became derogatory through the influence of white colonists and scribes.

Although it is presently impossible to substantiate the actual historical details whereby the Delaware became women, these authors convey a sense of the context within which the Delaware and Iroquois were interacting. The accounts suggest that after European contact, the Delaware nation became recognized as women by themselves, their Algonquian allies, and the Iroquois. Since an open conflict and conquest is unknown, some other explanation must be found. Heckewelder specifies Dutch intervention, and other authors cite political maneuvers. The Delaware became women before 1712, and although they were formally declared men in 1795, the women designation continues among modern Canadian Delaware and Iroquois. The designation as women seems to have been derogatory only in the eyes of Europeans. The Iroquois have denied its importance on numerous occasions, but the Iroquois have a long tradition of denigrating anything either Indian or European which is not Iroquois.

By Transformation

It is only recently that anthropological theory has advanced to a state where these data on the Delaware as women can be generalized as an example of the cultural process called [511] transformation.   Levi-Strauss (1968: 75) has called transformation the insistence on differentiation. A transformation is a process by which cultural features are reversed, inverted, segregated, or redefined on either side of a cultural boundary.

Both the Delaware and the Iroquois were prominent woodland societies during recent prehistory and contact. The Delaware were probably more important during pre-contact times, and the Iroquois were more important following contact. The Delaware and Iroquois share many cultural similarities. The most significant, for present purposes, is the observation by Fenton (1951: 48) that sexual dualism is fundamental in both Delaware and Iroquois. The following consideration of the sex categories among the Delaware and Iroquois will bear this out.

Among the aboriginal Delawares, the sex categories were complementary at economic, social, and cultural levels. Economically, the men did the hunting, stone knapping, woodworking, and protecting, while the women did the farming, cooking, and peacekeeping. Heckewelder (1876: 155, 157) noted that the men worked constantly at strenuous labor while the women worked periodically at difficult labor that rarely lasted over six weeks a year. Barnes (1968: 22) reported that the contributions of the sexes varied seasonally, with the men more important in winter and the women in summer. The sexes were so interdependent that celibacy was impractical. Delaware society emphasized the matriclan for purposes of descent, inheritance, and leadership. Women played an important social role, but men dominated politics and religion. In his analysis of the Big House Ceremony, the focal ritual of Delaware culture. Speck (1937: 34) concluded that just as sex categories pervaded this key rite, so they pervaded Delaware life and ideology.

Morgan (1972: 323) saw in Iroquois society "two great classes, male and female." Iroquois women played a vital part in economics and the society. They tended the fields, selected the life chiefs, and were elected Keepers of the Faith in equal numbers with men (Randle 1951). The sex categories were also culturally important. Hewitt, who was himself part Tuscarora Iroquois, first reported the male and female sides of the Iroquois confederacy (Fewkes 1922: 63). Speck (1945: 23n) also noted that the sex categories pervade Iroquois life and culture.

Obviously women did not have an insignificant, degrading, or ignominious status among the Delaware and Iroquois. Wallace (1947: 9) stated that "with maize as the staple crop and women as the cultivators... it is tempting to think that the high status of women in both cultures is ultimately a function of economic organization." He underscored this observation by noting that the wergild for a murdered woman was twice that for a murdered man throughout the woodlands. In light of these important similarities, how were the Delaware and Iroquois able to maintain different cultural identities? Since the sex categories are fundamental to both nations, they were likely sources for transformation. In this case the transformation took the form of segregation. Aboriginally, women had high status in internal societal affairs, and men dealt with externals. This pattern was expanded to the Delaware and Iroquois nations. Each society continued its organization of men and women handling external and internal relations, but at the international level the Delaware became women, and the Iroquois became men. Although this transformation may have occurred prehistorically, an incentive to either initiate or strengthen it was provided by the Europeans. The Delaware were located on the coast and bore the brunt of contact; it was easier for the Iroquois in the interior. Since the bulk of Delaware history has been characterized by many migrations occasioned by an expressed desire to minimize intercourse with whites, the status of non-combatant, neutral women would have been attractive to the Delaware. Iroquois vanity, if not superiority, would have espoused the status of men. Europeans were of [512] course oblivious to these cultural processes, though rather glaring in hindsight.

This is not the only example of man / woman transformation in North America. In addition to segregation, transformations can also take the forms of reversal and inversion. Miller (1972) reports an example of man / woman reversal. In New Mexico two societies, the Keres and the Tewa, are generally classed together as Pueblos. Yet the Keres and Tewa have different languages, social structures, and cultures even though they have been in contact for at least two millennia. Among the Keres, man and woman are the all-important, subsuming categories. Among the Tewa, the analogous categories are summer and winter. For the Keres, man is a marked category referring only to masculine qualities, and woman is unmarked, with both feminine and masculine qualities. Among the Tewa, however, the definitions of the sexes are the reverse: the woman is marked, with only feminine attributes, and the man is unmarked, with the attributes of both sexes. Thus, a Tewa man is told to "be a man and a woman" when he is being exhorted to behave in a manner befitting a Tewa male (Ortiz 1969: 36).

Reversals such as the above are horizontal processes while inversions are vertical ones. Such an inversion seems to be represented by the Pawnee and Winnebago. The Winnebago homeland was southern Wisconsin but by 1865 forced migrations and severe hardships brought them to live with the Omaha in Nebraska (Lurie 1971: 112n). The Pawnee were originally neighbors of the Omaha, but between 1873 and 1875 they were moved to Oklahoma (Weltfish 1971: 5). The decade between 1865 and 1875 marks the period of contact between these two tribes. The Pawnee divided their year between female farming and male buffalo hunting. Pawnee society was marked by elaborate rituals contrasting priests of the celestial or star bundles and doctors associated with terrestrial and animal spirits (Weltfish 1971: 182). The celestial had priority over the terrestrial because it was the source of the latter. It also was in the sky that Morning Star impregnated Evening Star to produce a girl and that Sun impregnated Moon to produce a boy. This girl and boy were sent to earth to sire humanity (Weltfish 1971: 101).

The Winnebago divided their year into seasons emphasizing male hunting or female gathering and farming. The former were more active in winter and the latter in summer. Winnebago society was divided into Earth and Sky moieties. The sex differences relating to earth and sky are given in an origin myth: "Earthmaker created four worlds, in each of which he placed men and women; ... the heavens we see represent the last man he created and the earth we are living on, the last woman he created" (Radin 1970: 329).

Both the Pawnee and Winnebago emphasize the vertical contrast between earth and sky; however, a transformation permits the differentiation of the Pawnee earth and sky, both of which contain men and women, and the Winnebago earth and sky, which are woman and man respectively.

Another possible example of a transformation involving man and woman is the Shawnee Supreme Being. Sometime after 1824, the Shawnee elevated a female deity called Grandmother to the position of greatest spirit. This change from a male to a female God is singular in the literature on American Indians. In discussing this change, the Voegelins (1944) suggest it may be attributed to Iroquois influence, analogy to the Virgin Mary, or influence from the Yuchi. However, the Shawnee and Iroquois are bitter enemies, Catholic influence was slight, and none of these sources in fact has a female Supreme Being. Rather, I think it significant that by the end of the 1700s the Shawnee were a decimated people who had placed themselves under the protection of the Delaware (Zeisberger 1910: 109). Historically and at present the Delaware have a strong belief in an all-powerful, male Creator. Historically and at present the Shawnee and Delaware have remained physically close. Considering these factors, it is likely that the [513] Shawnee might want to differentiate themselves from the Delaware and that a transformation to a female Supreme Being would provide such a solution.

As these examples attest, the transformation of man and woman is among the most readily recognizable forms of cultural differentiation and thus is by no means limited to the Delaware and Iroquois.

Summary

This article has been concerned with the historical accounts to the effect that the Delaware nation was designated as women and the Iroquois were designated as men. A review of previous opinions on this subject provided some background on the problem. Two major points of view were recognized. Morgan and Weslager were convinced that the Delaware became women as a consequence of being defeated by the Iroquois. Although there are references to such a defeat, no specific battle or incident has been identified. The other interpretation, that of Zeisberger, Heckewelder, Speck, and Wallace, is supported by historical and ethnographic evidence which indicate that the Delaware and Iroquois agreed on these designations. As women, the Delaware could refrain from constant involvement with European leaders. As men, the Iroquois acted as middlemen , for European (and their own) interests. This agreement suffered from European stigmatization of the Delaware's status as women and from European manipulation of the Iroquois. About 1755, pressure and treachery brought the retaliation of Delaware warriors upon both the Europeans and the Iroquois. After the American Revolution, the Iroquois found they had no position with the Americans and formally proclaimed the Delaware to be men, presumably in the hope that they would become allies. In fact, those Delaware who followed the Iroquois to Canada were adopted as Props of the confederacy. I know that the Oklahoma Delawares still harbor a bitter resentment of the Iroquois and their treachery.

The recognition of the Delaware as women and the Iroquois as men was then discussed as an example of a transformation. But this man / woman transformation is not unique. Other transformations involving reversal and inversion of man and woman were discussed for the Southwestern Keres and Tewa and for the Plains Pawnee and Winnebago. A similar transformation would explain the Shawnee shift from a male to a female Supreme Being.

In conclusion, transformation as a symbolic solution for the Delaware as women is much more informative than any of the previously suggested military or political solutions. The other analyses have added color and nuance to this problem, but only a structural solution could explain and generalize it.

Date of Submission: March 8, 1974
Date of Acceptance: March 20, 1974
American Ethnologist August 1974
Volume 1, Number 3: 507 – 514

Nora Dean's Personal Account
of the Unami Delaware Big House Rite

Abstract

Nora Thompson Dean attended full versions of the Unami Delaware Big House Rite between about 1909 and 1924 in addition to 3 abbreviated rites held during World War II. This paper presents her edited remembrances of this rite, in what is probably the fullest account extant.

Introduction

THE Big House Rite was the major annual ceremony of the Delaware Indians.

The last proper and complete rite was held by the Unami Delaware living in northeastern Oklahoma in the fall of 1924. The rite was briefly and incompletely revived during the Second World War. The rite itself represents the clearest lens by which traditional Unami Delaware continue to view their culture as an integrated whole.

Yet the published accounts of the Big House Rite, when checked with these traditionalist elders, have invariably proved to be misleading and occasionally erroneous. Of all the published accounts, that of Harrington (1921) seems the most reasonable, those of the educated Delawares (Adams 1890 and McCracken 1956) the most superficial, and that which Charles Webber gave to Speck (1931) the most uneven. Because Speck has become the standard reference on the rite, it is regrettable that he did not practice greater care in the collection and cross-checking of his information. Speck (1931: 85 upper note 2) even reported that the last Big House building ran north and south, rather than east and west as custom and memory demand that it did. With the exception of the unpublished ethnographic description of the rite which Truman Michelson collected from Chief Charlie Elkhair, there is no comprehensive account of the rite from the standpoint of a committed Delaware traditionalist.

To set the record straight, Nora Thompson Dean, a most articulate Unami traditionalist, decided to give her remembrance of the rite to Jay Miller, an anthropologist to whom she has given a Delaware name, and to Susan Roarch, a graduate student from Bryn Mawr, on July 24, 1974 between the hours of 9pm and 4am. For this article Miller has taken Dean's account and her discussions prior and subsequent to this date and has with Dean edited the text to provide the fullest possible description of the rite. It is also possibly the most accurate version available, based on comparisons of her memories with other traditionalists, with published sources, and with manuscripts. In all, Nora Thompson Dean has provided us with a document which is simultaneously personal, historical, and ethnographically detailed.

Big House Rite

"My parents, brothers, and I attended the Big House (*xingwikaon*) every year, I don't think we missed a year from the time the new Big House building was built, around what I believe to be 1909 or 1910, on up until 1924 when they had the last full rite.

Before they started the services, some men were usually sent around on horses to notify [40] people when the exact camping day would be.[13] The *məsinghɔlikan* (the impersonator of

---

[13] As traditional, the building where the services were held was built in the timber, near water,

the being called Masing dressed in mask and bearskin suit) would travel with these men. Sometimes he rode in a buggy. (Once the train that used to run out to the rock quarry scared the horses and they ran away with Masing in the buggy. Another time a new White settler couple had their team bolt and run away when they met Masing's buggy on the road. Generally, the team of the buggy that carried the Masing was kept from running away because of the blinders the horses wore.) These men go to each Indian home to tell them the exact camping day and to select the participants. The men usually had in mind who they wanted to be the assistants (*ʌškašʌk*). They tried to ask people who were 'empty' (without a supernatural vision). They once asked my father, but he couldn't find anyone to tend the stock on the farm so he had to refuse. My father was sent away to boarding school when he was young so he didn't have a vision. My mother did have one, so these men always asked her to recite on the last day with the other women visionaries. They picked three men and three women to be the assistants or helpers. The *təmíkɛt* (Enterer ~ Leader) had already been chosen. They tried to get someone who could afford to get food for the women assistants, who would cook it and feed it to his clanspeople (members of the matriclan of the Enterer) during the rite.

The assistants went to the Big House site several days before the camping day to prepare the area for the rite. They cleaned out the building and put hay on the floor for the people to sit upon. The hay forms a strip about four feet wide from the walls out towards the center.

There were twelve faces carved on the support posts and center post inside the Big House. There were three faces on the north side, three on the south, two on the west [b] door, two on the east door, and two facing east and west on the center post. There were absolutely no faces on the outside of the Big House whatsoever, despite the fact that some people think there were. The Wolf clan women sit at the north east corner, then the *təmíkɛt*, the Wolf clan men at the north west corner, the Turtle women along the west end, the Turtle men at the south west corner, then the two drummers, the Fowl or Turkey men at their right, and finally the Fowl women at the south east corner. So that the men and the women were seated separately. On the south side of the east door, the three men assistants were stationed and the three women were stationed on the north side. The men assistants took care of things on the south side, and the women were responsible for the north side. On the wall above the drummers on the south side hung a bucket filled with *wisahkak^w* (boiled and strained red oak bark infusion). From time to time, the drummers would get up and drink some of this to clean and soothe their voices and throats. In my day the two drummers were Willie Longbone on the east side and Jake Parks on the west. On the north wall behind the Enterer was hung a piece of white cloth, about four feet square, where the strings of wampum (*kekok*) hung the whole time until they were paid out on the thirteenth morning to the assistants.

I want to describe the drum that was used in the Big House. It was rolled up into a sort of a long shape. I would say at least three feet long or longer. It was a whole deerhide, stuffed with deer hair, and over the top there were two slats, very thin pieces of board. Sometimes during the daytime during the rite, men and boys would go inside the Big House and have what they call a trial sing (*ahkwɛtalamwin*), a sort of try-out singing of special Long-Winged Creature songs which refer to the Thunders.

On the first night and all the other nights of the service, the men assistants went around the church house and shouted "tamíkɛk^w," "tamíkɛk^w" at about dusky dark. They continued the shout, which means "all come in," "all enter." So we all went into [41] the Big House and took

---

and had a level cleared area for camping.

our proper seats. We brought in shawls and blankets to put on the hay. When we were all seated, a male assistant pulled closed the flap on the east door. It was canvas attached to a pole at the bottom to hold it tight. In the old days, my mother said that it was a deerhide. When everyone was seated why the *tamíkɛt* arose and addressed the people. He told us what we were there for: to worship the Creator. He gave thanks for our brothers and sisters, all of our relatives, grandchildren, the vegetation, the trees, the water, the rain, the stars, the moon, everything. He gave thanks that we would all live to meet again in the next rite. After his opening speech, he sat down. Meanwhile the turtle shell rattle with the leather thong handle (*šuhəníkan*) was placed in front of him, so he picked it up and started to sing his vision song. When he had moved out into the center, well, anyone could follow him that wanted to. While he recited, all the men must answer him, that is, repeat the words of his vision song. He started out with his dance, moving counterclockwise, and anyone could follow him except for children. They were not permitted to dance in the Big House. The women joined in too, but they formed a separate line of their own. From time to time, he stopped at different intervals during his recitation and he recited some more of the experience by which he acquired his vision. The men answered him, that is, they said whatever he said. Finally, he finished and went back to where he was originally seated. Whenever someone recited his vision song and experience (*wənjikanéi*), everyone in the Big House stood until he was through. You were not permitted to sleep or even doze in there. Because if you did, the assistants would come over and nudge your foot with their firesticks, which were long thin poles for tending the fires. They were warm from this use. After one man finished, the turtle shell was shoved toward the east until it reached another visionary. (I recall very well how afraid I was to make that turtle rattle because if you do why the drummers on the south side would beat the drum twice in answer to your shake [b] on this turtle. So when I handled it, I was very careful.) It continued on around, an assistant took it across the east doorway. When it reached a vision song man (*wənjikaneit*), he shook the rattle and was answered by the singer-drummers. Then he began his vision recitation. So this went on, in my day, until about 11:30 or midnight. My mother said that in the old days, there were so many vision song men that it lasted until almost daylight.

So that was the first night of the ceremony. The second night was the same and the third night. There was not too much variation in those first three nights.

On the fourth day, the hunters were called in, though I can not state too much about the hunters because they had discontinued the hunters in my day. I will repeat what my mother, father, and older brother told me took place long ago. The hunters were called in during the daytime and the drummers would sing a hunting song for them. They would pray for them. They would burn tobacco. The hunters were advised what to do and the women assistants gave each of them a sort of lunch (*nimɘwakan*), consisting of cooked meat and ordinary corn bread (*lɘnahpɔn*) in a little parcel. The hunters were gone about two or three days and just before they came back to camp they shot a rifle once for one deer, two shots for two deer, etc. The campers would notify each other that the hunters were back. The hunters went into the Big House to be prayed for and blessed again. Then they were released from this hunting. When the deer were dressed and butchered, some members of the older generation would receive the hides. But I can not elaborate too much on this hunting, because, in my day, they got beef from the butcher. Sometimes young men also hunted squirrels for the campers.

The fourth, fifth, sixth, and seventh nights were much the same as the previous nights.

On the ninth morning, the assistants opened the back or west door to carry out and dump the ashes from the two fires. They cleaned the Big House very well and called in [42] some "clean" (chaste) person to come and use the fire drill (*sʌŋhíkʌn*) to kindle a new fire. I never saw this because women weren't permitted to see this, only men and boys. The new fire was built in preparation for the service on the ninth night.

There were special events on the ninth night. On the tenth night they had a general cleansing called the *pilhəksútin*. The assistants burned cedar in the fires before the services and fanned the smoke around the Big House. Sometimes the smoke was so dense that you could hardly see across the room. The assistants brought out the paint dish, during, what I guess you would call now, an intermission, and the women assistants would paint us on the north side. The men assistants would paint the ones on the south side and also the two carved faces on the center post (*məsingsk^w*). I can recall that the faces were so high up that these men would have to jump two or three times to put the red on the left cheek. The old women made the red paint (*pekɔn*) from bloodroot. Men and women were painted on the left cheek but only women were painted down the part of the hair. After this was done, visionaries continued to recite. Later there would be another short intermission and maybe some of the old men would say "*hayuhpú*," "*hayuhpú*" which means "let's all have a smoke." Other old men would respond "*wɛhɛ*." Then they would all light their pipes and smoke. For smoking they mixed sumac leaves with commercial Velvet or Prince Albert tobacco. For offerings, they used commercial Bull Durham. This was sort of a rest period. Later they would bring out the twelve prayersticks (*mahtehikana*) and change the drumsticks. They substituted the drumsticks with the faces on them from now until it was over. The men assistants distributed prayersticks on the south side and women assistants did the same on the north side. These were distributed to a fast beat on the drum. They had to be evenly distributed, six on one side and six on the other. There were times I remember that the assistants had to re-gather and re-distribute the prayersticks. After all this, visionaries recited again. The ones who were given these sticks, held them in their right hands, and kept time with the drum [b] beat. Whenever the reciter paused to give prayer to the Creator, they said "hooo," "hɛɛɛ" and you were supposed to hold the prayersticks up in the air. I recall that one time I was given one of these prayersticks by Mrs Minnie Fouts. I was rather young and I just stuck it in the logs behind me. So she came up to me and said "Here, you're supposed to use one of these." I got it down again, kept time, and held it up each time they gave the prayer to the Creator.

On the tenth night, there was a wooden bowl inside the door on the right hand side. Everyone who entered the church door had to drop at least one or two wampum beads into it. The beads were gathered by the assistants and taken to the Enterer. The bowl was like a flat serving bowl a little under 12 inches wide at the top, about 4½ inches deep, and had a round bottom. Later in the night, the beads were scattered in the sacred area, between the center post and the east fire. No one was ever permitted to walk on that area. These beads were scattered in about a two foot diameter area. The assistants were called up to kneel, pick up the beads quickly in their hands, and put them into their mouths while they made a humming sound like "mmmm." Sometimes they would drop some out of their mouths, which caused a little quiet chuckle in there. This was called the *mawəsi*.

The eleventh night was a continuation of the usual pattern except that they had what was called the *wiltin*. It was actually held about three times during the twelve day service. They would call out men's Delaware names. If you were not inside of the church house, the men assistants were sent outside to call out the name. The man was supposed to say "*šɛwan*" (I am here) and the assistants would return into the Big House and say "*mɛči kɛnaxkumkuwa*" (Now he has answered all of you). Then they would call out another name. Sometimes they would name seven or eight men. These named men gathered in the Big House and one of them was selected to cut a small string of wampum placed again in the sacred area. He cut the string into as many sections as there were men named. Each man would take his share, file outside, line up facing east, and pray. Everyone was very quiet [43] inside while the men were outside praying. Things would resume much as before.

On the twelfth day it was time for the women visionaries to *ahtehumwi*. This is the time that they wear their finery: beautiful clothing, ribbon work, mocassins. The women would line up by the door and each lady would select a male visionary to dance by her side and join in with her song as she recited her vision. My mother usually selected a man called *nehəneyuxwe* (One Seen As He Walks), whose English name was William Wilson. He danced inside and my mother danced outside next to the hay. She usually made only one full circuit, pausing from time to time until she finished her recitation. Then the next lady would recite. In my day there were only about five women left: my mother, Sarah Wilson Thompson, of the Wolf clan; Lucy Wilson Willets of the Wolf clan; Lisa Falleaf of the Fowl clan; a woman called *Pawlinaw*, I think her English name was Mrs Blackwing, of the Turtle clan, and another woman whose name I forgot. That night the services are much as before.

On the morning after the twelfth night, we had the *təmahəma*, which means "the end" or "the conclusion." Something like that. In the morning we all went into the church dressed in our fine Indian clothes, moccasins, ribbon work, pretty Indian skirts, blouses, paint. Again the Enterer would stand and give thanks to the Creator that we had gone thus far with the services and he would call upon the Creator that we may meet again next year and pray together again. He prayed for the children, the grandchildren, continuing much the same for the rain, everything that grows on this earth, the vegetation, game animals, good crops, all wild things, and so forth. A Delaware's prayer is rather lengthy because we try to give thanks for everything we receive in our daily life. After he finished the prayer, one man took the rattle and recited his vision. As he did so, we all danced in toward the center post. Men, women, and children each started from wherever they were sitting and gradually danced to the center post. This was called the *ləntkan* (Common Dance). Sometimes you would not get to dance very far [b] because there would be quite a crowd in there. I remember that once the old women were crying and wiping their tears away with their aprons because they sensed the end of the Big House Rite. That was in 1924, the year I graduated from High School. When the man sang his last vision song, everyone raised their hands and said again "hooo," "hɛɛɛ." Then the assistants were given wampum. Not a yard length as they did in the old days because the wampum was becoming scarce then. Everyone filed out of the east door and we all went a goodly distance from the building, lined up north and south facing east, and the men shouted the prayer words. The old people would stand in the line, but the young knelt if they were agile. The men on the north side shouted "hooo," then a man shouted *natanuk*[w] ("watch out"), and the men on the south side would immediately respond "hɛɛɛ." This was done twelve times with the left hand raised to the Creator. After twelve times it was all over. Everyone in the camp, even the campers who did not attend the services, was supposed to get in the line.

Then the services were over and everyone packed up and went home."

Old Religion among the Delawares:
The Gamwing ~ Big House Rite

Abstract
Contrary to Anthony FC Wallace's famous argument that the Gamwing (Big House rite) was an 1805 "new religion" among the Delawares, a review of his sources, native testimony, and continuing cultural import suggests instead that it was their ancient integrative ritual, held to mark the conjunction of men and women, hunt and crops, and Creator and creation as a world renewal ceremony of universal thanksgiving.

As a trial formulation of his theory of revitalization movements, Anthony FC Wallace's (1956) article on "new religions" among the Delawares has had far-reaching consequences. In particular, Wallace's assertion that the Gamwing (Big House rite) was, to use a current term, "invented" by 1805 Indiana Delawares has been adopted by many scholars, including a Delaware woman who interviewed her own relatives about their memories of the ceremony (Jones 1973).

Yet the majority of scholars who have done fieldwork among Delawares agree that the Gamwing was an ancient expression of Delaware traditions, albeit modified over time as the Delawares came to terms with changed circumstances. To reinforce this majority opinion and, at the same time, to counter Wallace's claim, I will examine the chain of evidence leading to it, particularly works by John Witthoft, Alanson Skinner, and Frank Speck, and will also consider Vernon Kinietz's extreme position that the Gamwing was Christian-derived. In each case, sources for ritual details can be found in the culture itself, not only in outside or alien influences. Moreover, such influences had both Euro-American and tribal inspiration.

To date, however, no one has detailed the reasons for this continuity. [4] In this article I undertake to explain how the Gamwing was the Delawares' integrative rite, expressing community identity and cosmic harmony from ancient times. In intent and purpose the Gamwing derived from aboriginal contexts, especially the universal reciprocity between men and women.

Based on the self-perpetuating sense of community, the Gamwing relied on twin complexes of responsibility and revelation, each with a fourfold set of relationships. For responsibility, they involved a river, a clan, a town, and a chief; for revelation, a person, a spirit, a place, and access to some degree of power.

Responsibility had to do with public good and community welfare under the leadership of the chiefly family of a clan (or clan segment) associated with a specific waterway having a regional or capital town at its mouth.[14]1 The importance of this clan leadership was marked by a town hall or big house, which was sometimes also the chiefly residence (Brinton 1888: 40).

Revelation was basic to all other relationships within the Delaware cosmos, since it established the link between a human and a spirit that alone enabled the success of any undertaking. All human careers, rituals, and historical changes were validated by a personal

---

[14] These units of Delaware social organization have often been called phratries, because they included named subunits, but clan or matriclan is used here, in part to insist that these units were comparable to the three clans of neighboring Mohawks, Oneidas, and Mahikans. Thurman (1973: 87) regarded the units as "tribes," confusing their social purpose while denying the political (and tribal) importance of obligatory interclan marriages. Yet no one got these clans more confused than John Heckewelder, the Moravian missionary long associated with the Delawares.

vision quest that resulted in such a revelation. The encounter between the person and the spirit occurred at a specific locale, often a remote elevation, and conferred access to supernatural power, which ultimately derived from the Delaware Creator.

Celebrated after the annual harvest, the Gamwing expressed these themes of gender, responsibility, and revelation by re-creating the universe, according to the origin saga, first written down in 1679, which described how the Creator used a giant turtle and a cedar tree to make the earth and the first man and woman. Over the centuries, therefore, the Gamwing became the epitome of Delaware, self-designated Lenape, culture. When elders today are asked about traditional beliefs, activities, and institutions, their replies are based on memories of this ceremony, last held in 1924 near Copan, Oklahoma.

For twelve days Delaware families worshiped in a special building symbolic of the universe, renewing their spiritual ties with all of creation. As a community, people defined themselves as Delawares by joining together under the sponsorship of the Wolf, Turkey, or Turtle clan, inherited through the mother, and by witnessing how men and women evoked their visions − personal encounters with a manitu, or spirit power-in song, gesture, and dance. Simultaneously, the entire congregation symbolically rose each night through one of the twelve layers between earth and [115] heaven, finally reaching the abode of the Creator ("the one who thought us into being") on the last night.[15]2

Before settling in present-day Oklahoma or Ontario, the Delawares suffered successive uprootings as they were forced westward from ancestral waterways linked by the Delaware River, where those who became the Munsees were in the north (Grumet 1979, 1991) and the Unamis were to the south (Newcomb 1956a; Goddard 1971, 1979).[16]3 Each relocated community expected its new settlement to be permanent, but each lasted only a decade or two before

---

[15] The Gamwing descriptions abound, written both by scholars and by Delawares themselves, although these have been educated Christians. The Oklahoma or Unami version has been described by Harrington (1921) and Speck (1931,1937), although this "classic" version includes errors by Charles Webber (Miller1980a). Michelson (1912) recorded an account translated from the words of Chief Charlie [128] Elkhair. Related summaries have been forwarded by Herman (1950); Williams (1980); Grumet (1989); Miller (1994a); Kinietz (1946), using his 1938 Oklahoma fieldwork based on the 1823 Lewis Cass questionnaire for CC Trowbridge; and Newcomb (1956a), who combines prior sources with extended 1951-52 field-work. Big House music is analyzed by Robert Adams (1977) and texts and songs by Voegelin (1939, 1941) and Goddard (1979). Social context has been provided by Sue Roark-Calnek (1980), while Prewitt (1981) has examined population trends, rural farming techniques, the impact of boarding schools, and ritual for an environmental impact statement on the Copan reservoir. The most comparative treatment is Miller's 1980a).

Delaware tribal members who have written about the rite include Richard Adams (1890, 1904, 1906); McCracken (1956), then chair of the Delaware Business Committee; Jones (1973), daughter of Lucy Blalock and professor of Art at Bacone College; Dean (1984), more personally with illustrations; and Miller and Dean (1978). Gilliland (1947) left unpublished notes.

Munsee versions have been discussed by Harrington (1921), Michelson (1922), and Speck and Moses (1945), while Wampum (Chief Waubuno 1845) included a native account and Torry (1871) was an eyewitness, although neither was sympathetic.

[16] The problematic Unalachtigos, who were probably coastal members devastated by epidemics, are omitted for lack of data (Miller 19740; Hunter 1974; Welager 1975).

American expansion forced the Delawares westward again. As hostilities increased each time, Delaware concern over kwulakan, a taboo against anger instituted to prevent divine retribution (Miller 1975), eventually led to the decision to move. Of course, as "grandfathers" or "women" in the native system of international kinship, Delawares in advance of the frontier also drew on these respected roles to function as intertribal mediators (Hale 1987).

From Pennsylvania, the Delawares moved to Ohio, and from there, after the American Revolution, the majority of Munsees moved to Ontario, in three waves. Some Munsees stayed with the Unamis and moved with them to Indiana (1800-1820), then to Missouri (1821-29) and Kansas (1830-67), before finally settling in Oklahoma (Weslager 1972, 1978; Tanner 1987). A splinter group of Unamis left Indiana and crossed the Mississippi River, giving up their own Big House tradition and ranging through Missouri, Arkansas, and Texas before they were driven, with the Caddos, to central Oklahoma in 1859 (Hale 1984a, 1984b, 1987). All along the way, a few Delaware families remained in each locality after everyone else had moved on.

During each relocation the Delawares acted on their established beliefs. The Creator sustained them, along with the epic story of creation, and in each new town a big house was built to re-create the Delaware universe, particularly during the Gamwing, enacting the creation of the world on the back of a turtle, represented by the oval dance area, holding up the central cedar tree, which was the center post.

All of these beliefs – allowing for factors of time, place, and impinging forces – were logically developed in the Gamwing. Yet as a sustainer of Delaware identity over at least half a millennium it has been misjudged by many researchers. Most notably, Anthony Wallace regarded it as an invented tradition from 1805, when the Delawares were in Indiana. But Canadian Munsee Delawares, then separate, also conducted the rite as an ancient tradition. Wallace's argument was an aspect of his very influential statement about religious changes among the Delawares. [116]

Considering American (but not Canadian) Delaware materials as "a laboratory for a study of what might be called the epidemiology of religious movements," Wallace (1956: 15) examined their frequency, their association with possible "social deprivation," and their logical fitness with prior circumstances. By his count, the Delawares had experienced at least fifteen new movements over three hundred years, or one every twenty years, on average, roughly a generation apart. These clusterings defined six stages of change: 1600-1670 was characterized by politeness to Lutheran and Quaker overtures; 1670-1740 involved tepid conversions during a time of vast land loss; 1740-60 saw the missionary efforts of David Brainerd and the Moravians (United Brethren); 1760-1800 included major hostilities and religious revivals; 1800-1820, when Wallace placed the inception of the Gamwing, was "violently nativistic ... a transitional phase between acceptance of and trust in the Whites as friends, and acceptance of them as the fundamentally hostile powers that be"; and 1820-1900, something of a residual period, witnessed the acceptance of Christianity (Baptism and Methodism), along with the rise of peyote (in the Native American Church) and the Ghost Dance among modern Oklahoma Delawares (cf. Newcomb 1956b, Harrington 1913).

Within these periods, sharp decade clusterings occurred for fourteen of the fifteen movements: in 1740-49, three movements; in 1760-69, four; in 1800-1809, two; in 1830-39, three; and in 1880-90, two. Significantly, these "five decades of new religious acceptance followed some years after the years of impact of disaster, and they were not so much adaptations to the disaster itself as to the derivative, long-term cultural distortions which the disaster revealed and induced" (same: 19). For the Delawares, "the periods of maximum hardship for groups who ultimately accepted new religions were 1730-1740 (loss of lands and geographical displacement), 1754-1760 (the French and Indian Wars), 1775-1795 (Revolution and the conflicts for the Northwest Territory), and 1810-1830 (War of 1812, the loss of reservations in Ohio and Indiana, and displacement west of the Mississippi)" (same). Each movement was intended to restore morale, the moral order, and communal identity in response to social disappointments (anomie), or a "loss of confidence in a familiar and expectedly reliable pattern of social relations, rather than deprivation of food, shelter, and other economic wants" (same).

Throughout his study Wallace (same: 2.) was concerned with adaptive innovations, "which do not result in any approximation of a foreign culture," in other words, with creative solutions based on older traditions or, in terms of contemporary theory, with cultural inventions. In presenting a baseline for Delaware change, Wallace proposed an aboriginal pattern, [117] typical of the Atlantic slope homeland, of politically autonomous communities, each comprising people who summered in the same village (cf. Wallace 1947, 1949, 1957), but he doubted that a tribe existed in any overall sense. Living in scattered towns and camps, these Delawares were "matrilineal, and the women cared for the corn plots." Hence "the Green Corn ceremony, in the early fall, was the high point of the annual festival calendar" (Wallace 1956: 3).

According to Wallace (same: 3 #4), the major ritual series of the protohistorical Delawares did not include the Big House or Gamwing: "Witthoft in his study of Green Corn ceremonialism in the eastern woodlands found that the Green Corn dance, rather than the Big House ceremony, was the ritual described by observers of the Delaware in early contact times.... the Big House was a 'new religion' dating from 1805 ... a reorganized form of the Green Corn, with innovations both in ritual detail and in over-all pattern." During the succeeding decades many scholars have accepted Wallace's strongly worded claim that the Gamwing emerged from the Green Corn, despite his own references and Delaware statements about the continuity of both rites among the Unamis in Oklahoma (see Speck 1937: 79-90). Indeed, the chain of sources cited by Wallace to derive the Gamwing from the Maize rite calls his claim into question, for it seems that he misread Witthoft, who in turn had never finished reading a novel by Harrington.

In his famous study of the Green Corn throughout the eastern woodlands, John Witthoft did not derive the one ceremony from the other; on the contrary, he cautioned against doing so. Specifically, Witthoft (1949: 15) criticized Alanson Skinner, another anthropologist celebrated for his comparative Algonquian work, for having "carelessly equated such rituals." Moreover, while Witthoft (same: 16) was silent on the antiquity of the Delaware Green Corn rite, he erred in reporting that MR Harrington "included no data pertaining to such a festival in his published accounts" of the Delawares.

In Harrington's (1963: 135) superb novel set among colonial-era Delawares, Dickon, the protagonist, initially comments that "green corn time was always a happy time in Lenape land, with much feasting; yet I never saw a public dance to celebrate the occasion, as I hear is the custom among many other tribes." Later on, however, several pages are devoted to describing a Green Corn dance, after a woman has explained that "of course you [Dickon] would not know, because the Smearer's Corn Dance was over last fall before you came to the village, and nobody thought to tell you" (same: 182).Thus the plot of the novel accounts not for the lack of the ritual but for the initial denial of it. Once Dickon has been adopted and has spent [118] a whole year in the town, he observes both the Green Corn ceremony and the Gamwing (same: 48-53). By the end of the book Dickon has received a vision and has recited it in the big house (same: 223-26).

For Harrington as for other scholars, therefore, the Green Corn and the Gamwing were parallel, not derivative, rites. Most have agreed that the Gamwing, in some form, was aboriginal among the Delawares. In particular, Paul Wallace (1975: 66), father of Anthony FC Wallace, argued, "It is, of course, probably true that the precise form in which this twelve-day ritual has come down to us does not antedate 1805, when the revelations of a Munsee prophetess gave it final shape; but its central symbol, the World Tree (imaged in the Center Post), is very old." Yet the elder Wallace left unstated the role of the world-tree center post as the touch point of Delaware creation, the sacred spot between the post and the eastern fire marking the place where woman first appeared.

While Witthoft overlooked important information in Harrington and was himself misconstrued by Anthony Wallace, he did assemble useful comparative information that helps us interpret the Gamwing as a distinctively Delaware rite. For example, Witthoft (1949: 22) reported that William Fenton had discovered that an abbreviated version of the Green Corn rite was included in the Iroquois Midwinter rite (Tooker 1970; Speck 1949). This ceremony, as reworked by the Seneca prophet Handsome Lake, summarized Iroquois belief about the world and was analogous to the Gamwing. Thus, for the Delawares the Big House rite did much the same under the influence of different prophets at different times and places. While the Green Corn of necessity was a separate event, the Gamwing began to incorporate features of Maize preharvest and other rites, because it was the culmination of the ritual year, epitomizing and all-inclusive to encompass the cosmos. Therefore, during the nineteenth century the Gamwing subsumed some features of the lapsed Green Corn and, at the very end, actually reversed the process proposed by Wallace.

Since the Green Corn was a celebration of the maturing harvest, and since Mother Corn was believed by the Delawares to be extremely jealous, all of the foods served were from plant crops; meat was excluded. Therefore, when the serving of both meat and maize is mentioned, the likelihood is that the Gamwing rather than the Green Corn is being described.

Lastly, although Harrington's opinion seldom figures in arguments about the antiquity of the Gamwing, he did make the following observation:

> That these concepts are not new among the Lenape may be seen from the fact that most of the early writers who treat these people have [119] noticed such beliefs among them, which can be traced back as far as 1679....
>
> It therefore seems likely that the rites, in spite of the differences noted, probably have a common origin, and hence date back to a period before the separation of the Unami and the Minsi [Munsee]. Indeed we have an historical account which seems to refer to this kind of ceremony as early as 1683, while under date of 1779 there is a description of the rites practiced as enacted as late as 1920 (Harrington 1921: 192, 197-98)

So while Wallace presented his evidence for historical changes in Delaware religion carefully and well, his treatment of the Gamwing as a new religion of 1805 does not stand close scrutiny.

As Frank Speck, the best-known scholar of the rite and a mentor of Wallace, observed, the Gamwing was celebrated by all major groups of Delaware refugees, whether they went to Oklahoma as Unamis or to Ontario as Munsees. Further, their diverse observances of the rite suggest its great antiquity both in the homeland and in numerous resettlements:

For, indeed, the ceremony shows itself to have a complex capitalization, its ritual extending through every form of worship, including individual, family or "clan rites," that we have mention of in any of the Delaware accounts. The Big House capitulates the elements of certain minor feast ceremonies held on special occasions by families. The great annual ceremony seems to stand as an entity, one that does not submit to any assumption of recent origin in its present form of organization (Speck 1931: 17).

> While it is one truth that the annual Big House ceremonies of the various divisions of the widely diffused Delaware Nation show specific differences in their performance, it is also true that they coincide in the basic purpose of the performance and in the essentials of worship addressed to the Creator (Speck and Moses 1945: 83).

In contrast to Speck, whose opinion was well reasoned, other scholars prior to Wallace also argued that the Gamwing had been recently created by the Delawares. Vernon Kinietz (1940: 116), who compared chronological reports relating to the Delawares over four hundred years, even attempted "to give approximate dates to the addition or subtraction of the various [ritual] elements and to show the activating force and directional factor to have been contact with European civilization" (see also Kinietz 1946).[17]4 Yet while European, particularly Christian, practices influenced the Delawares and their rituals, so did contact with other tribes, such as the Iroquois, [120] Pawnees, and Osages. These influences were therefore not unilateral, as Euro-American bias (and ethnocentrism) has suggested. Both colonies and tribes contributed to the mix. Always, their influences were grafted onto traditions with roots in the aboriginal past, supporting "tradition" to enhance the Delawares' sense of ongoing community.

Kinietz (1940: 116) further argued that among the Delawares, repeated dislocation encouraged a "union for mutual protection," while missionaries "kept the attention of the Indians on religious subjects." This enabled native prophets to blend the missionary message with traditional feasting and dancing. "That there are many vestiges of their [the Delawares'] original culture remaining is due in no small measure to the effect of recurrent revivals." Among them Kinietz (same) identified the Big House ceremony, which "is now an annual affair, held in October, in a special building called the Big House and constructed of split logs and mud with two smoke vents in the roof and doors at the East and West ends. There are two images carved on the central post and single ones on ten wall posts."

While features were added to the rite, Kinietz thought that the masks or images on the post implied an ancient communal use for the building itself. He suggested that the twelve faces reported after 1824 might represent the Twelve Apostles of Christ, despite the internal logic or integrity of Delaware culture and the importance in it of the numbers 3 and 4 and their permutations, such as 7 and 12 (Miller 1980a), seen in the subsets of the Gamwing itself.

The Gamwing

---

[17] Speck (1948) was critical of Kinietz, who left academe shortly afterward. Indeed, scholars working on Delaware materials are a notoriously contentious lot, with personal agendas and narrow viewpoints. The lack of consensus among them has retarded a general understanding of recent advances or insights into Delaware traditions and their role in the Northeast and native North America, for which the comparative study of Algonquian world renewal rites has yet to be done (Schlesier 1990).

Close analysis and native testimony indicate that the Gamwing was divided into four periods, each three days long. Days 1-3 introduced the rite with nightly recitations. Delaware men gifted with a supernatural ally expressed this alliance in a song and dance that mimicked the encounter. Days 4-6 continued the recitations and added a ceremonial hunt for deer with which to feed the congregation. Special prayers that sounded like howling were offered at the meat pole outside by men whose names were called in public for this Summoning. (Because of their intimate association with a person, formal names were rarely and carefully used in public.) Inside the big house the ushers were called to the most sacred spot, between the eastern fire and the post, for a Gathering, at which they plucked up wampum beads in imitation of birds gobbling berries. Days 7-9 marked an intensification, when more elaborate facial painting, drumsticks, and prayer sticks were used. At the Measuring each owner of a whole turtle shell rattle received a string of wampum beads equal to its length. Days 10-12 were the culmination of [ ] the rite, and the Creator was reached on the twelfth evening after smoke from red cedar boughs had purified the hall and women had recited their visions for the only time during the rite. The congregation dispersed after prayers on the last morning.

The Gamwing was celebrated after the harvest to express general thanksgiving and the reciprocity of men and women. Once held in the home of a chief, the rite relied on a triple link of chief-clan-town, localized in the town hall that evolved into the log cabin-like big house of Oklahoma. Since each town was "owned" as the abode of a particular clan segment, each rite was also clan-sponsored.

Hints of these clan-based rites occur in the modern versions, expressing characteristics of the clans as Canine (Wolf = Summoning, howling at the meat pole), Fowl (Turkey = Gathering, berry picking inside), and Turtle (= Measuring, of whole turtle shell rattles). While historical origins for the three clans have been posited according to the first appearance of these terms in documents (Hunter 1974), it is important to note that three clans, identified with different species (turtle, wolf, bear) and habitats, were a northeastern feature that the Delawares shared with the Mahikans of the middle Hudson and the Iroquoian Mohawks and Oneidas (Trigger 1978: 200, 313, 467).

Moreover, almost every feature of the Gamwing has an obvious aboriginal source.[18]5 The building can be traced to the official residence of the chief and his family, the town hall ubiquitous in aboriginal North and South America. In New England one such large community building dated to forty-three hundred years ago (Ritchie 1969: 35). In the middle Atlantic one Dutch observer noted "rough carvings of faces and images ... in the houses of the chiefs" (Adrian van der Donck, quoted in Jameson 1967 [1909]: 302). Among Powhatans to the south, similar temples, with carved posts inside and outside, were ranked from that at Uttamussak, at the mouth of the Pamunkey River (Rountree 1989: 133, 134, 177; 1990). Similarly, the Iroquois league convened at the longhouse at Onondaga (Daly 1985).

However, specifically Delaware features of the building, such as the center pole, the double fires, and the clean, oval dance area, derived from the epic (Miller 1974a), first recorded in 1679 (Danckers 1966: 150-51), about how the Creator called up a giant turtle and placed a cedar tree in the center of its back. The tree sprouted up the first man and touched down to make the first woman at the point of contact between its tip and the earth.

---

[18] My argument about the Gamwing has parallels with revised thinking about the Midewiwin of the Ojibwas and Great Lakes (Hickerson 1988), which was recast, not "invented," at Chequamegon about 1700.

Indeed, so integral to their lives was the big house and the Gamwing that almost two hundred years ago, Delawares answering a questionnaire for CC Trowbridge and Lewis Cass were able to recall, on behalf of all [122] native survivors, that before they ever saw Europeans, a lethal darkness and stench had come upon them in a big house while they were engaged in an ancestral version of the Gamwing. Set against a festive background, this grim account conveys the impact of epidemics ravaging the East Coast.

What is the earliest incident they recollect in their history?

6. Previous to the discovery of America by whites they were in a large meeting house in their worship. The day of a sudden turned dark and a very bad smell was smelt apparently coming from the sea[;] shortly after they were all taken sick and a great number of them died, since that time all manner of diseases have been prevalent among them. Before that they had no sickness as they ever heard of (Weslager 1978:89).

While the building was the locus and focus of the rite, its context was the nodal town or clan capital of a regional community involved in the essential exchange of summer crops raised by women and winter game hunted by men (Miller 1974b; Grumet 1980). During the spring runs both men and women caught and processed fish. The culmination of the women's efforts was the Green Corn or Maize rite, and that of the men's was the Masing rite, featuring the masked incarnate of the spiritual keeper of the game.[19]6

In May 1745 David Brainerd, a famous Presbyterian missionary of New Jersey, encountered a prophet some distance up the Susquehanna River who wore, attached to a bearskin cap, a wooden mask, painted half black and half tawny, with an extravagant carved mouth cut awry, along with a bearskin coat and leggings, and who carried a turtle shell rattle. This prophet preached in a new house consecrated to religious use and decorated with diverse images (Harrington 1921: 41).

His building foreshadowed the Oklahoma big house, while his mask resembled, in dark and light colors, those worn by Ontario Munsees to portray Mazink, the spiritual patron of nature in all of its living forms. Among the Unamis, this being was called Masing and was embodied at ceremonies similarly dressed in a bearskin jacket and pants, carrying a rattle made of a snapping turtle shell, and wearing a wooden face mask painted half red and half black.

The creation of new sacred space, such as a temple, was so important for the reception of new beliefs that whenever the Delawares were exposed to native prophets or Christian sects, a new "church" was constructed to mark its introduction. After missionary attempts in Ohio,

---

[19] In terms of the struckon model of Delaware culture (Miller 1979), the Maize rite was exclusive, the Masing rite inclusive, and the Gamwing inclosive (all-encompassing). This logic explains why the Gamwing could incorporate other rites, while an exclusive rite like the Green Corn was too rigid to survive historical forces. The Masing rite did not survive in Oklahoma, either, except in the role of the Masing incarnate in the Gamwing. Regrettably, local pioneers quickly labeled this hairy, masked being a "devil" and urged the Delawares to abandon him. The mask and costume were sold to MR Harrington for the Museum of the American Indian, Heye Foundation. Transferring such powerful objects to whites served to protect the Delawares from supernatural retribution, believed to rebound on the "owner" of the objects.

Indiana, and Missouri, most Unami Delawares became Baptists or Methodists in 1832, while in Kansas some Canadian Delaware Moravians rejoined them. An [123] intriguing early Mormon visit led to the aged chief's promise, never to be fulfilled, to build a new hall:

> Six months after the organization of the Mormon church, on April 6, 1830, Parley Parker Pratt and other missionaries of the church visited some of the New York and Ohio Indians and continued to Kansas. Here they interviewed William Anderson, Delaware chief, to whom they explained the Book of Mormon. After much persuasion, he was induced to call the council into session, to whom the missionary, Oliver Cowdrey, made an address. The Delaware chieftain, as spokesman for his tribe, promised to build a council house in which the Mormons might instruct his people.... but the Indian agent ordered the Mormons out of the country (Foreman 1946: 58 #27).

For Delawares, the fundamental concepts that pervade the universe are gender and Mind, because the Creator, the apex of everything, functions through thought. Delaware culture derives from the basic equation of Woman and Man, mediated by Mind (Miller 1979, 1980a, 1980b, 1980c). In terms of expression, Woman is constrained, specific, limited, segregating, marked, and exclusive; Man is unconstrained, generic, unlimited, integrating, unmarked, and inclusive. Mind is open, permeating, limitless, congregating, and inclosive. For example, when the Delawares pray and give thanks to water, the form determines what kinship terms are used. Water in wells, cups, and containers is addressed as "Mother" and free-flowing water in rivers and lakes as "Grandfather." With the creation of space and time, the order of the universe was established, and the Gamwing celebrated all these works of the Creator. Held in early October, when the tree leaves changed color, the rite marked the transition from harvest to hunt, from the crops farmed by the women to the meat supplied by the men, encompassing the annual seasons and careers. In origin, therefore, the Gamwing was a community rite intended to express thanks, the reciprocity of men and women, the importance of personal revelations, and the linkage of chief, clan, town (hall), and drainage.

After Delaware survivors had left their native waterways and had begun to coalesce into the Unami and Munsee nations, the rite also unified newly formed communities. Even so, each new town seems to have been founded, occupied, and "owned" by a clan (Thurman 1973: 106-14), whose members, in consequence, took spouses from the other two clans if they married Delawares.

> Presumably the [Gamwing] ceremony grew longer as the originally separate rituals of each village gradually consolidated into a single, [124] tribal ceremony. As recently as 1805 the vigorous, leaping dance of the seventeenth-century was still performed by the reciter; but by 1824 this had been eliminated and a number of other changes had been instituted, all of them cosmetic rather than fundamental, which suggest some influence from Christian church services.... Virtually every action in the Big House was ritualized, and a number of distinct sub-rituals were performed that may originally have been independent ceremonies (Goddard 1978: 232).

After the Delaware majority had moved into western Pennsylvania, David Zeisberger (1885,1910) visited Goschgoschink, near his own Moravian mission at Lawunakhannek

(Heckewelder 1820, 1876 [1819]; Deardorff 1946). His visit precipitated a rearrangement of the interior of the big house, a change whose significance has never been noted by scholars.

Formerly, native leaders had placed themselves at the far end of the building, with men and women arranged in separate rows by clan along either of the long sides. Then, on 16 October 1767, Zeisberger arrived at the council house, where the prophet Wangomen preached, in the middle of the three neighborhoods constituting this town, founded by Munsees in 1765. In anticipation of his preaching, the natives of the upper and middle neighborhoods, "retaining the indispensable fire, which burned in the center of the building, seated themselves in rows, men on the one side and the women on the other" (De Schweinitz 1870: 330, 332). Since Moravian churches at this time divided men from women, and since "in the German Moravian scheme of church interiors the long communion table and the chair of the liturgist behind it were placed always by the longest wall and raised on a low platform two steps off the floor" (Gray 1956: 133), these Munsees instituted the layout of all later big houses.[20]7 In general, Wallace failed to note the vital Munsee influence on the evolution of the rite. Men and women were aligned with the western and eastern ends, respectively, as in the Ontario big house (Speck and Moses 1945). Important activities and people were located in the center or along the long sides of the building, near the center post and fires. The side-focused arrangement remained unchanged even while other features of the rite were modified or abandoned.

The rite became more consistently integrative during the 1760s through the efforts of Neolin (Beatty 1962), "the Delaware Prophet" (Hunter 1971), who made participation a means of proclaiming Delaware identity. While directing the Delawares toward practices reflective of aboriginal ones, he introduced purification features, such as emetics and the sweat lodge, and insisted on the use of the left hand as holy. Memory of [125] these practices survived among the Delawares for the next two centuries (Miller 1972). In 1805 Beata, a Munsee woman among Indiana Unamis who had once been a Moravian, received in a vision instructions to transform the rite further (Miller 19946). Initially taking place in the spring, the other season when men's and women's contributions overlapped, albeit to a lesser extent, her rite soon moved to the fall. Beata gave women a greater role, particularly at the borders, boundaries, or extremes, by allowing them to recite both at the beginning and at the end of services and to sit by the doorways. Subsequently, in Kansas, men began the rite, and women ended it (Miller 1989). This version was celebrated until 1924; then it was briefly revived during World War II to ensure American victory and the safety of Delawares in the armed services.

After the Unamis had finally settled in Oklahoma, native prophets again became active, particularly in the spread of the Ghost Dance. In 1880 John Wilson, whose father was Delaware and mother Caddo,[21]8 preached in support of the Ghost Dance, peyote use, and the local Catholic church. Better known as Moonhead, Wilson established the ritual and songs of the Big Moon peyote way (Speck 1933; Newcomb 1956b), which Wallace (1956) regarded as the syncretism of Christian and Delaware traditions, much as he viewed the Big House. Charlie Elkhair and other Delaware leaders also espoused other peyote ways, or moons, that eventually replaced the Big House (Petrullo 1934).

What finally doomed the Gamwing, according to modern elders, was rigid insistence on traditional purity. The primary food had to be venison, obtained locally until white settlers cleared the forests and game became scarce. At the heart of these rituals was the special

---

[20] Interestingly, clergy of Central Moravian Church in Bethlehem, Pennsylvania, now conducts services at the far end, like the officiants at other churches.

[21] Wilson also had French ancestry.

relationship between an individual Delaware and the spirit who conferred on him or her the power to pursue particular careers and to accomplish certain tasks. The recitation of the song and the miming in dance of this personal encounter was the basis of Delaware, and indeed many other Native American, religions (Benedict 1923).

For visionaries, revelations had to be received personally and directly. While other tribes now make the acquisition of spiritual powers hereditary, Delawares never allowed a child to claim a spirit solely because it had belonged to an ancestor, although the family-sponsored rites devoted to Bear, Otter, and Dolls did involve aspects of such a claim. Rather, each vision had to be personally earned according to a belief in self-directed revelation from an encounter with a manitu, or powerful immortal. The re-creation of this bond through the formalized recitation of a song, accompanied by gestures, lay at the core of every Delaware ritual. Once these revelations generally ceased, therefore, so did the ceremonies. [126]

Every generation had been expected to renew such alliances between humans and spirits (Roark-Calnek 1977: 152; 1978). Thus the Big House was an institutionalized elaboration both of Delaware genesis and cosmology, depicted in the layout of the space and the ritual process, and of revelations basic to the guardian spirit complex, relying on the personalized transfer of power between *manituwak* and humans. Among the neighboring Iroquois, its reflex was the ado-way, or personal chant, one of the four rituals emphasized by the prophet Handsome Lake during his revision of the Midwinter ceremony (Tooker 1970). Aboriginal origins of both rituals, therefore, are based on beliefs vital to the integration of the community and the cosmos.

Today, while the cultural mechanisms encouraging fasts and quests at puberty have lapsed, a form of revelation nevertheless continues to occupy a crucial role in Delaware religion, albeit within a Christian context.[22]9 This continuity has been overlooked, however, because Delaware Christians have been so openly hostile to the Big House that the underlying source of their diverse beliefs has been denied.

Whether Christians or traditionalists, Delawares emphasize the reciprocity of men and women. During the Big House it involved venison as a natural product from men and maize as a cultural one from women. Domesticated animals blurred this distinction and were unacceptable, although beef was served, with regret, during the last decades of the Oklahoma rite.

By giving thanks to the Creator and all of creation during the Gamwing, the Delawares made manifest their beliefs about their own world, which had been derived from the turtle and the cedar. Men and women were created by the actions of the cedar, and the entire universe was thereby engendered as male or female, specifically as man or woman, according to the actual Delaware words. All of life, regardless of species, had a basically human form − with head, hands, and legs − variously cloaked with a covering that made things appear different in nature.

The themes of genders, clans, seasons, and creations were always integral to Delaware society and culture. All four themes were expressed while the Delawares lived in their homeland along the Atlantic coast and their namesake river. With the arrival of Europeans, diseases, and pressures to move west, the Delawares, through a series of prophets, used the Gamwing as a means of preserving what was vital in their beliefs and lifeways.

Over the centuries aspects of other rituals, based in families, clans, and towns, were subsumed into the Big House rite. While its message always included thanksgiving and a prayer

---

[22] In a modern sense, such revelation refers to the personal relationship with Jesus espoused by many modern Delawares. While Nora Thompson Dean and a very few other Delawares were Catholics, most today are Protestants, and many are fundamentalists, although with an openness to native traditions at odds with mainstream American beliefs.

for long life, its specific injunctions ranged from the body purity of Neolin and the purging of aliens by [127] the Shawnee Prophet to the moral uplifting that called for sexual propriety, social responsibility, and abstinence from alcohol. Once the Delawares had been dispossessed, the Gamwing became increasingly a mark of their identity, and non-Delawares were forbidden to attend it, although spouses were allowed to watch.

Munsee Delawares took the rite with them into Ontario, where many eventually became Methodists; while the Unamis continued the ceremony as they were driven from Indiana to Missouri, Kansas, and Oklahoma, where their descendants now represent a variety of Christian denominations, the Native American Church, and other faiths but nonetheless continue as a community to uphold a distinctive set of tenets from their ancient past.

Asserting aboriginal beliefs about gender, responsibility, and revelation, the Gamwing reinforced the Delaware worldview as expressed by the big house itself, the oval outline as the turtle's back on the floor and the center post as the world tree. In other words, the Gamwing was as old as the mainstays of Delaware culture, anchored by Creator, cosmos, and creations, particularly gender, place, and power.

For these reasons, the claims of neither Wallace nor Kinietz can be sustained. The Delawares clearly maintained their cultural integrity despite impinging forces from other native or alien sources. The Gamwing had and has a logic and justification all its own, rooted in the ancient Delaware homeland and continuously revealed in history.

Thanks

In a study of thanksgiving, it is a genuine pleasure to express my gratitude to Nora Thompson Dean and Lucy Parks Blalock, who shared their experiences of the Gamwing, as well as to Raymond Fogelson, Helen Tanner, Ruth Hamilton, Ross Hassig, Harvey Markowitz, and, especially, Lenape Jim Rementer.

Ethnohistory 44 (1): 113-134 Winter 1997
American Society for Ethnohistory.

The 1806 Purge among the Indiana Delaware:
Sorcery, Gender, Boundaries, and Legitimacy

Abstract

In 1805-6, along the White River of Indiana, a Monsi Delaware woman briefly appeared as a prophet, preaching a revitalized "new religion" among Delawares. In the climax that followed her resignation, several Delawares were executed on the charge of witchcraft. The lives of four of the victims, one woman and three men, are sufficiently described in the records to indicate that their offenses included collusion with Moravians and other missionaries and with US government officials. Comparing living native memories of the events with Moravian contemporary accounts reveals fascinating differences of emphasis, but also supports the native justification that these punishments did indeed fit the crimes. These sanctioned killings defined boundaries of a renewed Delaware tribe by removing deviants who had overstepped these identified limits.

Driven from their homeland along the Atlantic coast and Delaware River, the Lenape people, better known as the Delaware, moved west into Pennsylvania and then Ohio, before settling, during the years 1800-20, along the White River between present Muncie and Noblesville, Indiana (Thompson 1937; Tanner 1987).   After the shattering experiences of depopulation, displacement, and disorganization, most Delawares were drawn together again in Ohio by the skillful leadership of Chief Newcomer (*Netawatawes*) and by the military successes of Captain *Buckongihilas*.

Following the American Revolution, however, whites coveted the Delaware's prime Ohio farmland. Despite early native victories over the forces of Josiah Harmar in 1790 and Arthur St. Clair in 1791, the intertribal confederacy was eventually defeated at Fallen Timbers and, under the terms of the 1795 Treaty of Greenville, survivors left Ohio for Indiana, where the Delaware settled on land made available to them by the Miami. Later hostilities between the two tribes over the ownership of these lands [246] helped to precipitate the crisis among the Delaware that climaxed in the purge of 1806.

At the same time, Christian missionaries attempted to discredit tribal beliefs and to impose Protestant ones. The turn of the eighteenth century was filled with religious ferment. In the "Burnt Over" district of western New York, American Christianity experienced a second awakening, both in terms of huge revival meetings for established religions and the rise of "new religions" such as Mormonism of Joseph Smith and Good Word of Handsome Lake, the Seneca prophet, who blended Iroquoian and Christian practices to encourage a prosperous native future.

The Delaware were less receptive to such preaching than most tribes because they still mourned the 1782 massacre of a hundred Delaware Moravian converts at Gnadenhutten, Ohio. Former converts who sought refuge among their Delaware kin constantly warned everyone to beware of conversion because "all that the missionaries wanted was to tame them preparatory to another massacre" (Stocker 1917: 67). Indeed, most Delawares, based on their own experience, believed that the role of Christianity in American expansion was to soften up converts so that they could not defend themselves during the coming slaughter (Wallace 1956).

Moving west from New York and north from Kentucky, a few missionaries sought out scattered native communities. Quakers moved to Fort Wayne in 1801, while a Presbyterian missionary settled at Lower Sandusky, Ohio, in 1803. There, in 1805, he intervened to prevent the killing of four Wyandot women accused of witchcraft by the Shawnee Prophet (Tanner 1987: 103), who was at the forefront of the nativistic movements of this time, particularly that of his brother, Tecumseh (Tekumtha).[23]1

Although the Shawnee brothers were the most famous revolutionaries, many other local prophets were active among their own tribes. Of these, the Delaware were distinctive in having as their primary reformer a woman, a Monsi apostate who had been baptized by the Moravians as Beata. Her call to revival was insistent for several months, but then she faded into obscurity. Once the Delaware had decided to purge their ranks of deviants, they summoned Tenskwatawa to act as leader to sanction the executions, which occurred during 13-17 March 1806. Having attained political cohesion in Ohio, the Indiana Delaware sought tribal integrity by defining themselves in terms of participation in a ritual, an ancient thanksgiving rite called the Gamwing, or, more recently, the Big House Ceremony. By attending and celebrating the same ritual, Delawares embodied themselves as a cohesive whole in sacred time and space. While the Gamwing had long been the summary of their seasonal rites, Beata's preaching made it the communal basis of Delaware tribal [247] identity, shared alike by members of the three clans (Turtle, Wolf, and Turkey) and of the Monsi and Unami subtribes (Harrington 1921; Speck 1931; Miller and Dean 1978).

To accomplish this, the Delaware purged deviants who were beyond the pale of the newly defined tribal community, whose boundaries were defined on the basis of unquestioned loyalties to the Gamwing and to the "purity" of ancestral traditions. European goods and fabrics were rejected, and skins were to serve again as clothing. Dignified and solemn feasts were to be held, without white interference. For their past transgressions and current unwillingness to give up white attitudes, each victim, in turn, was accused of committing sorcery and executed by young Delaware men who had taken control during a crisis in leadership. In the aftermath of these deaths, most Delaware were cowed into their best behavior, fearful that any anger, jealousy, or selfishness would result in further witchcraft accusations, and their own executions. Malevolent intent was not eradicated and some modern Delaware continue to fear the use of witchcraft, but, as a result of the purge, the Delaware believed that whole communities were no longer threatened, only individuals and families.

According to the Delaware, witchcraft has always relied on the use of sacred bundles, passed through matrilines, containing objects required by the visions of past owners, along with many strings of wampum beads. This wampum was hoarded by gloating owners, but also was used to bribe a promise of silence from anyone who found them out. With these powerful items, witches, known as night walkers, had the ability to send members of a household into a deep sleep so they could steal any possessions they wanted. These malevolent bundles were personal possessions, unlike the important tribal and family bundles that sanctified leadership and hosting

---

[23] *Tenskwatawa*, the Shawnee Prophet, and his brother *Tecumseh* (Edmunds 1983, 1984) mobilized an intertribal offensive against American encroachments. The brothers lived with the White River Delawares from 1798 to 1801, before settling at Greenville, Ohio (1802-7) and then Prophetstown, Indiana (1808-07). The latter town, at the confluence of the Tippecanoe and Wabash Rivers, was attacked on 7 November 1811 by a force led by William Henry Harrison. After this skirmish, the brothers moved to Canada, where Tecumseh fought for the British and was killed on 5 October 1813 at the Battle of Moraviantown. Ironically, that town (on the Thames River in Ontario) had been founded by Christian Delawares who were spared massacre in Ohio. The Prophet was in Canada until 1826, when he rejoined Shawnee, then living in Kansas; where he died peacefully in 1837.

responsibilities for various personal, clan, and communal rituals.

Both witchcraft and sorcery are constant features of life in close communities, expressing the dark side forcing cooperation. Such beliefs urge members to be cooperative and friendly in order to avoid any direct conflicts. In general, sorcery is defined as an innate malevolence passed through families, while witchcraft, as with the Delaware, was transmitted through talismans that happened to pass from mother to daughter. Sorcerers are more vulnerable because their family tendencies are well known, while witches are harder to identify.

Overt accusations and subsequent punishments or executions occur under specific conditions of stress. According to Deward Walker (1989: 3, 7), who summarized the characteristics of malevolent magic in the Americas, witchcraft was "the aggressive use of supernatural techniques," and Africanists have shown "that witchcraft and sorcery perform what [248] we describe here as a governing function, in that they maintain social and ecological equilibria of various kinds." Further, periodic witch-hunts "have an obviously inhibiting effect on acculturational and other cultural changes." A better understanding of the Indiana Delaware situation is provided by Kai Erikson in his famous study of Puritan persecutions during the "crime waves" of Antinomism propounded by Anne Hutchinson in 1637, of Quaker intrusions during 1656-65, and the witchcraft trials of 1692 (1966: ix, 92, 114, 137). In each case, internal boundaries were clarified by attacks on deviants.

The deviant is a person whose activities have moved outside the margins of the group, and when the community calls him to account for that vagrancy it is making a statement about the nature and placement of its boundaries. It is declaring how much variability and diversity can be tolerated within the group before it begins to lose its distinctive shape, its unique identity. The occasion which triggers this boundary crisis may take several forms – a realignment of power within the group, for example, or the appearance of new adversaries outside it – but in any case the crisis itself will be reflected in altered patterns of deviation and perceived by the people of the group as something akin to what we now call a crime wave (same: 11, 68).

As we shall see, the Delaware were being pressured from both within and without their society. Military, missionary, and mercenary agents of American expansion were eroding Delaware attempts at cohesion, while disease, dissension, and disparity of ages tore at their sense of community. By purging the witches, the Delaware established their boundaries and strengthened their cultural reintegration. Epidemics resulted in greater numbers of young people, hearty survivors who used the purge as an opportunity to move into positions of leadership.

Unlike the Cherokee example made famous by Raymond Fogelson (1984: 261), in which an apocryphal revolt against over demanding priests served to epitomize inherent social tensions between hierarchy and equality, the Indiana purge was a historic event, but it too became symbolic for recent Delaware elders, who used it "to encompass and make intelligible seemingly impersonal, inevitable, and insidious processes of change through the invocation of a real or fanciful, dramatic, epitomizing event... [involving] human motivation and causation." While there are excellent contemporary sources for the White River events in the Moravian mission journals and diaries left by Abraham Luckenbach, John Peter Kluge, and their families (Gipson 1938; Gray 1956), we begin with the account by [249] Nora Thompson Dean, a Delaware elder who traced family back to Indiana and further east (Miller 1971-; Hunter 1971, 1974a, b, c).

Revival

As a child in Oklahoma, Nora Dean was told that the ancient Delaware led a hard but happy life. In particular, they were free to pray the way they wanted. Then whites came from across the water and tricked them out of their homeland, forcing the Delaware westward, accompanied by Nanticoke refugees. Traditionally, the Delaware avoided contact with this other tribe because of their powerful witchcraft that could exterminate entire towns.

When the migrants reached the White River, a few people went to the creek to water their horses. Among them was a Nanticoke woman leading a horse with a huge bundle tied on its back. Soon, the bundle cried like a baby, so the Delaware knew it was full of witchcraft. The woman hushed the bundle by saying that it would eat soon. A few days later, all the babies got sick and many died. Alarmed, an old man called a council to seek the cause, with the old woman the prime suspect.

A fire was built and two men dragged the old woman before the fire and told her to confess. When she denied owning a witch bundle, they burned her "a little" until she admitted that the bundle was inside a hollow tree. They retrieved the bundle and the old man ordered her to throw it into the fire, but, again and again, she refused. Finally, they threw both the woman and the bundle into the fire and burned them up. The Delaware then burned other people, men and women, who were actually innocent, including *Kaltas* (baptized as Ann Charity), an ancestor of Nora's mother. Left in a strange state of mind, people stayed up all night to reflect on their deeds. They watched for signs.

The next morning began cloudy, then bad things began to happen. Thunder and rain filled the sky, the ground trembled, and a great wind blew down many trees. Everyone screamed and was afraid. Finally, the rain stopped and the world was still. The wise men met and decided that the people had done wrong. They asked the children, both boys and girls, to pray to the Creator for forgiveness, because youngsters were pure innocents while most adults were corrupt.

An old man had previously left the proceedings and gone into the woods. There he met Masing, a supernatural being with a masklike face, wearing a bearskin outfit, and carrying a turtleshell rattle, who held up his hand, shouted "hoo, hoo," and gave the man a song. Returning, the old man explained his vision to the assembly, particularly the children, who [250] then began to pray, using the new song. These innocents were so pure that they began to rise up into the air. An old woman shouted for people to gather up soiled menstrual garments and throw them at the children. As each child was hit, he or she settled back to earth. Seven boys, however, rose into the autumn sky, where they can still be seen as the constellation known as the Pleiades. The community memorialized these events by building a longhouse and decorating it with Masing-like faces on the inside, which Nora said were "like they had done long ago when they lived in the East." Every fall, people prayed in this big house for twelve nights to thank the Creator and to ask for long life. During the rite, Masing came back to visit in the form of a man dressed in mask and bearskin.

In contrast to this account of witchcraft, execution, and repentance, the historic sources portray events that seemed disruptive at the time, but became integrative over the long run. Eventually, events occurring over several years were conflated into a single dramatic narrative. For example, while there is no mention of a Nanticoke woman at the major purge of 1806, in October 1802, two women, a Nanticoke and a Mingo Iroquois, were killed to counteract an epidemic (Gipson 1938:195). Thus, while not strictly chronological, the accuracy of Nora's account is confirmed.

In the four years between these two events, witchcraft accusations were broadened to involve Moravian converts, such as Ann Charity and Joshua, and aged leaders, such as *Tatapaxsit*, who cooperated too closely with land-hungry government officials, such as William Henry Harrison. Also implicated were Chief *Hackingpomska* and a Delaware man named Billy

Patterson. In the aftermath of the 1806 purge, William Anderson emerged as the foremost chief of the Delaware, guiding them through resettlements in Missouri and Kansas.

Captain Pipe

The most contemporary native account of the purge is the early 1824 description given to CC Trowbridge by Captain Pipe, the third Monsi Delaware of that name, who was on a visit to Indiana from Upper Sandusky, Ohio (Kinietz 1946: 92).

> They believe in witches and wizards and attribute their powers to the use of certain medicines, said to have been procured of the Nanticokes who had it from a naked infant found by them on the Sea Shore. In 1810, the prophet when preaching against the use of this medicine pointed out five or six men and women on white river as the possessors of it. These persons protested their innocence and were put to [251] the torture, where they were exhorted to save themselves by delivering the means of destruction which they possessed. Seeing no other prospect of escape from death, they professed a knowledge of the arts and promised compliance, but after release they were not able to produce the cause of the difficulty, and they were by common consent condemned to death by burning.

Though the dates are imprecise, both Pipe and Nora attributed the initial deaths to Nanticoke malevolence, agreeing that the slain Delawares were hapless victims of the outburst, unable to prove their guilt or innocence.

As the contemporary documents suggest, those killed for their deviancy were hardly innocent bystanders. Each committed antisocial acts that upset other Delawares, and their executions set new boundaries for acceptable Delaware behavior, fostering an ongoing community cohesion. The following discussion is divided between women and men because boundaries among the Delaware, as other tribes, have much to do with gender.

The Women

Women participated on both sides of the purge, as leaders and as victims, reflecting the crucial role they have always played among the Delaware. Indeed, gender was an important aspect of the boundary crisis in Indiana. Delaware were matrilineal by village and clan, and women had a more prominent role in the revised version of the Gamwing, both starting and ending the service (Miller 1989). Because Beata was the acknowledged instigator of the religious revival, the meager historical records about her are reviewed first.

Beata

In his journal, Abraham Luckenbach, Moravian missionary at White River, referred to the "woman teacher" as Beade, baptized in Friedenshutten, but the use of voiced dentals (d for t) was typical of his German dialect. Hence, the Monsi woman was properly Beata, the name usually given by Moravians to girls who die in infancy, a parallel to the use of Beatus for boys.[24]2 The registrations for the Moravian mission of Friedenshutten (also called Wyalusing or

---

[24] Important background information on these women and other leading participants occurs in

Wialusing), Pennsylvania, occupied from 1765 to 1778, indicate that three Beata were baptized there, but two died within a year of birth. The third Beata was a daughter of Moses (Fliegel 1970: #221) and Juliana, baptized by Reverend John Jacob Schmick on 8 May 1769.[25]3 On 3 March 1770, she was very sick. This early brush with death was [252] probably taken to mean Beata was spared for some special purpose, providing a good omen for a later career as a prophet. Further, her family's stay at the mission until 1773 may have provided parallels between its features, the new community hall Beata ordered built, and the buildings at later Delaware Big House encampments. Just as they continued to do in Oklahoma, the Delaware set up tents around the Big House where Beata preached.

According to Heckewelder (1820: 94), the settlers of Friedenshutten erected tents for themselves and log houses for their missionaries and for the church. The town was regularly laid out, with the chapel "an ornament to the place" (same: 119). It was also at Wyalusing that Joshua, martyred in 1806, built and played a spinet. Presumably, the log church was like that of other missions; for example, the chapel at Schoenbrun was 40' by 36', while that at Gnadenhutten was smaller. "Both were built of squared timbers, and a shingled roof, with a cupola and bell" (same: 128). Except for the cupola and bell, this building was very like the Oklahoma Big House. Notably, the chapel and tents had the appearance of the Oklahoma grounds when campers were in residence for the rite. As the Delaware were fond of recounting word pictures of their past experiences, it may be that this arrangement had its origins in such memories.

During a period of pressure for land cessions, rampant epidemics, disparities of age, and faltering native leadership, Beata preached a return to the old ways, which was endorsed by the Delaware chiefs. The focus of her teachings was a renewed Thanksgiving Rite conducted in a calm and prayerful manner. Beata's first reported vision came in February 1805, when two shadowy men, whom she later identified as angels, said "We came to tell you that God is not satisfied with you Indians, because at your sacrifices you do so many strange things with wampum and all sorts of juggling, and also do not keep separate spoons with which to stir the sacrificial meat and to dip it out." Having said this, they threw down seven wooden spoons and continued: "You Indians will have to live again as in olden times, and love one another sincerely. If you do not do this, a terrible storm will arise and break down all the trees in the woods, and all Indians shall lose their lives in it" (Gipson 1938: 333).[26]4

As word spread of Beata's message, replete with domestic images[27]5 such as spoons, the Delaware gathered to hear her preach, even during severe rainstorms. They came, not to Monseytown where she lived, but rather to the larger town of *Woapikamikunk*, where a new hall had been specially built, presumably to create an undefiled sacred space for holding the

---

Moravian records indexed and inventoried by Fliegel (1970). By convention, each person named in the records also has an identifying number.

[25] On the 1772 list of residents, Moses is located at one end of town, in a long-house with clapboards, but by 1773, he and his family had left the community (Anonymous 1772).

[26] By preaching against the use of wampum, Beata may have been avoiding its association with witchcraft, suggesting a substitute for supplies that were surely dwindling after a century away from the coast. Or she may have been [264] following a 1779 Delaware decision to rely on the written record, since wampum no longer was a traditional pledge of sincerity, particularly when whites were involved (White 1991: 383).

[27] One angel tries to predict that a baby will soon be born who will immediately tell people how to live in the old way, but the other angel rejects this sign. Even so, word of the baby was circulated, adding to the domestic, maternal, and female images in Beata's message.

sacrifices she instituted. The larger town was also the residence of Captain *Buckongihilas*, the aged Ohio war leader who lent his stature to Beata's reforms. During these gatherings, Beata warned that if her words [253] went unheeded, a storm would soon destroy forests and people. Despite this threat, the Delaware continued to fall short of her injunctions. Beata received an explanation for the lapse in a vision on 14 March 1805, when an enormously tall man appeared to her, identified himself as the Devil, and said he had kept her so confused she "could not think properly" (Gipson 1938: 339). Now, he urged, it was time for her to return to her first vision because she would be successful.

Hearing the explanation, the chiefs again called for people to gather and begin a series of sacrifices. Those gathering pledged to renounce "all evil, drinking, fornication, stealing, murder, and the like" (same: 354).

> On such occasions, the Chiefs addressed their people, both the men and women, and, although they themselves did not abstain, strictly prohibited the use of strong drink, fornication, adultery, stealing, lying, cheating, murder, and urged hospitality, love, unity, as things well-pleasing to God.... It is customary among them on these occasions to erect tents around the outside of the Council House (Stocker 1917: 153).

An eight-day sacrifice was held during April to pray for a good corn harvest. Unfortunately, its intent, "so as to enjoy a long life," came to naught when Buckongihilas died on 2.4 May 1805, a devastating blow to both Beata and her reforms.

In January 1806, Beata had a vision from God, who offered her a small white "light" to swallow and absorb as a good spirit. On her third attempt, she consumed it and "consequently spoke only the word of God" (Gipson 1938: 403). Thereafter, Beata acted as a judge, pronouncing to the community all offenses, such as witchcraft, which had been committed in strictest secrecy. After a brief time, however, dispensing justice took its toll on Beata. Despite the strong Monsi tradition of female prophets, Beata relinquished the role on the pretext that she "did not want to keep the office any longer, because it was too hard for her, being after all a woman" (same: 620).

From this moment, when she disappears from the documents, the Delaware experienced great upheaval. About this time, they became aware that their chiefs had signed an agreement with United States officials in 1804, ceding land around Vincennes. The Miami claimed ownership of that land, contested the agreement, and reestablished their rights in a treaty of 21 August 1805. A contributing factor in this reclamation was the wasteful practices of Delaware hunters, who killed animals, marketed the hides, and left the flesh to rot (White 1991: 490). Times were very unsettled. Even as the Miami were agitating to get their land back and [254] killing a few Delaware, rumors of another outbreak of smallpox began to spread.

Deprived of their judge, distrustful of their chiefs, and threatened by repeated epidemics, the young men seized authority as the largest constituency with the least fault among the Delaware. Some of this ascendancy was a result of the American Revolution, which "diminished the power of chiefs and increased that of the warriors and the war leaders" (same: 435). One of these young men, William Anderson, had recently become leader of the Turkey clan, and was fated to become the most important Delaware leader after they moved across the Mississippi River. (The place of his village is known to this day as Anderson, Indiana.)

On 13 March 1806, the young men rounded up suspected witches and began to torture them to confess. They also invited the Shawnee Prophet to come from his home in Ohio, to help identify the individuals who were causing their misfortunes. When the prophet arrived on 15

March, the accused were placed in a circle around him so he could specify their crimes and punishments. Most of the executions took place over the next two days.

Of the four best-known victims, two were Moravian allies, Ann Charity and Joshua, a second-generation Mahikan convert. The other two were traditional leaders, *Tatapaxsit*, chief of the Turtle clan, and William Patterson, his nephew, who were sympathetic to Delaware conversion. If the Moravian sources are read from a native perspective, the punishments did indeed fit the crimes. From a Delaware viewpoint, these victims were guilty as charged.

Kaltas (Caritas, Ann Charity)

The first prisoner executed was Ann Charity, a woman of about seventy, who had long been associated with the Moravians. The documents do not specify the charge against her, but it seems significant that a woman was the first victim in the aftermath of a woman prophet's resignation. Because native men and women operated in separate though mutually dependent realms, women wielded the greatest influence over their own concerns. Therefore, Ann Charity was probably an outspoken critic of Beata, and as a Moravian, had probably been preaching conversion to her own relatives in opposition to the message of the apostate Beata. Ann Charity also may have used her familiarity with European housekeeping to insult or to badger more traditional Delaware women. Since Benjamin Mortimer (Olmstead 1991: 114) estimated in 1799 that 232 former Moravian converts were living with relatives, most of these along the White River, Ann Charity typified a significant portion of the local population.

Ann Charity (Fliegel 1970: #243) was known as "an active [255] industrious woman, and admired for her cleanliness, both in dress and in household affairs" (Gipson 1938: 415 #3). As a child she lived with the family of John George Youngman, Moravian missionary to the Mahikan and later the Delaware (same: 415; Heckewelder 1820: 419). She was baptized as Caritas at age fourteen, on Christmas Day 1749 at Gnadenhutten, Pennsylvania (Hunter 1974a, b).[28]6 Her grandfather was Salomon (Salomo in Fliegel 1970: 361 #133), a Delaware leader in the region at the Forks of the Lehigh and Delaware Rivers (Hunter 19740). Although he was born at Rocky Hill, New Jersey, in 1672, his parents lived at Pennington, New Jersey. His boyhood name was *Keposh*, but after he died and miraculously returned to life, he assumed the name of *Tammekappei* ("Step Aside ~ Stand Off"). This resurrection was precipitated by a Delaware

---

[28] Fliegel (1970: 157) lists the following people as Ann Charity's siblings:
Ludwig (#176), aka Captain John Thompson, *Gulpikamen*, ? - 1781, married to Christine (#184), then to Lucia (#288), ? - 1772; Leonard (#213), ? - September 1773, married first in 1750 to Lucia (#288), who then married Zacharias (#210), before he was murdered in March 1763; Esther (#208), baptized 22 August 1749 at Bethlehem, died 21 December 1749; Anna Maria (#327), baptized at Bethlehem 28 February 1752, married to Tobias (#326), died 28 October 1753; and Jonathan (#173), baptized at Bethlehem 18 April 1749, married to Verona (#177), before she died on 17 March 1776. Jonathan returned from the Jerseys on 22 October 1753 and 22 August 1767, and claimed title to Jersey land on 20 January 1764.
Ann Charity briefly married Johan Jacob (#324), son of *Teedyuscung* (Gideon), in 1754; in 1760 she married David (#374), also called *Mamsochalent*, baptized 17 March 1754, died 1797; David's brother was *Newallika*, "Four Steps," Augustus (#760), baptized 17 March 1755, died 1769 (Hunter 19740). She and David moved to Ohio in 1772, and settled at Gnadenhutten, Ohio, in 1774, where they remained until the mission survivors scattered in 1782. After 1801, she relocated among her relatives on the White River.

chief, perhaps *Nahnquei* ("Growling" as a Dog), who abandoned his wife. When Salomon married her (*Oqehemochqua*, she died in 1748 at Nazareth), the old chief bewitched him. Salomon died, but after four days, his hand feebly lifted the cloth covering his face. When fully recovered, he told of visiting a man wearing white robes in the sky, who commanded that he return to life and take the new name.

Salomon, baptized 13-14 January 1749, had an older brother, Abraham, living at Cranbury, New Jersey; a younger sister, *Tauinechqua*, near Pennington; and at least two living children, *Memeniscunt* (Thomas) at Nazareth, Pennsylvania, and a daughter, *Pnedchaechqua*, at *Tunkhannock*, Pennsylvania. The Moravians heard that Salomon died in the spring of 1756 at Tioga (present-day Athens), Pennsylvania, and recalled that he was a man respected over a long life. His large family, often linked with the Moravians, had high status, which lends support to the claims of the White River Delaware that Ann Charity had access to supernatural powers, in both ancient and introduced forms. Certainly she belonged to a large and important family, well known for their miraculous abilities; however, such attributes doomed her.

Ann Charity certainly had a bundle, which was kept by her descendants until a decade ago. On the White River of Indiana, however, Delaware anxiety crystallized around a belief that such bundles were being used to weaken, infect, and kill Delaware upholding their ancient religion. Although bundles had been given to the missionaries when their owners converted, and were no longer in Delaware possession, they were believed to be still effective, though now used perversely in the interests of white malice. According to Drake (1852: 88):

> The tragedy commenced with the old woman. The Indians roasted her slowly over a fire for four days, calling upon her frequently to deliver [256] up her charm and medicine bag. Just as she was dying, she exclaimed that her grandson, who was then out hunting, had it in his possession. Messengers were sent in pursuit of him, and when found he was tied and brought to camp. He acknowledged that on one occasion he had borrowed the charm of his grandmother, by means of which he had flown through the air, over Kentucky, to the banks of the Mississippi, and back again to its owner, and after some consultation, he was set at liberty.

Drake based this account on his November 1821 interview with Anthony Shane, a mixed-blooded Shawnee (Draper 1821), who actually said that "an old woman called *Caltas*, chief among the women" was the one killed first. "They washed her for four days, calling on her each day to deliver up her charms and medicines, and just as she was dying, she explained that her grandchild had it, who was then hunting." They located the grandson, who admitted using the charm to fly to the Mississippi River and back in a day.

This original text adds two points for discussion. Ann Charity, or *Kaltas* (as Nora Dean knew her), was a leader among the women and was killed by washing, not burning. This was confusing until I discussed the text with Delaware elders, who thought that she was probably scrubbed with water mixed with woodash ~ lye. Thus, she would have been both burned and washed at the same time. Since one of the major criticisms of her was that she kept house like a white woman, a skill she learned from Moravians, her fastidiousness was turned against her to make the punishment fit the crime.

The Men

Most of the victims of the purge were men, and their deaths were politically motivated.

Older chiefs were particularly singled out, because these upholders of ancient traditions and community well-being had failed in their duties. They had not taken care of the people and their needs, especially in relation to the land.

Joshua

Witchcraft is understood as an extremely antisocial activity, so Joshua (1741-1806, Fliegel 1970: 230-32 #130) was guilty of the crime for which he was executed. As a second generation Moravian, the son of the famous Mahikan convert also named Joshua (same: #12) and his wife Salome, he held significant positions as national helper and translator, [157] until his scandalous conduct exposed him to charges of witchery. A complex individual, Joshua led an uneasy existence, caught between native and Moravian worlds. Although his talents ranged from that of musician and translator to skilled handyman, his life was filled with grief and discord during three marriages. In particular, his behavior between his second and third marriages made him a prime candidate for suspicion.

Joshua married Sophia, daughter of John *Papunhunk* (first Susquehanna convert, baptized by Zeisberger [Gipson 1938: 54]) in 1764; she died 2 February 1801. He then married Abagail on 31 December 1801; she died 20 March 1804. He married his third wife Peggy, a Monsi born in Esopus, on 6 January 1805 (same: 320). All of these marriages were marked by tragedy. Many of his ten children died young, including his daughters Anna and Bathseeba, who were massacred at Gnadenhutten, Ohio. Moravian records note that Joshua was censured several times for scandal, superstitious practices, and drunkenness; although, as early as 1762, he was absolved and readmitted into communion. His marriage to Abagail was particularly unhappy; she left him at least once, and after she died in 1804, Joshua became very disruptive. He was excluded from communion for heavy drinking on 21 June 1804, sold everything to pursue heathen women on 4 July 1804, and was indiscriminate in his advances toward women in general.

Of great significance is the accusation by senior converts John and Catarina Thomas that Joshua used witchcraft to kill their child (Fliegel 1970: 19 May 1803; also Gipson 1938: 231). As a grieving father who had lost many children, Joshua might be expected, in the native view, to seek the death of other people's children in revenge for his own losses. Further, his attempts to break up other marriages to get a wife of his own added to suspicions. These kinds of deliberate antisocial activities were prime evidence of a witch; that he was also a prominent member of the White River Moravian Mission made his situation even worse.

Since Moravian converts had access to two sources of potency, one native and one European, they were doubly dangerous. Joshua knew both systems of belief since, at least once, he took an ill son to a native healer (Gipson 1938: 113). Certainly, the very range of his accomplishments gave evidence of control of great power. According to the Shawnee Prophet (same: 414), however, Joshua was not a witch. Instead, he had "an evil spirit in him by means of which he could bring about the deaths of Indians." This was a kind of sorcery uniquely his own. Joshua also commanded a range of technical skills. At Wyalusing, he built and performed on a spinet, having learned music at Bethlehem in 1756-58. He was literate in both English and German (Heckewelder 1820: 414-15), [258] and fluent in Mahikan, although his Delaware translations were criticized for being a mixture of Monsi, Delaware, and Mahikan (Gipson 1938: 381). He was also skilled as a cooper, carpenter, gunsmith, and canoemaker.

Throughout Native America, the greatest manifestation of contact with the supernatural is music. When human and spirit became linked in a vision, their bond was the song given to the human. Such songs were the basis for the revelations recited in the Gamwing ~ Big House Rite (Miller and Dean 1978; Speck 1931; Harrington 1921). Interestingly, the belief in the spiritual associations of song was close to that of the Moravians, for whom music was an all-pervasive bond between nature and grace (Nelson 1963:173).

With obvious proof of his religious endowments, Joshua was open to criticism by both Moravians and natives. His repeated falls from grace were symptomatic of the degree of his distress, and his unhappy domestic life may also have been a consequence of this. Above all, his role as intermediary, translator, and musician led to a double faultfinding of him. When conditions became critical among the Delaware, Joshua was the most vulnerable victim available, and he paid with his life. It was, after all. Chief Anderson who told Luckenbach that Joshua had been killed, making it clear that he approved of the execution (Gipson 1938: 623).

Tatapaxsit

As the oldest Delaware chief in Indiana, *Tatapaxsit* was also a prime target for community fears. He was open to witchcraft accusations by virtue of his great age and seniority. In the native view, old age might be a well-earned reward, or it could be achieved by siphoning off the lives of others through witchcraft. In any case, great age was a proof of personal reserves of power: only through awesome supernatural protection could old age be achieved with faculties intact. Thus, it was believed that successful leaders were accomplished sorcerers (or allied with such), who were expected to direct their malice against critics and those who disturbed the peace of the community (same: 367). For example, when *Buckongihilas* died, *Tatapaxsit* was suspected of willing his death (same: 358).

Tatapaxsit himself contributed to community unrest by dispensing (and perhaps selling) alcohol, though he officially preached against its use (same: 190, 218). He also angered his grown family and others when, on 2.2. March 1803, he took a young woman as his second wife. Political and spiritual coercion may have convinced her family to compel the woman to marry a much older man. If she was the daughter of George Girty, as [259] I suspect, the chief may have intended this marriage to provide him with important white allies.

Tatapaxsit was most incriminated by his mark, first on the list, upon the treaty negotiated by William Henry Harrison on 18 August 1804. Article 1 specified a land cession for the Vincennes area "between the Ohio and Wabash rivers, and below the tract ceded by the treaty of Fort Wayne, and the road leading from Vincennes to the falls of Ohio" (Kappler 1903: 70-71). What the Delaware later claimed they were signing was conveyed in Article 4, "the said United States will in the future consider the Delawares as the rightful owners of all the country which is bounded by the White River on the north, the Ohio on the south," and Article 5, "stipulation that the United States will treat with the Piankeshaws for the acknowledgement of the title of the Delawares, etc." (same: 71). Unfortunately, these claims could not be sustained, as witnessed by the first article of a treaty negotiated a year later, on 21 August 1805, in which the Delaware "for the sake of peace and good neighborhood, relinquish their claim to the Vincennes in favor of the Miami." Significantly, all of the Delaware signers of this later treaty − *Hackingpomska*, William Anderson, White Eyes, and Beaver − survived the purge because they took proper steps to lead the Delaware into an acceptable compromise.

However, by 1806, there was increasing evidence that the senior chiefs were not performing their duties. They were supposed to safeguard the welfare of the community with the help of their supernatural allies, but continued disease and death proved that Delaware leaders were either ineffective or had turned malevolent. Several disasters contributed to the climax.

For example, on 1 April 1803, the Turkey clan hosted a sacrificial feast, as it did every third year, but provisions were so scarce that the participants were asked to bring their own food. This was an appalling breach of the ethic of generosity expected of hosts. Furthermore, although the rite was dedicated to achieving longevity, it ended in disaster: "the chief who had given it died during the night after a two days' illness, without anyone being present, and that in spite of the fact that he had just held a festival in the interest of long life" (Gipson 1938: 221). In societies where people thrive on warm, close relations, a death alone was dreaded. Thus, the indications were all bad when this chief died. Apparently, it was at this juncture that Anderson assumed the leadership of the Turkey clan.

Buckongihilas died 24 May 1805, and on 7-8 June many Delaware became ill, with at least six dying; this led people to remark that "last year we had two sacrifices and prayed for long life and but two people died. This year we are sacrificing all the time and all the more of our number [260] died" (same: 359). Other deaths came during subsequent months. In the same period, the Delaware's right to live on the White River was openly questioned by the Miami and other tribes.

In this growing uncertainty, *Tatapaxsit* and his wife moved to the Moravian mission during Christmas (same: 399), possibly for safety, but the Delaware made them go home. On 3 July 1805, the young men successfully agitated to have *Tatapaxsit* deposed as Turtle chief, but his age and ability entitled him to continued authority as an elder. During this crisis of leadership, the young men came forward in the spring of 1806 to take control and, in the face of accumulated evidence, those suspected of damaging the community were executed in a desperate attempt to exorcise the ill-fated Delaware communities.

Both *Tatapaxsit* and *Hackingpomska* − Wolf chief, shaman, and drunkard (same: 546; Ferguson 1972: 54) − were condemned. Only the former was executed, however, largely because of his closer ties to the Moravians and his own personal conduct. *Tatapaxsit* was slain at the Moravian mission on 17 March, his own son administering the killing blow in retaliation for the disruption caused by *Tatapaxsit* taking a second wife, and his body was burned, an insulting gesture to the deceased (Gipson 1938: 218, 622.).

Billy Patterson

Tatapaxsit's nephew, Billy Patterson, was killed next, although the charges against him were largely guilt by association. When the chiefs denied the validity of the 18 August 1804 Vincennes land cession, they sent Patterson to Fort Wayne on 5 April 1805 to ask William Wells to intercede with William Henry Harrison on their behalf (Esarey 1922: 121-122), but the effort was unsuccessful.

According to Dunn (1909: 67), Patterson died "Bible in hand, praying, chanting hymns, and defying the powers of evil until his voice was stifled." While the deaths of Joshua and Patterson may be linked here, the Shane interview (Draper 1821) implies the latter's death was a turning point, at which the Shawnee Prophet was repudiated and the Delaware again took charge of their own affairs, shamed into doing so by a brother and sister, presumably *Tatapaxsit*'s recent wife, related through their father to the famous Girty family.

The next day Patterson and Tatapaxsit's wife were brought into the council and seated together. They killed Patterson and while walking around the King's wife preparing to do the same to her, her brother, a young man of about 20, rose, took her by the hand, and led her out [261] of the council to the astonishment of the others. He returned and said the Prophet was a devil come among them and we are killing each other. This man was called George Girty, and he put a stop to the Prophet's influence among the Delawares (Draper 1821).

If Patterson were the son of *Tatapaxsit*'s older sister, he would have been heir to the Turtle chiefship. Ferguson (1971: 66, 78) says he was a mixed-blood, but this may not have been a factor in his murder. After all, both Anderson and some of his grandchildren had white fathers. Moreover, William Patterson (*Mehshaquowha*) became head chief (1831-39) after Anderson died (same: 169). While it is unclear how Billy and William were related, it is more likely that they were siblings rather than father and son, so as to account for a matrilineal succession.

Other leaders were able to ransom themselves during the days following the executions, and, eventually, the young upstarts consoled them with gifts and wampum. Despite these witch-hunts and killings, hard times continued. Famine and disease returned, together with disruptive alcoholic binges. By August, Tom, a black man, and his native son-in-law had taken over Joshua's house and were drinking an herbal concoction to encourage visions of the future (Gipson 1938: 446). At the end of August, a great festival was held, led by a man dressed in a bearskin and mask, as earlier directed to do so by Beata.

> On an occasion of this sort, at the direction of the prophetess, an Indian dresses himself in a bearskin; over his face, he wears an ugly mask, so that a disguised Indian like this makes an altogether horrible appearance. During the festival this fellow has oversight of the Indians because they are of the opinion that he knows everything and is able to bring to light all of the bad things done in secret. For this reason, he frequently goes from one Indian to the other and looks into their faces while he performs all sorts of ceremonies (same: 451).

Certainly, until the Big House Rite ended in 1914, this masked being, known as Masing, continued to play a supervisory role.

It is not clear how long the furor lasted. Certainly, the young leaders would have benefited from a close association with the Gamwing, which the Delaware regarded as the ancient wellspring of their traditions. It was likely, however, that the rite was waning by the end of the decade, only to be revived by massive earthquakes in the central Mississippi valley. The shocks began at 2AM on 16 December 1811, with a severe series occurring from 23 January through 4 February 1812. In Louisville, Jared Brooks counted 1,874 shocks between 16 December 1811 and 15 March [262] 1812 (Penick 1981: 140). The last severe tremors came at 4AM on 7 February 1812 (Douglass 1912: 212-214, 224). These earthquakes had a profound effect on natives, some of whom attributed them to Tecumseh sending a sign to members of his confederacy. Moreover, while more native people died than were recorded, in the official counts of deaths, they outnumbered others two to one: six natives, two women, one black. Within the area of disturbance, natives were the majority population, since they had been encouraged to settle there by Spanish officials seeking allies against Plains raiders (Penick 1981: 109, 121).

With the reformation of the rite after the earthquake, certain changes were made. As initially urged by Beata, and based upon earlier clan ceremonies, the Thanksgiving Rite was held every spring, in counterpoint to the other major rite, the Green Corn (Maize), held every fall. Eventually, however, the Big House Rite came to be celebrated in the fall, providing a thanksgiving for the bounty of harvest and hunt. The Green Corn Rite continued to be celebrated just before the harvest, until it lapsed after the Delaware moved to Oklahoma in 1867. When Oklahoma Delawares traced the origins of their Big House Ceremony, they attributed its renewal to the warning sign of an earthquake that went on for most of a year, during which the Delaware gathered to pray and to worship continuously (Speck 1931: 8i).

In the aftermath of the purge and revival, William Anderson, who became a leader before the coup, emerged as the dominant chief among the Delaware. He embarked on a lifelong strategy of consolidating the nation by gathering together widely scattered Delaware and relocating them onto productive lands. To do this, the Delaware moved to Missouri and then Kansas, where Anderson died, before settling in Oklahoma, then known as Indian Territory.

Conclusions

Comparing the oral tradition provided by Nora Dean with the contemporary Moravian accounts and that of Captain Pipe, obvious discrepancies occur, but these derive more from different cultural emphases than from factual errors. Each account presents its own perspective, while all but ignoring that of the other culture.

The oral memory emphasizes the increasing strength of witchcraft, particularly by Nanticoke, and the consequences of infant deaths. From other sources, we know there were Nanticoke among the Delaware in Indiana, as indeed their descendants still are in Oklahoma (Newcomb 1956: 70) [263] and that babies were dying, but the Moravians were silent on these factors. Once the Nanticoke witch was killed, the Delaware were caught up in the momentum and killed members of their own nation, including Ann Charity – the only person to overlap the different accounts. The oral tradition mentions natural forces turning against the Delaware, and a subsequent time for remorse and absolution.

The Moravian written sources give details leading up to the purge but, at the critical moment, these dwell upon the Moravians' own terror and inability to comprehend what was happening around them. The victims were specific individuals at the extremes of traditional society, tainted by their involvement with conversion schemes, land sales, and prominent whites such as William Henry Harrison, George Girty, and William Wells. Far from being senseless or random, the victims' crimes justified their punishment from a native perspective, although succeeding generations have permitted well-deserved grief to enter into the oral accounts, allowing Delaware to confess the error of their overzealous reaction to great stress and unsettling conditions. To their credit, the Delaware have tried in the ensuing years to balance necessity with remorse and cruelty with compassion.

Thanks
For sharing my torment with drafts of this paper, I would like to thank Helen Tanner, Ruth Hamilton, Ross Hassig, and John Sugden. For aid above and beyond the call, I thank Ray Fogelson and Bill Fenton.

Ethnohistory 41 (2): 124-266 Spring 1994

Delaware Traditions From Kansas
Nahkoman to Isaac McCoy

Abstract

Delaware traditions collected in 1834 are published for the first time. They are particularly informative for the active role of women in ritual and for me memories of technology and subsistence from the Atlantic shores of their homeland.

Among the many peoples who moved into the Plains were the Delaware (Lenape), who fled the Atlantic and moved west through Ohio, Indiana, Missouri, Kansas (where this record was made), and finally settled in Oklahoma over a century ago. This engaging account of their traditions occurs in the papers of famous Baptist missionary, Isaac McCoy (McCoy Collection, Kansas State Historical Society, Reel 8: Frames 617-620). It is important for several reasons.

Beginning with a parable about the introduction of alcohol, which so ravaged Native. American populations, the story specifically mentions the annual worship of thanksgiving (Gamwing or Big House Rite), which provided cultural cohesion for the Delaware until the present generation (Miller and Dean 1978, Miller ms). It was last held in full form in 1924, and was revived briefly during World War II. Though best known from Speck's (1931) somewhat flawed account, many aspects of its historical form remain unknown. Thus, the summary account of the Kansas rite is the gem of this document. Last, the memories of precontact economy and technology, reported over a century after the Delaware left the shores of the Alantic and their namesake river, provide further testimony of the native love of place, particularly a sanctified homeland. The reference to the feather blanket recalls the turkey-feather cloaks reported in the earliest historical accounts of the Delaware.

It was while in that holy land (ironically, near modern New York City) that the Delaware genesis was first recorded. The Creator placed the earth on the back of a turtle, a cedar grew at the center and created the first man and woman, the parents of all life (Miller 1974). In the Big House, the oval floor represented the back of the Turtle and the center post the Cedar.

This saga was the basis for the annual ceremony, the ancestor of the modern Big House Rite. Certainly, such a building (rotunda ~ town hall) had been a feature of Northeastern communities since the Late Archaic (cf. Wapanucket # 6 at 4300 years ago, Ritchie 1969: 32), as were fall harvest ceremonies. In origin, the gamwing was a community rite held in the fall after the harvest to express general thanksgiving and the reciprocal relationship of men and women. Such a rite would have been celebrated in the fall because this was the season when harvest and hunt overlapped, allowing both men and women to contribute their economic staples. The time was decided by the leaf-color change of deciduous trees.

Early sources refer to the annual worship as Cantico and Gamwing. According to Brinton (1884: 41), Cantico, a jollification, assimilated to Latin *cantare*, actually comes from the Lenape term "*gentkehn*, to sing and dance at the same time." Zeisberger (1887: 72) lists "*n'gamuin*, to feast," and the Brinton-Anthony dictionary (1888: 95 #9) has "*Ngamuin*, to keep a feast in Indian style." As applied to the annual festival in the Big House, therefore, the term Gamwing probably signified "the Feast of feasts."

Held in the home of a chief, the rite relied on a triple link of chief-clan-town. There are hints from different areas of Native America for an equation between the cosmos, the settlement, its community house, and its leader. For instance, among the Californian Yuki (Foster 1944: 177-178), each new chief was confirmed in office by the building of a new rotunda whose central support was a tree carefully cut down while the new chief stood securely within its branches. The evidence that the Delaware may have also made this equation rests on the fact that, once the Delaware had moved to Oklahoma in 1867, the traditionalists built two Big Houses in succession, each during the tenure of a different ceremonial leader, first Colonel Jackson and then Charlie Elkhair.

Since each town was the abode of a clan segment, each rite was also clan dependent. Features of the ancestral clan-based rites that carried over into the revised rite included the Summoning, held at the meat pole where men formerly howled like wolves and later recited the prayer words ho and ha in exchange for wampum; the Gathering, when ushers squatted and tossed wampum beads into their mouths while humming; and the Measuring, when turtle shell rattles were matched with strings of wampum. They can be associated respectively with the Canine (Wolf), Fowl (Turkey), and Turtle clans. (The abundance of wampum was an index of their ancient coastal habitat where shells for making beads were plentiful.)

Participation was based on personal contact with a supernatural (*manitu*), providing a text, song, and array of gestures evocative of that patron. The original recitations were, therefore, much more animated than the modern, more staid ones, probably after influence from Protestantism.

When the Delaware left the homeland and began amalgamating, the rite took on added significance for unifying the newly-created settlements. Even so, these towns seem to have been founded by clans.

The rite became more integrative in 1760s Ohio through the efforts of Neolin, the Delaware Prophet. He made participation a means for proclaiming Delaware identity. In the process of directing Delaware toward practices copying aboriginal ones, he introduced features emphasizing purification, such as emetics and the sweat lodge. Memory of these survived among Delaware through the next two centuries. Also, it was probably Neolin who introduced priority of the left into the rite.

The modern rite can be traced to the efforts of a woman, baptized by Moravians as Beata, who returned to her ancestral faith and preached, in late April of 1805, a renewed acceptance of former traditions, particularly the Gamwing. Nothing has previously been reported about what we know of her life from the Moravian records.

Beata (Flege 1970: 60 #616) was baptized by Rev Schmick on 8 May 1769 at Friedenshutten (also called Wyalusing), a day after her mother Juliana (#615), the wife of Moses (same: 292-3,#221). On 3 March 1770, she was gravely ill. Among Moravians, children who die in infancy are named Beatus~Beata, so it is significant that this girl was near enough to death to receive this name. The only other Beata in the Friedenshutten records both died within a year of birth. On 6 February 1773, Moses and family were asked to leave the town (Fliegel 1970: 293), subsequently Beata is called an ex-convert receiving visions from "demons".

Her efforts were noted in the diary and letters of Moravian missionaries trying unsuccessfully to establish a mission among the Delaware along the White River of modern Indiana (Gipson 1938). Descriptions of the ceremony itself were provided by Abraham Luckenbach (Gipson 1938: 611-12) and by two responses to the 1821 questionnaire sponsored by Lewis Cass and collected by Charles Trowbridge from Captain Pipe and Agent John Johnston (Kinietz 1946: 93-97 #41). Lewis Henry Morgan (1959: 57) provided an account of the ceremony in Kansas, from William Adams, a Delaware ordained as a Baptist minister and unsympathetic to the ancient religion.

Starting as a spring ceremony, the other season when men's and women's contributions overlap, Beata's rite soon moved back to the fall. She gave women a greater role, serving to define its limits, by performing at the beginning and end of the services, and by sitting near the doorways.

Beata reworked ancestral features to institute a new Gamwing directed toward general thanksgiving and culture renewal. She gave women a stronger role, which subsequently eroded, and combined aspects of clan-sponsored rituals (Summoning, Gathering, Measuring) to create a synthesis of more timely relevance for harried Delaware.

It is important that this Kansas version came from Nakoming, an acknowledged chief, and, therefore, represents the synthesis of a participant, if not leader, in the rite. McCoy (Schultz 1972), though a missionary, had little hostility toward native traditions. He gave paint and native-style apparel to his converts, feeling that fashions and dress were not mandated by God (McCoy 1840: 64, 88). Since McCoy believed that ancient ceremonies had little influence on morals, they were permitted until the natives themselves decided on their own to give them up, realizing that "Religion consisted of a right disposition of the heart, rightly influencing actions" (same: 88, 505). McCoy had long been interested in a mission among the Delaware, first proposing one in 1818. Before the Delaware moved from Missouri to Kansas, McCoy surveyed the new reserve. He, therefore, had a long and supportive association with the Delaware, whose leaders were willing to share privileged information with McCoy.

Nakoming became head chief in Kansas in 1839, after the death of William Patterson. He was long an important leader, famous for his extensive travels and war record. During the 1828 Battle of Blue River, avenging a "Pawnee" attack on soldiers from Fort Towson, he received a poison arrow in the thigh, which gradually made him blind. A special 1833 act of Congress provided him with a pension (Foreman 1930: 274). Catlin painted his portrait before he was incapacitated by 1842, although he did not pass the head chiefship to Captain Ketchum until 1849 (Ferguson 1972: 170).

I suspect his increasing handicap encouraged him to be more reflective. Certainly, his statement of the ritual, though brief, is brilliant, confirming my own analysis of the rite as based on the complimentarity of the sexes (Miller 1979, 1980) and the priority of the left (Miller 1972). Further, his account, unique among all of them, specifies that the women went first. The Oklahoma ceremony ended with recitations by women. Nakoming's report has particular appeal, however, because we know that it was a woman who instituted the modern form, although it progressively lost major features until the 1924 finale. The significance of this 1834 account, ergo, is that it shows the transition between the 1805 Indiana revision by Beata and the recent male-dominated rite of Oklahoma. It may well have been the case that the men had already assumed the beginning recitations at this time and Nakoming was giving McCoy his memory of Indiana and Missouri practices.

My own additions to the text are placed between brackets [].

From Capt. Nahkoman − Delaware Chief
Written down the day after conversation at McCoys Nov 22, 1834
To be filled up with other matters when they can be obtained

The name of the Delawares is Lenappe which [is] the name for mankind as English speak of man in distinction from beasts. Other tribes are distinguished by particular names as Putawatomie, Miamis, &. The same as white people distinguish people of different nations as Dutch, French, &.

The Indians claim to be grandfathers of the following tribes −. The following tribes are, address each other by the appellation of Sister −. The following call the Delawares uncle −−. [Left blank in the original, a, Speck (1931: 33) for application of kin terms to named tribes.]

By other tribes the Delaware are called Waupunahka because they came from the sun rising [East].

They formerly lived upon the Atlantic ocean. They are sure then none lived between them and the great water, because they have no traditions coming from the east side of them.

Previously to the appearance of white men, at one of their grand annual festivals, which is also a matter of worship, the principal man upon the occasion, who was a conjuror, exhorted them to continue the exercises longer than was customary. Before the conclusion of the additional time, he fell into a very singular and frantic frame, such as never before -first [he] became merry and loquacious, then became cross and troublesome. They got him off from the company about half a mile where, in reeling to and fro, he fell and they let him lie and sleep. From his nap he arose and was in all respects restored in a talkative mood. He told the company that another people were coming. They were not coming out of the earth, nor from above, nor out of the water, but they were upon the water.

When the whites first landed almost the first thing which they offered the Indians was whiskey. When the conjuror had scented it as the wind blew from the vessel to them, he said these were the people of whose coming he had fore told and when he saw the bottle that there was the article the drinking of which would produce such effects as they had witnessed in him at the festival. That they might have full evidence of the truth of all he spoke, he would drink some of the article.

He accordingly took three drams which produced precisely the effect which he had predicted.

The Lenappe Indians not only esteem themselves entitled to the general appellation of man, But they consider their religion a thing sacredly belonging to themselves. Nations of Indians with whom they were most friendly, and with whom they mingled much, were never allowed to become acquainted with their religious ceremonies. The house of worship was a sacred place which others were not permitted to enter.

Since the coming of the whites, their prejudices have so far relaxed that a few white men have sometimes been admitted to be present at their annual worship.

The annual festival or time for worship occurs in roasting ear time, or about the time the corn begins to harden in the ear. The women bring to the place corn, and the men bring twelve deer. Of late years we have been much concerned lest the Deer should become so scarce that twelve could not be obtained. No domestic animals could be substituted for the deer. [During the last Oklahoma rites, beef was served.]

Fire used at the festival must not be such as is common -made with flint and steel - because the Lenappe originally had no iron, consequently they used fire procured in another way. "We always procure fire for the occasion, as our forefathers did, by rubbing sticks together." This process of obtaining fire is not as difficult as might be sup [5] posed [because the pump fire drill was quite effective].

If a white person is allowed to attend worship he is placed at the door, but not allowed to mingle with the worshippers within. All who enter the door of the house of worship are required to turn immediately to the right, then he moves, he moves around to the left and must in no case go back the way he came. Every movement must be in that direction around to the left.

The females alone, without any male mingling with them, employ the first night and half the following day in worship. The principal of whom then delivers a speech to the men, in which the latter are addressed by the title of our sons. They are told that we the women are ofthe earth, and you are born of us. Therefore we have gone forward first in this worship. We have our separate and distinct spheres in which severally to act, and it is right that each should faithfully perform its relative duties. It is ours to furnish the corn, it is yours to provide the meat &&.

The men follow and perform similar ceremonies. Throughout both branches of the services, they are reminded in exhortations that there is one God, and one only, who is the creator of all things, and who has control of all things. -There is but one road to him. It is necessary that each should faithfully discharge the duties of life, that they may find their way to God. They are also reminded by their exhorters that the God will be much displeased in sins [?] committed by them during their worship. Evil thoughts must be banished from them. The sexes must be kept entirely apart and neither can [?] indulge thoughts of marriage during their continuance in worship.

The smoke of their kettles of boiled flesh and com ascends toward God.

McCoy inquired respecting a sacred bundle which report said was kept by the principal priest, or principal cantor. They said there was such a thing, but it was merely a medicine prepared from a plant known only to those principal persons who led[?]the worship. Its uses were to prevent drowsiness in time of worship. When, on account of long continued exercises, some would become sleepy, they applied some of this medicine to the left side of the face and body, and on the left arm. It was put upon the left parts because they were nearer the heart. When it is used at all, it must be applied to everyone, even to white men who may have been admitted as spectators. But as for the latter, it has not been seen to take effect, and even some other Indians, after receiving it, would become sleepy after this touching and would be carried out of the company, and so would lose the benefit of the worship.

I [McCoy] told them that we could see in many places along the coast where the Indians ate oysters and I remarked that the natives at that time probably obtained food from the waters and the woods in abundance.

They said it had not been long since old people among them could tell of the Indians collecting oysters and such things when the tide was low. In low tide also there were {places} holes of water [tidepools] left in which they caught fish with ease.

Still, their people, they observed, were subjected to much inconvenience procuring subsistence. They had no iron tools to make a hoe. They had to bum down a small tree and then bum it off at a suitable length. Then to reduce [it] to a proper thickness and shape, fire was applied to the side of the stick and as it became charred; it was scraped with a rough handstone and so, with much labour, reduced to a bow.

The arrow point was made of flint stone broke into shape by the use of other stones, and feathered with the oosing [oozing] which exuded from the pine tree.

For an ax they brought [it] into suitable shape by other stones and for a knife they used a flint. For a graining knife to take off the grain of deer skins in scraping they used the small bone of the foreleg of a deer.

Game was abundant because they killed only what they needed for food and raiment. Since skins have become an article of traffic with the whites, game has rapidly diminished, because it is often killed merely for the sake of the skin, which is sold.

Formerly, when a man desired a very fine pair of leggings, he would kill a couple of otters and, skinning them whole, would draw one onto each [6] leg with the tail hitched to his belt, and so he fancied himself fine.

Blankets were made by sewing any kind of furred skins together which made a light and warm blanket. Some who were fond of curious blankets would construct one of feathers. This must have appeared singular enough. Were one to see a person at this day in the woods and they with a blanket on made of feathers, one would be at a loss to determine what kind of an animal it was.

Acknowledgements

Thanks are due the Kansas State Historical Society of Topeka for permission to publish, Susan Box of the Bartlesville Area History Museum and Archives, Mrs Argie Thomas for her Baptist bounty, Blue Clark for haven, the Dunn family for support, and the Delaware elders who put and keep me on the right track.

Plains Anthropologist 34 (123): 1-6
Journal of the Plains Anthropological Society
Volume 34 Number 123: 1-6 February 1989

Kansas Munsee: A Lost Tribe

Unfortunately, among the general public any reference to a loat group of people conjures up only romantic notions. To the scholar, however, the reference aeans data for use in theories and analysis. If there is any romance, it is the romance of science. The report of a lost tribe or new data are vital in the social sciences. The physical sciences have the advantage of a concise, logical language (mathematics) for organizing their data and analysis. Because social scientists deal with people, who are as yet unpredictable, they must be ready to pivot and reorganize existing data as new events occur. The report of possible new data is among the most important of these new events. That is what an account of a lost tribe is about, the likelihood of new data on that group, on other groups, and on mankind generally.

In the case **of** the Kansas Munsee, they are a lost tribe on two counts. First, until a very few years ago they had not been constituted as a tribe in some while. Second, their existence has gone largely unrecognized by the anthropological profession. Ignorance of the Kansas Munsee has meant ignorance of a whole sector of Delaware society: the sector of Moravian or Christian Delaware.

I had originally gone to Ottawa, Kansas, looking for historical records on local Delaware settlement. Kansas had of course been one of the temporary locations for the Delaware between their leaving the East coast and final settlement in either Oklahoma or Canada. Most of the Unami bad settled in the former and most Munsi in the latter. However, while the Unami were settled in the vicinity of Fort Leavenworth, Kansas, [2] they were rejoined by a group of Christian Munsee who had come down from Canada.

The return of the Christian Munsee is something of a surprise in Kiev of their treatment by Americans. These Delawares were the descendants of the original Moravian converts and were closely associated with the ministry of the Reverend David Zeisberger. More than just descendants, they were in fact the survivors of the senseless, brutal massacre at Gnadenhutten, Ohio, on March 6, 1782, There about 90 Christian Delaware were clubbed to death by the American Militia. A decade later, May, 1792, Zeisberger moved the colony to Fairfield, Ontario. It was from Fairfield, with some coning by way of Green Bay, Wisconsin, and the Stockbridge Delaware, that the Moravians came when they settled Westfield, Kansas, in 1837. Later when the other Delaware moved to Oklahoma, the Munsee settled with the Chippewa in Chippewa Hills just outside of Ottawa, Kansas.

It was there that I visited with the Christian Munsee on my way to work with my Uhami kinspeople. Since I aa not at liberty to use people's names, the account has to be somewhat impersonal.

It was while I was researching in the Ottawa Carnegie Library that I encountered my first proof of living Munsee. The clue was the volume of relevant xeroxed material on file. As it turns out, the Christian Munsee are currently engaged in a legal battle to prove they are Delaware! Although every Jersey school child knows that they are, the law is more obscure. Currently the Delaware tribal roll is being revised before the allotment is distributed. To get on the roll the Christian Munsee must prove lineal descent from people on the 1800 tribal roll. Hence the need for the documents. Later when I cross-checked the case with the Unami, [3] they denied that the Kansas Munsee could appear on the roll because they have long had their own treaties, rolls, and allotments, which other Delaware did not share. At present, the outcome is pending.

Of greater significance here is the unbroken line of Moravian ministers associated with the Christian Munsee. The exact succession i« unclear, and very likely will remain so until it is rooted out of the Moravian archives in Pennsylvania. For it was there, I was told, that the church records were sent. They are so comprehensive that the three books begin with entries by Zeisberger and end with those of Reverend Joseph Romig, the last of the line. Bomlg published the only account of his followers: "The Chippewa and Munsee (or Christian) Indians of Franklin County, Kansas" in Collections of the Kansas State Historical Society, Volume XI, 1909-1910. There he tries to list the succession of ministers by name, beginning with Reverend Vogler, who came with the Munsee to Westfield, and Reverend Micksch, who is probably buried there, through four others until Romig took over until 1871 and then again between 1900 and 1905. Between 1871 and 1900 there were three ministers. Ronig also had the distinction of being father-in-law to William Killbuck, the Christian Munsee missionary to Alaska, somewhat in the tradition of the Mohigan missionary Samson Occun. The Moravian charch was torn down during the Depression, around 1932, by a white man named Young. Some Munsee were sparked by tribal pride to try and save it. Edith Killbuck, the daughter of William, was also asked to help although she was then living in Arizona. But the search for the papers to prove tribal ownership of the church lands was futile. Presently the Munsee belong to several Christian denominations. The last tie to the Moravians is the Munsee cemetery atop one of the [4] highest of the Chippewa hills. I was told that when it was founded, evergreens were planted in the shape **of a** cross **at** its middle. Knowing this, it was easy to verify it when I visited the cemetery.

The loss of church and pastor has not meant that there is no sense of continuity. Unbelievably, I was shown three pieces of wood taken as mementoes from Gnadenhutten. I know nothing else about them, but realizing that wood does not long survive in the East, they must be old. There are also hand written documents in existence. I believe the University of Kansas Library was also given one of the gospels that Zeisberger printed in the Delaware language.

As for precontact Delaware survivals, there are few. I did learn two things from an elderly man who remembered that this grandmother told him 1) the Munsee came down from Canada originally, through the east, and settled at the foot of the Alleghanies before they moved west, and 2) in Kansas the Delaware occupied a peninsula at the confluence of the Missouri and Kansas Rivers at the site of the present Old Soldiers' Home on Fort Leavenwortb. These statements are amazingly accurate considering they are at least 145 years old. Incidentally, he was unaware of any larger affiliation for the Munsee until the Delaware tribal roll case began. This is another indication of how estranged the Christian Munsee and Oklahoma Unami have become. Yet they are less than a day apart by car.

The last Munsee speaker was Sabilla Elliot (also Caleb, Nathan, and Wilcoxson) who came to Westfield in 1837 and died near Ottawa at 91 years of age in 1907. She is warmly remembered for her stories and kindness. It is a pity her traditional knowledge, to which all attest, was lost. [5]

On the whole the Munsee seem to have preferred to marry other Muneee. There **are** also numerous Munsee-White marriages, but very few Munsee-Chippewa marriages. Bonig found none in his day, but since then I have discovered three. One of these may be significant since it involved the granddaughter of the Munsee leader and the grandson of the Chippewa chief. These marriage patterns seem to indicate a continuance **of** Munsee ethnic pride.

In his history of the Delaware (1972, Rutgers Press), Weslager has very little to say about the modern day Kansas Munsee. His and ay closest ties are with the Oklahoma Unami, and I guess we both assumed that the Kansas Munsee had been long assimilated into the white population. Happily our assumption was wrong. The last recorded event for the Christian Munsee was November 8, 1900 when they were given title to their land and their funds were divided up at about $494 per person. In the photo of this event, the Moravian chapel is in the background. The photo is kept by the Munsee themselves. But left on their own, the Munsee have not gone away, and are in fact reviving as a tribe. If nothing else is learned, and I very much doubt that, something more has now been said of the Munsee, the Delaware, and the bogus idea of the American melting pot.

Delawares and Pawnees: Earth and Sky on the Plains.

Abstract

Complex interactions involving war and ritual have characterized Delaware relations with Pawnees, including the famous destruction of an earthlodge village, and these continue to this day.

Delawares entered the Plains after being driven across the eastern Woodlands from their ocean and river homelands. Moving across Pennsylvania, they regrouped in Ohio under the venerable leadership Newcomer (*Netawatwas*) counseling with clan leaders and Moravian converts. After Ohio came the religious fervor of Indiana, followed by a decade stay in Missouri, four decades in Kansas, and now 14 decades grappling with Oklahoma Cherokees. Chief William Anderson became national leader in Indiana and died in late September of 1831 (G Foreman 1946, 58 note 32) soon after Delawares settled on prime Kansas forest land, where they stayed from 1830-67, near what became Ft Leavenworth (started in 1827, Barry 1972, Cole 1912).

Delaware scouts and mountain men were famous throughout the Plains for the distinctive aroma of their tobacco smoke. Francis Parkman (1964) remarked that Kansas Delaware in 1846 were regarded as the most adventurous and dreaded warriors on the prairies, successfully taking on Sioux, Comanche, and other tribes.

Kansas Delaware hunted by treaty along an outlet to the west, 150 miles long and ten miles wide into the Plains bison range (Abel 1904) claimed by Pawnees, who lived and farmed in Nebraska but hunted in Kansas and southward.

Anderson immediately sent wampum to the Pawnee through their agent John Dougherty, who reported in October of 1831 that the gesture was "well received by the Pawnee and that they would be glad to become acquainted with the new arrivals" (G Foreman 1946, 56). Anderson had been dead for a month, and instead of a diplomatic response, hostilities began. In 1833, this same agent rode into the Skiri town to try to save a Cheyenne woman from the Morning Star sacrifice, with the same result.

Delawares prospered but at a cost to their traditions. After years of being faithful to their own religion, especially the Gamwing or Big House Rite, and hostile to Christianity, Kansas Delaware began to convert -- even as they began living on homesteads much like rural whites. Such private abodes placed individuals outside of the public gaze that had enforced community solidarity and shared sentiments (Lutz 1906, Farley 1955, Unrau 1979). Mormons, Baptists, and Methodists preached among Delawares to mixed results (below). In the 1840s, Kansas Churches themselves split over the issue of slavery.

In August 1833, Delaware baptisms began, during a time of hostilities with the Pawnee. Delaware were served from the Shawnee Baptist Mission before a Delaware Mission was started by Ira Blanchard. William Lykins gained respect for this mission by inoculating Delawares and Shawnees during a smallpox epidemic.

Watomika (Jacob Beshor, James Bouchard) left Kansas for college in Ohio to become a Presbyterian minister, then converted and join the Jesuits in St Louis and served in California during the Gold Rush (Miller 1989a).

In Kansas, on 21 November 1834, *Nahkoman* ("Answer"), who became head chief in 1839, described a Delaware Gamwing to Rev Isaac McCoy, a famous Baptist missionary, who wrote them down the next day (Miller 1989b, George Catlin painted his 1842 portrait now hanging at the Gilcrease Art Center in Tulsa). In 1849, Captain Ketchum became head chief until he died in 1857 at the age of 77 (Ferguson 1972: 170). The Conner brother, John and Jim, Ketchum nephews, became head chiefs in turn.

According to Frank Speck (1931: 17), "The Delaware Big House stood about six miles east of Lawrence, Kansas" (also repeated by Muriel Wright in McCracken 1956, 184, # 1a). In 1859, at that location, William Tomlinson (1859: 34) spent a night with Delawares in a clearing to attend what he called a "war dance", though, since both men and women danced, it was some other occasion.

Lewis Henry Morgan gathered kinship schedules from Kansas Delawares, though his key sources were Delaware Christians. Rev William Adams described the Gum-mween, while his son Richard C published an account in the 1890 census.

Morgan's oldest source was Sally Journeycake (Morgan 1959: 56-57), driven out of Ohio in 1833. She was born in Ohio in 1797, daughter of Mary Castleman, who was captured as a girl, and of Abraham Isaac Williams.[29] Sally married Solomon Journeycake, a leader of the Ohio Sandusky Delaware. Their son was Rev Charles Journeycake, ordained in Oklahoma as a Baptist preacher in 1872, and, from 1877-93, serving as the last Delaware principal chief. His death led to the creation a business council (Weslager 1978a: 237).

Kansas and Texas Delaware men spent considerable periods away from home, roaming along the frontier (Dodge 1882, Newcomb 1978). In 1837, eighty-seven served as scouts in the Seminole Wars in Florida. Others were scalp hunters in Mexico until 1850, tracking Comanche and Apache raiders in the employ of James Kirker, who glutted the market for native scalps (Gregg 1974, 228, note 4). Black Beaver (C Foreman 1946), a famous Plains Delaware guide, led James Audubon and others to California.

During the 1857 summer campaign against the Cheyenne, Fall Leaf, a Munsee with many Unami descendants still living in northeastern Oklahoma, returned with gold nuggets that helped precipitate the 1858 Colorado gold rush (Stone 1956: 227).

John C. Fremont had Delaware scouts on his expeditions of 1842, 1843, 1844, and, briefly, the ill-fated one of 1845. During the expedition of Captain Wilkes (1845: IV, 471), Horatio Hale reported "From some of the officers of the Hudson Bay company, I learned there were many Delaware and Shawnee 'Shaved Heads' among the Blackfeet.[30] Tom Hill, a famous Delaware, was present at the 1847 Whitman Massacre in Washington State. An unnamed Delaware man lived briefly on the lower Columbia River among Wishram Chinook traders. Big Nicholas[31] helped instigate the 1848 Taos Rebellion that murdered Gov William Bent, then retired to Kansas to serve on the tribal council, moved to Oklahoma, and is buried in a cemetery at Nowata.

During this period, the Pawnee men were equally adventurous, though at considerable cost at home, where they suffered the incongruity of being victims of Osage, Sioux depredations in their own homelands but victors on horse raids and skirmishes in the Southern plains and

---

[29] This sketch of Sally Journeycake's life is based on unattributed notes in the Bartlesville Library and Archives.

[30] The reference here was to the high foreheads, produced by shaving the front hair to the crown of the head, favored by older Delaware men as a mark of wisdom and maturity. This hair style was traditionally worn by councilors at formal assemblies.

[31.] Reported herein strictly for the sake of historical accuracy, his name was really "Big Nigger", when the N-word was in blatant usage.

146

Southwest. A long line of Quaker agents, pacificists all, did nothing to serve their defensive needs.

In 1832, a party led by Captain Shawannock, a son of Chief Anderson, sacked the Grand Pawnee village in retaliation for the killing of three Delawares. This was the Clarks Site on right bank of the Platte River, burned while most residents were away on their summer hunt. It was rebuilt the next year in time for a visit by Commissioner Henry Ellsworth negotiating the treaty the ceded all Pawnee lands south of the Platte. With him were Washington Irving, his nephew and secretary John Treat Irving, and several Europeans (Wedel 1936: 31). During this 1833 treaty conference among all the neighboring tribes, Delaware acted as mediators (except from Shawanuk's bravado), continuing their long diplomatic tradition. Hostilities resumed, and, on 1 December 1835, a Delaware hunting party returned with 11 Pawnee scalps.

For some time I pondered how Shwanuk escaped revenge for his arson, but, looking at the record, it is clear that almost everyone had burned a Pawnee town. The most amazing was a single Oto chief in 1806 to precipitate a war with his own disobedient people (Hyde 1974: 135), who paid off this arson with gifts.

Delaware / Pawnee warfare, moreover, had further consequences, particularly in terms of the "medicine bundles" and rituals of each tribe. Since these activities served to control life-giving power, bundle keepers acted deliberately.

In Oklahoma, traditional Delawares celebrated seven major rites. The Gamwing was the culmination and condensation of the six others, divided between Family and Tribal rites. The Family or Grease Drinking Rites, held in the spring, honored (1) Otter, (2) Bear, and (3) special Dolls. Tribal Rites, held throughout the farming cycle, honored (4) "Indian Football" games played men against women, (5) the Məsing^w, a masked bear-like being, and (6) Green Corn (Preharvest Maize).

For the Otter Rite, the singer wore a slit otter pelt with the head resting on his chest. This hide also served as the outer covering of this bundle.

Pawnees are even more famous for their bundles because they have cosmic, political, social, and cultural ramifications. Some bundles include the full garb of a warrior, featuring a collar of otterskin. This is a special use of whole skin, though otter fur also served for turbans, quivers, garters, anklets, and belts. A meteorite dedicated to Evening Star was kept in an otterhide bundle, while the Morning Star bundle's warrior garb include an otter pelt belt with 65 scalps along one side (Murie 1981: 70, 114, 119)

James Murie wrote that

> A warrior's regalia consisted of a whole otter collar, a sacred pipe, an eagle feather, soft down feathers, a buffalo-hair rope, paint, and native tobacco. The otterskin was split through the middle so the warrior could put his head through. The head of the otter usually hung on the back. On the right shoulder the warrior wore a swift hawk and on the left hung Mother Corn. On his breast were two flint arrowheads, each encircled in a ring of sweetgrass (Murie 1981: 137).

Throughout the Americas, otters are powerful beings. In the Northwest, River Otters are still regarded as mind-reading supernaturals (*kushduhkah*). Everywhere, their dexterity on land and water gained them special regard. It is therefore not surprising that both Delawares and Pawnees honored these aquatics. What is fascinating is the Pawnees gave them war associations, with the head over the shoulder to literally "watch the warrior's back", with the Delaware assured family health and wellbeing by the care and feeding of this being and its bundle (Miller 1974b).

As further indication that such a deliberate reversal is not accidental, there is another intriguing Delaware and Pawnee parallel of a most unusual kind.

In the Gamwing, two drummers sat behind a deerskin folded inside out with slats along its surface. This instrument is uncommon so it is startling that young Pawnee used an impromptu one when a young warrior rushed into the circle of warriors, "folded his buffalo robe into drum shape and placed it upon the six willow sticks he held .... The warriors gathered round the robe and sang the wolf songs, beating time with the sticks" (Murie 1981: 139).

Again, in these examples, intertribal reversals abound because what is inside and life-giving for Delawares is outside and death-taking for Pawnees.

The Kansas Delaware were directly in the path of whites moving west and their land was again chopped away in sections. By the 1854 Kansas-Nebraska Act, the Delaware lost their hunting outlet and their reservation was reduced to ten by forty miles, with land held in common. In 1860, this Diminished Reserve was allotted, with each Delaware receiving 80 acres. The remaining land was sold off to the Leavenworth, Pawnee, and Western Railroad for $1.25/acre. After delays caused by the Civil War, this money was used to buy Cherokee land and citizenship in Oklahoma.

Today, Delawares and Pawnees are friends. During the 1970s, I often spent 4th of July with Nora Dean's family at the Pawnee Homecoming. By contrast, I never went to Tahlaquah, the Cherokee capitol while she was alive.

A Birthday Peyote Meeting
Vincenzo Petrullo
Jay Miller, ed

9:00 PM

Because we were not sure of our way, we arrived a trifle late at the meeting place, and unfortunately the service was already in progress.[32]1.

One of the Indians not attending the meeting escorted us to the door of the tipi, and in so doing gave us our first lesson as to the direction we should walk during a meeting. He approached the tipi from the left, making what seemed to us an unnecessary circuit of it. I was told, however, "The Indian always goes that way, believing things go around to the left the way the sun goes in the sky. The world, too, goes that way." He added, cynically, "White man believes things go any which way, just so long as he gets there."[33]

At the door of the tipi, our guide spoke to the fire chief, who in turn made our presence known to the leader, and, after a few minutes conversation, we were admitted and shown to places on the north side. The seating of worshipers is at the will of the leader. I was told that the seating is guided by the desire to distribute the good singers around the circle in order to make the overall singing better. The only fixed positions are the leader, who sits directly behind the center of the altar facing east, the drum chief, who sits at the leader's right, the cedar-man, who sits to the left of the leader, and the fire chief,[34] whose position at the immediate right of the entrance is ideal for his duties of tending the fire, bringing in wood, and carrying in water at midnight. Visitors are usually seated at the left of the tipi entrance, considered the place of honor, as they are the first to partake of water and of breakfast, we were not seated in this usual place because one of the worshipers asked that I be seated next to him.

The leader of the meeting, who did not speak English, asked one of the worshipers to tell us that they would now start over again. He translated for us the speech made by the leader explaining the purpose for which the meeting was being held. He ended by saying he was glad we came. We all pray to the same God, and if we all pray for the boy, whose health was the concern of the gathering, he felt that our prayers would be heard, and that they would do good.

9:15 PM

The leader then said we would make cigarettes and pray for the boy. He passed pieces of corn husk to his left.[35] Following the wrappers, the leader passed a beaded tobacco pouch, filled with " Bull Durham". Each worshiper, as he received the pouch, took from it the bag of commercial tobacco, poured some of it on a corn husk, and rolled up a cigarette.

---

[32] According to Henry Murdock, "The meeting is held at night because it represents this world. This world is dark – we do not know where we go, moon and Peyote are our light. Day is as it will be in the next world – light. We will know no sickness, no hunger, no fighting."

[33] I suspect the meaning of the altar may also be the reason for moving to the left, as this would be in harmony with man's journey through life from birth to death.

[34] It may be well to explain how the officers for the meeting are appointed. Should the host not wish to act as leader, it is customary for him to do so, he asks a friend to act in that capacity. The leader chooses his assistants; the cedar man, drum chief, and fire chief.

[35] Usually the strips of corn husk were rolled. At this meeting the corn husk had evidently been purchased from a store, as it was in a waxed paper envelope.

9:20 PM

    The fire chief than took a glowing poker[36] and passed it to the lady sitting at the left of the entrance. She lighted her cigarette, and passed the poker to the left. When it made the circuit and all cigarettes were lighted, everyone began to pray in undertones. The prayers were interspersed with puffs on the tobacco and gestures of the hands, as if emphasizing a point in a petition to the Creator. The prayers were made in great earnestness and solemnity, though not in a fearful manner. They conveyed more of a sense of one who has approached near to the deity, with whom a close and friendly relationship is maintained.[37]

9: 45

    The leader stamped out his cigarette on the floor and the others followed his example. The fire chief then arose and, collecting all the butts from the left side, up to and including the leader, deposited them at the north side of the altar moon. Then, proceeding to the left from the cedar man to the door, he gathered the rest of the butts and put them in a pile at the tip of the south horn of the moon.[38]

9:55 PM

    The leader took from his box a green bandana handkerchief and spread it on the ground in front of him. On the bandana he placed a whistle made from the wing bone of an eagle, a feather fan, a peyote staff, and a gourd rattle.

    Then the cedar man approached the fire and, taking cedar needles from a pouch, sprinkled them on the fire. The drum chief and leader now approached the fire and the drum chief passed the drum through the cedar smoke while the leader did the same with the staff, rattle, and whistle. This was to make the paraphernalia ready for use – a kind of purification ceremony.

10:00 PM

    When the leader and drum chief had resumed their places, the leader explained about Peyote. He said,

> "This herb has been given to man by the Creator to be the teacher. He meant man to eat the herb so he would know. He wanted everyone to eat the herb when it is passed. When the herb is passed, take two. When we want more of the herb, ask for it. If you want to smoke and pray, ask for tobacco."

    The Peyote, in two cloth sacks, one for green and one for dried plants, was passed to the left starting with the leader, each worshiper taking two.[39] Having finished passing the Peyote

---

[36] A stick about a foot and a half long.

[37] It is possible that this sense of nearness to the Creator is due to their belief in Peyote, One of the functions of Peyote is to bring the worshiper into close contact with Him.

[38] At another meeting attended the procedure followed in the gathering of the cigarettes was slightly different. The cedar man gathered the cigarette butts from his own left toward the tipi entrance and placed the pile at the north point of the moon. The fire chief gathered the butts from the left of the door and placed them at the south tip of the horns on the moon.

[39] The dried Peyote is prepared for the meeting by washing it in warm water to remove dirt. Before eating the dried button, many Indians pick off the center fuzz. The green Peyote, ell

around, the singing was begun. The drum chief inspected the drum to see whether the top was wet; if he found it dry, he either picked it up and shook it, or placed the drum to his mouth and sucked water into the drum head. In the meantime, the leader had taken the staff in his left hand,[40] and the rattle in his right.[41] The drum chief began in a low, slow drumming while the leader shook the gourd rattle to indicate the rhythm of the song. The drum chief gradually assumed the rhythm of the song and the [3] leader began to sing. The end of the song was indicated by a lateral motion of the rattle, at which sign the drumming changed to the original low, slow beat to await the start of the next song. After singing four songs, the drum chief and leader exchanged paraphernalia, and while the leader beat the drum, the drum chief sang four songs.[42] The staff then passed to the cedar man, who sang four songs to the drummed accompaniment of the leader.

The cedar man, when he had finished singing, passed the staff to the man to his left, who sang four songs. In like manner, the staff was passed around the circle. As it came near, the Indian sitting next to me leaned over and whispered that he wanted me to drum for him[43] while he sang. When I hesitated, he reminded me that I had promised to do so when I was at his place, so I consented. When it came time for Henry [Murdock] to sing, he spoke to the leader asking permission to have me drum for him.[44] The leader nodded his consent and so the drum was passed to me and I did my best.

11:00 PM

The circuit of the tent was completed in about one hour. The singing during this round was much slower than was the singing during the latter part of the meeting when the worshipers were under the influence of Peyote. Also the procedure was more formal, that is, the drum and staff go around the tent in an orderly succession, the man at the right of the singer always doing the drumming.

When the drum had again reached the leader, he took from his satchel a red cloth and, placing it beside the handkerchief, put several fans on it. The cedar man approached the altar and again sprinkled cedar needles on the fire. The leader held the fans over the fire and also fanned himself. Replacing the fans, he passed the staff and rattle through the cedar smoke while the drum chief did the same for the drum. The worshipers were free to approach the altar and fan themselves in the cedar smoke.[45]

---

   masticated, is spit into the palm of the hand and then rolled into a compact pill and swallowed.

[40] The staff is held while you sing to give you strength. It should be remembered that the staff is held at the place of the five crosses. Either a fan or bunch of sage is also held in the left hand with the staff. The reason for this I do not know.

[41] Each worshiper usually sings four songs; I noticed, however, that some of the younger men sang but two.

[42] There was a woman sitting next to the cedar man. Women do not sing because "it is not woman's place to sing."

[43] This was Henry Murdock.

[44] Visitors and women cause this rule to be broken, however. In such cases, the man to the singer's left does the drumming.

[45] The only reason for this act that I was able to discover was "cedar is medicine — "it makes you feel good." The actions of worshipers often imitate a person bathing. The hands are held over the fire and rubbed together as when washing, and then are passed over the face,

The second round of singing was begun as the first, by the leader.[46] I noticed that the cedar man asked his neighbor the time; Henry, sitting next to me, did likewise. It was approaching the time for the midnight water and they were desirous that the ritual be carried out on time. The fire chief, with a whisk broom, began to sweep the floor; he started at the drum chief and, breaking the ceremonial rule,[47] swept the floor between worshipers and the altar to the left of the tipi door. Then again, going right, he started sweeping from the cedar man to the right of the entrance. The space between the earth altar and the crescent of ashes[48] was also swept.

11:55 PM

When the drum was about a quarter way around the tipi, the leader gave the signal and the drum and staff were immediately passed to him. When leader had received the staff and rattle, he handed the eagle wing bone whistle to the cedar man. [4]

The leader began a song, during which the cedar man blew a number of blasts with the whistle,[49] several times. The fire chief meanwhile had left the tipi. On the second song of the leader, he reappeared bringing with him a pail of water. The leader put down the staff and rattle and rolled a cigarette which he gave to the cedar man who took it to the fire chief. The man sitting to the right of the fire chief took the poker from the fire and held it for the fire chief to light his cigarette.

This was a very solemn part of the meeting as was shown by the attitude of the worshipers. Prayer was offered by a close friend of the father. He very much loved the boy for whom the meeting was being given, so the prayer should have done some good since it was the prayer of a devoted friend.

The fire chief now offered a prayer, when he finished, the drum chief took the cigarette to the leader, who gave it again to the drum chief, who puffed and handed it back to the leader, and he, in turn, gave it to the cedar man. He took a puff and returned it to the leader, who smoked, offered a prayer, and stamped out the cigarette. The fire chief dipped a cup of water from the pail and poured it on the ground in the shape of a cross,[50] then passed, first the cup and, second

---

head, and body.

[46] In a way, the drum chief starts the second round, for he sings twice during the first, once immediately following the leader, and again when the drum reaches him in making the circuit of the tipi.

[47] There was one other exception to the rule of passing to the left. If, in leaving the tent, going to the left would necessitate passing in front of someone either praying or singing, it is permissible to move toward the right. The leader, when granting permission to leave, indicated the direction you should go.

[48] As ashes are formed by the fire, they are shoved back into the moon and banked so as to form a second crescent.

[49] The following reason for blowing the whistle was given to me. "Water is here in this world for us. It shows the Creator's love for us. Animals and all need it. Eagle is the chief of all the birds, that's why. All birds and everyone else are welcome to water is what the blowing of the whistle means."

[50] I was given two explanations for this act.

"All things come from the earth. The earth is our mother. She sent out plants and things for us to eat. Water is life, it makes you live. So we pour water on the earth, to make things live." (George Kisketon)

"There's a people way back who have died. The Bible teaches they go to Heaven, but we

the pail, to the person on his left, who took a drink and started them on their circuit around the tipi.

The time had now come to offer prayer at the cardinal points. The leader passed the staff and rattle to the cedar man, while he took the eagle wing bone whistle and left the tent. During his absence, the cedar man sang, accompanied by the drum chief. The leader without went to each cardinal point,[51] prayed, and blew the whistle. When he returned to the tent, the cedar man put cedar on the fire, through which the chief passed the whistle.

When the leader resumed his place, the singing began as before. There was now a decidedly less formal atmosphere about the meeting. For example, if I desired a particular man to drum for me, I got him to come up and change places with the man on my right so that he would be in the proper position to drum for me. This seating arrangement was temporary, however; the man returning to his old place when he had finished drumming. When people desired to pray or eat more Peyote, they either asked the leader to have it passed or went to the leader and helped themselves.

4:30 AM

The singing was now on the third round. Many worshipers were visibly under the influence of Peyote. Prayers were now broken by spasms of sobbing. The actions of such individuals were similar to what had in the past been termed "sinners laboring under deep conviction of sins." The singing had changed. The beat was more rapid while the rhythm was more jerky and less smooth. In the beginning, only those immediately around the singer would join in singing a song, but frequently now, the [5] whole body of participants would join in a song. The increased volume of the singing and accelerated tempo gave the impression of unrestrained barbaric abandon.

4:50 AM

There was present at the meeting a sick man. During the course of the meeting, he frequently had violent coughing spells. The fire chief placed a lard kettle filled with water near the fire to brew Peyote tea. When the tea was ready, he took it to the sick man, who drank two cups. The remainder was placed on the red cloth before the leader.

5:00 AM

The fire chief left the tipi and returned with a shovel to fill it with ashes to start the kitchen fire to be used for making breakfast.

5:12 AM

The music began the fourth round.

5:20 AM

The fire chief swept the floor in the same manner as described above.

5:30 AM

The ash crescent and fire was pushed back further within the altar.

---

are taught that people must remain here somewhere and must be judged before they can get to a heaven. The water poured on the ground goes to these spirits" (Henry Murdock)
[51] The order is East, South, West, North.

5:45 AM

The leader gave a signal and the drum was passed to him. The morning call for water was about to be given. This call was given in the same manner as that at midnight. On the second song by the leader, a pail of water was brought in by a woman.[52] The ceremony of offering prayer was carried out as at midnight except that the cigarette was lighted by the fire chief and then handed to the woman.

6:03 AM

When the company had finished partaking of the water, cedar was placed on the fire and the woman who brought in the water, taking up the pail, passed it through the cedar smoke. Then she asked a woman sitting at the left of the cedar man to aid her in preparing breakfast. The woman consented and they went out together.

The wives and children of those attending the meeting began to come in to partake of the meal. The boy for whom the meeting was given came in and sat beside the leader, his father.

6:20 AM

Breakfast arrived. Never was I more pleased to behold a meal, not because I was hungry (the unsettled condition of my stomach made food far from desirable) but because it marked the approaching end of a vigil now almost nine hours in duration. The five vessels containing the breakfast were placed in a [6] straight line from the altar to the tipi entrance, in the order in which they were to be eaten: first, the pail of water, next, a bowl of parched corn, then, a bowl of boiled rice and raisins,[53] followed by a bowl of meat,[54] with a bowl of candies and cakes at the last. Each of these foods has a symbolical significance — water is your life, all life, corn and meat mean strength and courage, while fruits and sweets are love and sweetness.

6:23 AM

The fire chief now placed on the fire the piles of cigarette butts, so our prayers would ascend on the smoke to the Creator.

6:29 AM

The leader sang three songs accompanied by the drum chief after which (6:35 AM) a general putting away of the paraphernalia ensued. The drum chief took apart the drum, pouring the water from the inside over the altar. The leader put the fan, cloths, and eagle bone whistle into his metal box, also removed the Peyote button from the altar and placed it in the box. All of the worshipers at this time packed away their fans and drum sticks.

---

[52] Sister of the boy for whom the meeting was dedicated. It is customary for a female member of the family to bring in the morning watery. "It means more to have a family member bring water and pray for you. Women raise us from the time we are babies. They raise us up. When we get to be men, they still raise us, wash our clothes, feed us. They love us. So their prayers, they do good." (Henry Murdock)

[53] Rice and raisins come under the category of fruit. Sliced peaches is the more usual dish.

[54] The meat had been jerked, pounded in a mortar, and then mixed with sugar.

6:45 AM

The leader asked one of the men to say grace. He prayed for five minutes.[55] Cedar was now thrown on the fire to purify the food – although the food was not actually passed through the smoke. Breakfast was now ready to be eaten. The food was passed in the prearranged order, beginning with the person at the left of the tipi door, each using the common cup and the spoon in each dish. When all had eaten, the people slowly filed out, and the meeting was over.

---

[55] At one meeting, a fifteen minute grace was said.

Structuralist Analysis of the
Delaware Gamwing ~ Big House Rite[56]

A decade ago when I began research among the Delaware, they had already been the subject of countless historical treatments mining the rich records that catalog their involvement with the Dutch, Swedes, English, Germans, French, and eventual Americans. Yet, missing from all of these works was any systematic sense of the Delaware as a distinctive entity in their own right. Oh sure, there were Delaware individuals and Delaware events, but only the more prominent or obvious ones. Some authors (the more ethnohistorical ones) were also aware that there was a vague something called "culture' mucking up the reported interactions between the Delaware and others. (For example, it is all well and good to know exactly that the Delawares and fledgling Americans signed the first of many Indian treaties on 17 September 1778, or that the Delaware shifted from maize to wheat farming by 1869; but these facts alone tell us very little about the complexities and subtleties of Delaware culture which made these events possible).

Even the anthropological compendia summarizing Delaware ethnography produced through 1956 fail to tell us much about Delaware culture as an integrated conceptual system.

The problem throughout Delaware research has been that authors have not reflected on their data sources, not appreciated the kind of sophisticated analyses these data deserve, and not grasped or even attempted to go beyond mere description to present the internal logical consistency that serves to integrate, maintain, and reinterpret this or any other culture. All humans are capable of highly abstract, symbolic, meaningful, and satisfying thought; all cultures serve to focus and to articulate specific limitations on such thought; and all cultures include particularly gifted intellectuals who monitor and adapt these cultural patterns in ways congruent with their own status and the social circumstances of the moment.

Yet most sources, especially those with an historical orientation, have ignored, denied, or side-stepped the importance of culture for a fair reading of the Delaware record.

This paper is an attempt to discuss Delaware culture as it has been preserved and formulated by the Delaware themselves and "acted out" by them in their major religious ceremony, the *xingwikaon* ~ the Big House Rite. The Big House is the summation of Delaware uniqueness and their abiding strength through the past several centuries. Only after we understand the Big House Rite as the lens on Delaware culture can we honestly return to the historical record and be assured that the Delaware can then be regarded as full participants in Delaware ethnohistory. [108]

Contemporary Delaware traditionalists with whom I have worked in Oklahoma continue to use this rite as they experienced and remember it as a lens for interpreting their aboriginal culture and society. In fact, the claim to being a Delaware traditionalist is based on fluency in the Delaware language and participation in the Big House Rite. The full form of the rite was held annually until 1924 and briefly revived in abbreviated form during World War II. This paper will describe the Big House Rite based on several published sources and my own field data. I will be particularly concerned to present the rite in terms of the features common to all of the sources and of the features unique to a single source. This presentation will then serve as my data base for a structuralist analysis which is intended not only to account for the common

---

[56] The term "structuralist" in this title is intended to avoid confusion with the so-called structural studies of the British school. My intellectual influences are Americanist and structuralist.

pattern, but also for the variations reported in various sources. An additional concern of this paper will be an attempt to sort out the diachronic dimension of the rite and the relative merits of structuralist over historical interpretations. In this regard, I will be particularly concerned to distinguish what seem to be clearly historical errors in terms of dates or events from the more general disagreements among informants and sources which are less likely to be informant errors and more likely to reflect intracultural variation.

I ~ Background

The original homeland of the various communities and tribes of the Delaware nation was the drainage of the Delaware River on the Atlantic slope of the United States. Most descendants of these aboriginal Delaware now reside in Ontario, Kansas, and Oklahoma. The consequences of their movements, with its associated disruptions and pressures, has yet to be fully explored, but any analysis of Delaware materials must include an awareness of this historical dislocation. Summary histories of Delaware movements have been provided by Weslager (1972) and Spicer (1974). Miller (1975) presents data from contemporary elders which indicates that the successive movements of Delaware were both the result of supernatural prohibitions on inter-human hostilities as well as the consequences of Colonial American avariciousness. The recognition of this supernatural factor is an example of the kinds of data still retained by Delaware traditionalists which encourage a reconsideration of usual historical interpretations. Delaware social disruptions have meant that any attempt to reconstruct aboriginal Delaware society is likely to be more conjecture than fact. On the other hand, culture (in as much as it is a conceptual, integrated configuration) is more likely to have adapted to the vicissitudes of time and events, and thereby, modern Delaware culture is probably more faithful to its precontact antecedent. We will return to this possibility in the conclusion.

Scholarly consensus suggests that Delaware society was once divided into 3, or perhaps 4, tribes known as the Monsi, Unami, Unalachtigo, and possibly the Unalimi (Weslager 1972: 47, Figure 9). Miller (1974c) has countered that fieldworkers among the Delaware have been able to substantiate only the Monsi and Unami both as tribal and dialect groups. The other two tribes are mentioned only in historic documents. Interviews with Oklahoma elders have further suggested that there may have been a third Delaware tribe called the Winetkok, who historically merged with [109] other remnant tribes to form the conglomerated tribe known as the Nanticoke, which has maintained close geographical and cultural ties with the Delaware down to the present. At least the Monsi and Unami tribes were characterized by 3 matriclans, usually called Turtle, Turkey, and Wolf in the literature; although Turtle, Fowl, and Canine are better translations of the Delaware matriclan names (Miller 1973). Our accounts of the Big House Rite are limited to the Unami and the Monsi. I will focus primarily on the more numerous and detailed descriptions of the Unami rite since I have also been able to check details of this rite with Unami speakers in Northeastern Oklahoma. Another small group of Unami speakers, currently living near Anadarko in central Oklahoma, abandoned the Big House Rite when they joined the Caddo and adopted a Plains orientation in the 1800's. Reference to the Monsi rite will be reserved for the analysis section, where it will serve as a basis for a comparison of sequence and meaning in these two forms of the rite.

The last "real" Unami Big House Rite was held in the fall of 1924 at the site of the Big House building (after which the rite is named) on the Little Caney River near Copan, Oklahoma. McCracken (1956: 185) reported the date as 1927, but all available information indicates this is an error.   Newcomb (1956: 110) and living Unami say that three abbreviated Big House meetings were held during the Second World War to pray for the world and the safe return of American servicemen.   During the last service, the assistants (*ashkasak*) were children.[57]2 These meetings witnessed considerable friction, especially between Peyotists and others.   Among the reasons given for the lapsing of the Big House Rite are this kind of friction, the lack of new visionaries, and the related growth of evil and impurity in the world.

Elder Delaware remember two Big Houses used in Oklahoma.   Both were on the Little Caney River near Copan, Oklahoma, which was the locality with which Delaware traditionalists identified.   In the past generation there seems to have been a distinction between the Delaware traditionalists centered around the Caney and Big Houses and the Delaware Christians centered around Lightning Creek, the payment grounds, and the Baptist Church.   The traditionalists identify the Old Big House, built after they entered Oklahoma or Indian Territory from Kansas, with the traditional elected Chief, Colonel Jackson (died 1904), and the New Big House with the last elected traditional chief, Charles Elkhair (died 1935).   According to Rohn and Smith (n.d.) the Old Big House (site 34Wn46) was used 1867-1902 and the New Big House (site 34Wnl9) dated 1902-24, although McCracken (1956: 184) and Michelson (ms) report that the building was remodeled and roofed with handsplit shingles in 1913.   Throughout this paper, my sources will refer to the New Big House Rites under Chief Elkhair.

In summarizing the various theories, Newcomb (l956: 64ff) has argued that the Big House Rite was synthesized in the early 1700's when a Delaware tribal society was emerging from scattered, autonomous towns.   The rite was said to be a national ritual which developed from clan ceremonies, which themselves represented family privileges to particular [110] feasts and dances.   Wallace (1953: 3, note 4, 10), following Witthoft (1949), saw the Big House Rite as emerging on the White River in Indiana Territory as a reorganization of the aboriginal Green Corn Ceremony, stimulated by the visions of a Monsi woman, an apostate from the Moravian community at Friedenshuetten.   In her visions, angels told her to have the people recite their guardian spirit visionary experiences in a large house built for this purpose in the spring of 1805. Since the Green Corn dance was held in the fall, after the corn was ripe, the Big House Rite apparently began to be celebrated in the fall as a ceremony of thanksgiving.   Kinietz (1940) called attention to what he considered white and Christian influence in the rite, the number 12 for the 12 apostles is frequently mentioned.   Speck (1937: 11) thought the number 12 was derived from the lunar cycle.

While the Delaware probably long have had rituals perpetuated by clan families, such as the Doll and Otter Dances, I think this historic origin unlikely.   Miller (nd.b.) argues that the presence of 2 large, deep, contemporaneous sites along the Delaware River suggests considerable political cohesion.   I also believe that an annual tribal rite was pre-Columbian.   Speck (1945: 76) noted that standing posts with embossed human faces were widespread among Atlantic Slope peoples.   This distribution suggests that the annual rite may have focused on an earlier parallel of the Big House center post as found in the historic rite.   However, a Delaware did tell Speck (1937: 19) that the 12 carved faces inside the Big House were a "fault" or "imperfection" added shortly after contact, as was the appearance of the Masing impersonator, wearing mask and bear skin, during the rite.   This implies the Delaware regarded the rite as changed historically.   I too regard the ethnographic rite as a historic synthesis but based on a precontact ritual, much like the argument for a historic synthesis of the Midewiwin of the Ojibwa (Hickerson 1970: 63) or, more especially, for the Midwinter Rite of the Iroquois as revised by the Prophet, Handsome Lake

---

[57] The singular form is *ashkas* and the plural is *ashkasak*.

(Tooker 1970: 153). Incidentally, these previous theories indicate some of the reasons for the differences between historical and structuralist interpretation. When scholars resort to history, events are studied chronologically as a series of constants, changes, or additions. Yet a structuralist analysis looks first for the particular culture pattern in order to detail the inter-relationships which will be responsible for the rejection, addition, interpretation, or integration of items. For this reason, this article concentrates on the ethnographic evidence for traits, events, categories, and relationships to the virtual exclusion of earlier historical sources.[58]3 Diachronic problems can best be considered after the structuralist analysis has been completed, as I will do after the section on the analysis.

II ~ Sources

There are six primary sources on the Unami Big House Rite, both published and in manuscript. These sources vary in quality but a comparison of all of them permits a sorting out of consistent features and variations. Such a comparison permits me to discuss each of the sources critically. [111] The most rich and satisfactory published account, which includes a survey of earlier descriptions, is that of Harrington (1921 – hereafter MRH). Almost all of the MRH account is duplicated in the other sources, was affirmed by living Delaware elders, and has an internal consistency which supports credibility. The most troubling account is that of Speck (1931 – hereafter FGS) because it includes errors of fact and other data which seem to have been idiosyncratic to his source, Charles Webber. Miller (1976) has expressed skepticism of the cultural competence of Webber. Modern elders deny that Webber was ever a regular or frequent participant in the rite. The FGS account has to be augmented by comparison with other sources, informant statements, and a later reconsideration (Speck 1937). Among the errors attributable to Webber is his statement that the Big House building ran north and south since the evidence of photographs, informant statements, and ritual requirements indicate that the building ran east and west.

Earlier information is included in a manuscript of information collected by Trowbridge in 1823 when the Delaware were settled in Indiana (Weslager 1972: 494ff). An important source is the fieldnotes of Truman Michelson, which include an account of the rite from Charlie Elkhair collected in 1912 (hereafter CE). As the last traditional chief, Elkhair was long an active leader and participant in the rite.[59]4 I originally regarded the CE description as the most complete and reliable, but conversations with living elders have suggested to me that since the account is in English, which Elkhair spoke poorly, there is some likelihood, however slight, that his translator, Silas Longbone, could have influenced the description. It is nonetheless detailed and informative, including some significant variations from other accounts. Of equal value is the account of the final twenty years of the rite provided by Nora Thompson Dean in 1974 (Miller and Dean 1978 – hereafter NTD). Least informative are the publications by educated Delaware

---

[58]   Summaries of the ethnographic data found in the early histories of travelers and of missionaries, especially Zeisberger and Heckwelder, can be found in Kinietz (1946) and Newcomb (1956). Kinietz documents the historic changes by chronological trait summaries, while Newcomb is more systematic and integrative.

[59]   Speck (1931: 115, #3) says Elkhair had been chief since 1898, but I was told that Jackson was chief until his death. According to his gravestone, Colonel Jackson died in May 1904. Adams published a November 1903 Big House speech by Chief Jackson (Weslager 1972: 75).

on the rite, Adams (1890 and in MRH) and McCracken (1956). These later two accounts are superficial and include some misinformation presumably attributable to Traditional / Christian factionalism. I also have brief statements and comments about the rite given to me by other Unami in Northeastern Oklahoma. By relying on all these sources, it is possible to provide a full description of the sequence of events and variations in the Unami rite. Speck and Moses (1945) and MRH have summarized the Monsi Big House Rite which will provide comparative data for our analysis. The MRH account is particularly insightful for meaning and symbolism of the rite.

Before trying to piece together a consistent account of the rite, I will present a composite discussion of the Unami rite based on all of the sources.

III ~ Composite Description of the Unami Big House Rite

Preparations. CE set the beginning of the rite in the previous spring,[60] since it is then that the crops are planted for which thanks are returned in the fall rite. NTD began her account in the fall when the leaves turned colors and the officials were selected, apparently by ability or vow. These included the host ("Leader, Bringer-In, or Enterer" = *tamikət*) who conducted the service; the man who would primarily [112] impersonate the Masing; and 2 horsemen. The horsemen and the Masing visit several weeks before the rite to tell Delaware families the day selected for everyone to set up camp at the Big House site. NTD also said these men also selected the ashkasak, the ritual attendants or helpers. MRH: 84 says the Host selected the 3 male *ashkasak*, who in turn selected the 3 women. FGS: 58 said the 6 *ashkasak* consisted of a male and female pair from each of the 3 matriclans. In a letter in the Michelson manuscript, Silas Longbone also said the 6 ashkasak were paired by clan. NTD said that in her experience the *ashkasak* were not clan linked, nor could they be a married pair. Generally they were older men and post-menopausal women, who like all the campers had to be chaste, as Newcomb (1956: 65) also reported.

Before the campers arrived, the *ashkasak* cleaned and repaired the Big House itself and the surrounding area. All sources but FGS say the long axis of the rectangular Big House ran east and west. Tom Wilson, who lived near the Big House (although he sparsely attended the rite), said me that during these preparations the west door was used to bring in the hay, which was scattered around the inside walls for people to sit on. Otherwise the west door was nailed shut for most of the service. NTD described the hay strip as 4 feet wide, leaving an oval clear area in the center. In this area was the center post, an east fire, and a west fire. The most sacred area of the interior was between the center post and east fire. On the center post and wall supports were 12 carved faces, the right half painted red and the left half black according to MRH: 83 and FGS: 37. There were 3 faces on the north support posts, 3 on the south supports, 2 on the west door supports, 2 on the east door supports, and 2 on the centerpost, one facing east and the other west (e.g., photos in FGS: 34-35). For the period before 1763, Newcomb (1956: 65) describes a center post with faces which faced north and south. These faces represent the 12 Keepers of the Heavens, who are related to Masing (MRH: 31). The Creator, to whom this rite is addressed, sits in the 12th or highest heaven. CE referred to 12 tiers and NTD to 12 levels. Each

---

[60] I am tempted to suggest that the spring "Delaware football1" games, held around planting time to encourage the crops, were vaguely the first event of the Big House Rite. The games are played men against women, indicating the same cosmic symbolism of the sexes found in the Big House Rite.

Sky Keeper passes upward the prayers of humans until they ultimately reach the Creator.

All the accounts say that the rite lapsed long ago and then a continuous earthquake occurred. CE said the earth shook for a whole year until the chief revived the rite in 2 joined bark houses while a new Big House was built. After 6 months the shaking lessened. The new building was finished in the spring and used continuously until the Delaware heard the voices of the Sky Keepers outside. After a while the old men asked if anyone had a vision or "gift" from these beings. A young man did, so he and 2 old men went out to talk with the Keepers. They were told to hold the service and to plant crops. When they had done so, the earthquake stopped. The next fall they were to continue the rite and to perform it annually forever after that. The Keepers promised to drive deer near the Big House during the rite so that the hunters could kill them to feed the participants. Thereafter, the faces of the 12 Sky Keepers were carved inside the Big House so that the Keepers could put their power into the carvings. This was the change some Delaware believe occurred about the time of White contact (Speck 1937: 19). [113]

Within the Big House, people were seated by matriclan and sex. Silas Longbone sent Michelson a seating diagram in which the Turtle clan occupied the entire west half, the Canine clan occupied the northeast side, and the Fowl clan occupied the southeast side. Within these clans the Turtle women sat along the west wall with the Canine and Fowl women just inside the east door, with their respective men to the west. However, Longbone leaves no room for the Host and Singers. The more detailed diagram in MRH: plate VII is usually cited and agrees with that given by NTD. The Canine women sat in the northeast, the Canine men in the north center, the Turtle women along the west wall, the Turtle men in the southwest, the Singers in the south center, then the Fowl men and finally the Fowl women beside the east door on the south. The Host sat north of the center post before the Canine men. Adams (MRH: 119) places the Turtles on the south, the Fowl on the west, and the Wolves on the north. These various seating arrangements may be explained by the fact that the clan of the Host sits on the north, while the other 2 clans sit on the west or south (MRH: 93). While the clan seating shifted, the division by sex is constant. Most sources report that clansmen as a group and clanswomen as a group sit side by side, although Trowbridge (in Weslager 1972: 495) said the women sat behind the men. Inside the Big House, NTD said women ashkasak were responsible for the north side and men ashkasak for the south side. Outside the Big House, however, this was reversed because the women ashkasak camped on the south and men ashkasak on the north. Newcomb (1956: 65) reported that women camped on the north of the Big House and men on the south, although all other sources indicate people camped by families.

A child could briefly sit with the clan of either parent (MRH: 211). Tom Wilson told me much the same thing. However, NTD was adamant that a child sat with its matriclan. When I checked again with Wilson, he told me how, as a child, the ashkasak had once allowed him to sit with his father for a brief period before they escorted him back to his mother. Hence, a child belongs rightfully with his or her matriclan but can visit that of the father. Newcomb (1956: 109) found that many acculturated Delaware claimed descent from the clans of both mother and father. A similar change could have affected the last performances. Newcomb (1956: 64), MRH: 82, and FGS: 115 report that the form of the rite depended on the clan of the Host that sponsored the service. They cite this as evidence that the Big House Rite was a historic fusion of clan rituals. For example, the Canine form lasted 8 not 12 days (Newcomb 1956: 65). Adams (MRH, 120) says each clan had a 12 day rite which it performed once every 3 years while the other two clans held 6 day services or all 3 clans conducted a 36 day rite. Others (NTD) assert that there were no variable seating arrangements or clan forms. Other Delaware have suggested to me that the clan versions of the rite were invented to prolong informant fees. Both FGS: 85 and NTD agree that the families of the Host could be served 3 meals a day in the Big House by *ashkasak*, who also ran a food stand during the day. The ashkasak sold chili, candy, and fruit for wampum beads. They charged 25 beads, the equivalent of 25¢, for a meal (MRH: 110) and a few beads for a snack (NTD). [114]

Near the south center wall were two Singers. Although FGS: 117 noted that cranes were an early colonial ecological casualty, both he (FGS: 115, #1) and MRH: 85 call the Singers "cranes." Yet while collecting zoological taxa from NTD, I learned that the Delaware word which they translate as "crane" presently refers to Canadian geese.[61]6 The Singers are called Canadian geese because they are always a beat or two behind the person reciting a vision, much as Canadian geese repeat the call of their leader in sequence. The drum used consisted of a deerskin folded into a rectangle about 3 feet long with the hair side in. Along both the top and bottom of the long axis there were 2 slats (see sketch, MRH: 94). For the first 8 nights the Singers used drumsticks decorated with an incised X, but after the 9th night they used 2 slat drumsticks, one with an embossed face and the other with an embossed face and breasts (MRH: 102), both used facing upward. Hanging over the Singers was a small wooden bucket containing a suffusion of Red Oak (w*isahkakw*) to keep their voices clear and throats soothed. During the day young and old men would gather in the Big House to try out the drum and songs not related to visions. There was a special category of "Long Winged Creature songs", intended for the Thunderers, that were sung at this time (NTD).

The Host or Bringer-In stood just north of the center post. He was the senior visionary who conducted the rite. According to NTD he was selected from several eligible men without consideration of his clan. However, most other sources report otherwise. On the wall behind him was a 4 foot square of white cloth upon which was hung the wampum strings used in the payment of participants. At the beginning and end of each evening the Host seems to have deferred to the traditional chief, Elkhair, while the latter was alive. Then the Host reminds the people that they are gathered to worship and thank the Creator. He gives thanks for everyone's relatives, vegetation, trees, rain, stars, and much else he can think to name.[62]7 He asks that all those present live to meet again the next year. He prays for everything good and the perpetuation of the rite (MRH: 87-92, 113). He extends his kind thoughts to the people and everything else (CE). When he finishes, 2 *ashkasak* leave to cook a deer over the outside fire for the morning meal. Meanwhile, a turtle shell rattle (see MRH: 93) is placed before the Host, who begins the recitation of visions that characterized each of the 12 nights of the service. He picks up the rattle and stands. While he gave the narrative, he shook the rattle from side to side, then he would break the narrative by shouting "kwi" and sing a few lines of his vision song while shaking the rattle up and down (NTD). The narrative and song alternated until he ended with a song. Voegelin (1941) records about 15 vision songs.[63]8 During the recitation all the men, women, and children stood in place. As described by NTD,

---

[61] The word for crane is *kakos* while the word for Canadian goose is *talked* (NTD). It is the latter word that FGS: 115, #1 and MRH: 85 used to refer to the Big House Singers. Since NTD actually owns a Canadian goose, George by name, she was able to give me the name and a living example of it.

[62] Canadian Munsi used 13 mnemonic wampum strings to represent earth, plants, streams and waters, corn and beans and vegetables, wild birds and beasts, winds, sun, moon, sky, stars, thunder and rain, spirits, and the great spirit (MRH: 141). This is also Iroquois practice.

[63] A recent analysis of Delaware and Big House music is the thesis by Adams (1977).

he starts out with his dance, moving counterclockwise, and everyone but children may get up and dance behind him. Women form a separate line. From time to time he stops and tells some more of how he got his vision. All the men repeat after him, that is, they say whatever he says. Finally the man finishes with his vision recitation and he returns to where he was originally seated. Then the turtle shell rattle is [115] shoved toward the east. (I recall very well how afraid I was to make this turtle rattle because if you do, why the Singers on the south side would beat that drum twice in answer to your shake on this rattle. So when I handled it and passed it on, I was very careful not to shake it.) It went on around until the ashkasak took it across the east doorway. Maybe there would be some man on the opposite side would then sing his vision song. He would shake the rattle and the Singers would answer him. Then he did the same as the first reciter. So that went on, in my day, until about 11:30 or midnight. But my mother said that in the old days there were so many men that it lasted until daylight.

Other sources add to this account. During the intermissions between the recitations, two *ashkasak*, with a turkey wing fan held in the left hand, would sweep figurative obstacles from the cleared area and people's lives. A man and a woman *ashkasak* started from the east and west sides alternatively (CE), or according to NTD, the man sweeps from west to east and the woman from east to west. Toward morning, when the rattle had completed its last circuit, the people raised their left hands and prayed "*Ho*" 12 times (MRH: 229).

This then is the basic pattern for recitation repeated by each male visionary during the services each night. In addition, special events occurred on particular nights or days.

<u>Night One</u>. On the first day the Big House was readied by the *ashkasak*. Just before the service a ritually pure man kindles a sacred fire with a pump drill starter. Speck (1937: 21) and NTD insist that no women or children were allowed to be present in the Big House when the new fire was being made. FGS and NTD were referring specifically to the new fire on the 9th night so MRS: 87 may be correct when he reports that the first fires were made by a man and a woman ashkas. About dusky dark, the men ashkasak go around the camp calling people into the Big House. When all are seated on shawls and blankets placed on the hay, an ashkasak closes the canvas (earlier deerhide) flap on the east door (NTD). Then the Host begins his speech of thanks to the Creator and all else. When he finishes his vision recitation, 2 women *ashkasak* leave to cook the deer stew for the morning meal. Inside others recite their visions until the rattle has finished its last circuit. Then the chief, not the Host, asks that the stew be brought in (CE).

<u>Second and Third Nights</u>. The sacred fire continues in use and recitations are repeated. Apparently when the Delaware were in Indiana, a new fire was kindled each day to prevent its secular contamination (Kinietz 1946: 93). Adams (MRH: 120) reports "On the third day of the dance all men, both married and single, are required to keep out of the company of women for 3 days at least." This may have been a special injunction on the already continent camp. [116]

<u>Fourth Day</u>. On this day the hunters are sent out. This event had lapsed by the time of NTD, but CE provided a full account. At noon as many men who want to hunt enter the Big House. They elect a leader and eat lunch. Elsewhere in his description CE said the hunt leader should be an *ashkas*. After eating they line up east to west facing north with the right foot of each lightly atop

the left foot of the man or boy next to him. Each hunter holds his gun upright with the butt resting between his feet. In this pose, the Host instructs them, especially the leader. While this occurs, the Masing impersonator, wearing a mask like the 12 carved faces and a bear skin, enters the Big House and stands near the center to listen. During his instructions, the Host places 12 pinches of tobacco in the fires. The 2 Singers are also present to sing about the Sky Keepers to encourage them to drive the deer into the paths of the hunters. The texts of the departing and returning hunter's songs appear in Voegelin (1941: 52). The hunters are gone for 3 days. The leader carries a brass kettle on his back for them to cook in. While the other hunters can return to bring in their kill, firing 1 shot for each deer killed, the leader cannot return until noon on the third day. When all have returned they are fed in the Big House. Over lunch they discuss the hunt, the successful hunters and the reasons for lack of success by others.

In contrast to CE, MRH: 97-100 says the hunt leader was selected by the Host and paid a yard of wampum. The hunt leader then selected the other hunters. They were fed at noon and given lunches by the women ashkasak to take along. In the line, the hunters stand on their left feet and barely touch the ground with their right toes. During his instructions, the Host places 6 pinches of tobacco on the west fire and then 6 on the east one, praying to the Masing to drive deer close to the Big House. The Masing sees them off and then dances in the Big House as the Singers sing for him. On the 7th day of the rite the hunters return and are fed in the Big House. The successful hunters were announced. The deer were skinned and hung on the meat pole east of the Big House.

FGS, 141 adds only that the Masing costume was hung on a branch some hundred yards from the Big House. There it was out of reach of dogs and accessible to men other than the primary impersonator if they wished to wear it. NTD was careful to point out that both the hunters and the Masing were missing in her day.[64] However, her parents gave her details on these past events. She duplicated the previous accounts but added that tobacco was only burned when the hunters' departed, not when they returned. The women ashkasak gave them a lunch of cooked meat and corn bread. After the deer were dressed, the hides were given or promised to old people.

<u>Fourth, Fifth and Sixth Nights</u>. These were taken up with vision recitations. On the 4th evening, 6 men were given a yard of wampum to divide among themselves in return for their praying "Ho" 12 times at the meat pole (MRH: 99). Another yard of wampum is unstrung and scattered in the sacred area for the ashkasak to pick up as they pray "Ho." More details on these 2 events come from FGS: 143 and NTD. The first event is a *wiltin*. The Delaware names of worthy men and boys are called out by the *ashkasak* to come to the Big House and share a yard of wampum. [117]

In return they are told to go out to the meat pole and shout "Ho" 12 times to pray that the hunters will be successful. The second event is a *mawąnsi* (pronounced nasally), which means "to gather or pick (as with berries)". The beads were scattered in the sacred area and the ashkasak were called upon to kneel there and pick up the beads and pop them in their mouths while they hummed. If they dropped any beads there would be a quiet chuckle (NTD).

---

[64] The Masing costume was sold to MRH by its Keeper in about 1908. Delaware leaders were upset by this loss. Some modern traditionalists feel that since none of them know how to properly care for the Masing costume in terms of its requirements of food and ritual, it is safer to have it in the Museum of the American Indian in New York where it is less likely to cause harm to them.

<u>Seventh Night</u>. While the other accounts do not indicate major events in the rite until the 9th night, CE includes them both on the 7th and 9th nights. Otherwise the 7th day is devoted to welcoming back the hunters and the 7th night to recitations. Because of its uniqueness, I will quote from the CE account,

After the 6th night meeting, they "make everything new". The meeting is then generally ended; straight business now takes place, wants and wishes. They build a fire by a revolving stick. (There is a wheel with buckskin strings, by pulling up and down revolves the shaft of mulberry. This shaft rests on a block of mulberry.) After the fire is built, before starting of the meeting, new hay is spread where the people sit down along the edges inside, then they repaint those 12 false faces. Everybody then comes in; 12 sticks of sassafras about 1½ feet long are distributed. There are a few turtle shells, stripped (prairie turtles). Those are distributed. They are lined up in a row right in front of the leader of the meeting (he will be on the north side of these shells). The leader takes a string of beads, fully a yard long, called wampum. He measures the length of the back of the turtles. He cuts the beads so as to correspond. Then the nearest relative walks up. Then they take beads off each turtle shell and then he or she takes those beads. He or she hands the turtle shell to the leader of the meeting, keeping the beads. Those attendants ashkasak (sweeping, getting wood, etc.) are 3 men and 3 women. They are called up by the leader. A yard of beads is to be poured out in the center of the church building. Those 6 attendants all kneel down and kind of hum, pick up beads with the left hand and place those beads in their mouths. After the beads are so gathered, they go to the door where they are supposed to stand (on the east end of the building). There they count how many beads each got. After that the meeting starts in for that night. The headman he shakes one of the turtle shells (they have shot or rocks in to make a rattle). It is answered by the singers accross [sic] the building by 3 strikes on the deer skin (on the south side; the building runs east and west.) The leader tells the people what he saw when a child. This will be about some animal who turned into the appearance of a person. He will tell what this animal told him. What help will be rendered him . . . The new fire will be used till the 9th night, when a new fire will be used till end, till 12th night. [118]

<u>Eighth Night</u>. This was spent in recitations.

<u>Ninth Night</u>. On this night the Big House was refurbished according to MRH: 101-104, FGS: 147-153; and NTD). On the 9th day, the *ashkasak* open the west door, remove the ashes of the old fires, and deposit them on the ash heap outside the door. Then without women and children present, new fires are kindled with the fire drill. That night the Singers replace the plain drumsticks with the drumsticks carved to represent a human pair, one with a face to represent a man and another with face and breasts to represent a woman. Everyone who owned a turtle shell rattle brought it into the Big House to have it placed before the Host, who matched its length with a string of wampum. The owner kept this string. Prayersticks (6 plain and 6 striped) were distributed among the audience by the ashkasak to a rapid drum beat. Both drumsticks and prayersticks are used every night from this time on. If it so happens that the plain sticks do not fall opposite each other (or on opposite sides of the house), they must all be picked up again and

redistributed. After this, those who have received a stick raise that instead of their hand, when they repeat the prayer word "*Ho-o-o!*" and carry it when they dance" (MRH: 103) The <u>wiltin</u> with 6 men paired by clan is also repeated each night thereafter until the end (MRH: 104), The prayersticks are distributed by *ashkas* traveling in opposite directions (FGS: 149, #3). Speck (1973: 18) says that symbolically the decorated sticks represent the beginning prayer "Ho" and the plain sticks represent the ending prayer "Ha", both of which represent the cries of innocent children during the earthquake that forced the revival of the Big House. During an intermission, the ashkasak brought in a bark dish of red paint. The women ashkasak paint those on the north side and the men ashkasak paint people on the south side and then the black side of the faces on the center and side posts (NTD). The centerpost faces were so high that the men had to jump 2 or 3 times to paint the diagonal line on the left cheek (NTD). The people were also painted on the left cheek and women were painted on the part of the hair. Then someone recited his vision. When he was done, the ashkasak swept away obstacles and the old men smoked as usual. Then the prayersticks were passed out and the drumsticks changed. A man *ashkas* passed out prayer sticks on the south and a woman *ashkas* passed them out on the north (NTD). Then the recitations continued until the end.

<u>Tenth Night</u>. Other sources continue the usual pattern of recitations, but NTD specified that there was also a general cleansing ceremony. The people stood and the men *ashkasak* burned cedar in the fires and fanned the dense smoke throughout the Big House with a small blanket. The *wiltin* may also have been held.

<u>Eleventh Night</u>. Recitations continued but NTD adds that a wooden bowl was placed on the right side of the door. As everyone entered they would drop 2 or 3 wampum beads into the bowl. When all were seated, an *ashkas* took the bowl to the Host, who later used them for a *mawạnsi* "gathering" for the *ashkasak*. [119]

<u>Twelfth Night ~ Day</u>. The women visionaries recite. According to CE, cedar was burned before the service. Two men *ashkasak*, one with a bark dish of deer marrow and one with a dish of red paint, painted the faces, drumsticks, deerskins taken by the hunters, and turtle shells. Then 2 women *ashkasak* painted the people, 1 puts grease on the left side of the head and the other paints a diagonal red line on the left cheek. The women reciters are told to go outside and get ready. The women visionaries line up with a man on either side of the woman leader at the head of the line. The men cry "*k^{w}iya*" and the women respond "*Hu*" 12 times. The flap is raised and the Singers beat the drum. As they enter, the men cry "*Ho*" and everyone holds up their right hand. The woman leader, accompanied by 1 of the men, sings 6 songs. Then the turtle rattle is passed and all other visionaries must sing. The second woman then sings 4 songs, the third woman 2 songs, and other women can either not sing or do 1 song. They finish about 12PM. The *ashkasak*, first the men then the women, now sing. If any are unable, they hire a substitute for a yard of wampum. The Host announces that this portion of the service is over and the leader of the 2 men with the women ends with 12 songs. He dances 12 steps to the east door. All follow him out crying "*Hi*" with the right hand upraised. Outside all those who sang are given deer meat in baskets. The *ashkasak* are called back to sweep the Big House with the turkey wing fan in the left hand. Some of the *ashkasak* can leave the Big House during this if they wish. Then the Host begins the rest of the service with his own recitation. Afterward, other men recite until the rattle reaches the Singers, who place it at their spot until the next day.

According to MRH: 105, 2 women ashkasak begin painting on the north side at the east door and finish by painting the carved faces. Every woman who sings receives cooked deer meat from the fattest and largest buck the hunters brought in. The 12th night is open to women and young men or boys with a vision but who were too young to recite on previous nights (FGS: 155). The rattle seems to be used by seniority, with the oldest woman going first. While the woman recites, adults line up behind her with men on the outside and women on the inside. (Substitute reciters might also be hired.) The old women are the ones generally given the deerhides from the hunters.

When NTD was a girl, women recited on the 12th morning before noon. Women wore their finery with ribbonwork only for the last services. Each woman selected a man to dance beside her on the inside and join her recitation. They would only make 1 circuit each time. Only 5 women would recite while NTD attended the rite, 1 of whom was her own mother. On the 12th night the men repeated their recitations. The service resumed the next day with everyone in their finery. Women could also wear paint if they wished.

Thirteenth Day. The fires were removed and the interior cleaned (CE). The meeting continued until the rattle reached the chief, who sang 12 songs. On the 10th song everyone stood and formed concentric rings moving in toward the center post. On the 12th song all raised their left hand and cried "*Hi*" then "*Ho*." All are then told to be seated [120] while a woman ashkas passed out 2 to 3 beads to each person to extend thanks to the Creator. The other ashkasak bring in the deerhides and pile them in the center. The chief asks who was the hunt leader and which hunters killed deer, so that the oldest members of their matri-clans can be given a hide. The remaining deer meat is distributed first to the relatives of the Host, then the elders present, and then to the others as far as it will go. To the Singer's drum beat, a man ashkas will start in the east and another will start in the west and collect the deerhides and prayersticks from the north or south and pile them in the center. Then the 6 *ashkasak* are given a yard of wampum each as the chief thanks them for all their work. If the *ashkas* sweeps for 12 rites he or she has swept their way to heaven after death. The *ashkasak* go outside while 4 or 5 relatives hold their wampum. Inside the Big House, the chief thanks the people. Then all file out and line up north and south facing east, raise their right hand, cry "*Ho*" 6 times while kneeling and 4 times while standing. Then a man on the south end will cry "*Hi*" and another at the north end will answer. Their neighbors pass these cries through the line and when they reach the middle the rite is over. The previous description is that of CE.

MRH: l06ff says that on the 13th morning, 2 men sing 12 songs to close the service with the women forming an inner circle and the men an outer circle around the center post. MRH also explains why 4 or 5 relatives must hold the wampum for the *ashkasak*, it is a single 6 foot strand. The strand is divided near the outside cooking fire. At noon on the last day, the people line up with the hunters carrying the deerhides from the kill. Later the hides are given to the elderly for moccasins.

For FGS, 159 the rite resumes with everyone in fancy traditional dress. The men cry "*k*^{w}*iya*" and the women respond "*Hu*." Elsewhere Speck (1937: 18) records that people placed in their mouths the few beads, which symbolize the heart, given them by the women *ashkasak* before they lined up outside.

According to NTD, when the service resumed on the 13th day, the Host prayed, gave thanks, and wished that everyone would be able to return the next year. He gave thanks for everything. Then 1 man took up the turtle rattle and sang as the men, women, and children danced toward the center post. On the last song, everyone shouted *"Ho"* then "Ha" with hand raised. The *ashkasak* were paid with what wampum was available. Everyone lined up and agile people knelt down while a man on the south end cried *"Ho"*. Another man would shout *natanuk*[w] ~ "watch out" so they all would shout *"Ha"* at the north end. This was repeated 12 times with the hand upraised. Then the rite was over.

IV ~ Consistent Pattern

Based on a comparison of the sources for the composite description, it is possible to piece together a coherent account of the rite. I am assuming that if only one source mentions an event but that event fills in a gap in the sequence of events of the rite, then barring any extenuating circumstances, that report can be used to piece together the consistent pattern. [121]

In the fall when the leaves turned colors, officials were selected for the rite. These included the Host, Masing-Impersonator, and six *ashkasak*. People were notified by messengers of the day to begin camping at the Big House site. The participants and campers were expected to be chaste. The *ashkasak* had cleaned and prepared the Big House building and environs. The west door was kept closed. Hay was scattered around the edges inside, but a central oval area was kept bare. In the middle was the center post. During the service, the Host sat on the north and the two drummers sat on the south. Clansmen and clanswomen sat separately, but there is disagreement on the location of the clans.

The service was conducted much the same each evening. After a speech of thanksgiving by the Host, a turtle shell rattle was passed counterclockwise around the audience until it reached a male visionary, who shook it, received answering beats from the drummers, and began his recitation. During the narrative, he shook the rattle from side to side, and during the song, he shook it up and down. Those who wished, if they were adults, danced behind him. The audience stood during each recitation. Between recitations, the *ashkasak* swept the length of the building with turkey wing fans. Old men might smoke. After the last recitation, everyone used the prayer word *"Ho"* 12 times with their left hand raised.

This type of service continued for each of the 12 nights, together with some features particular to some nights. New fires were kindled by a chaste man on the first and ninth nights. Hunters left on the fourth day and returned on the seventh until their participation lapsed and meat was purchased from a butcher in NTD's experience. On the 4th and after the ninth nights, the *wiltin* and *mawąnsi* might be held. The ninth night also included the elaborate addition of decorative paint, turtle shell display, anthropomorphic drumsticks, and prayersticks. Women visionaries recited on the twelfth evening or thirteenth day but men recited after them on the twelfth night or thirteenth morning. A woman recited with a male visionary accompanying her on the inside, nearest the center post. For a female visionary, the right hand was raised. People wore their finery for these last recitations. The rite concluded with the "Common Dance" performed as concentric rings around the center post moved toward it. Then deer hides and wampum were distributed and the ashkasak compensated. Finally, everyone filed outside, lined up from north to south, and passed the prayer words along until they reached the middle for a total of 12 times; after which the rite was completed and the Delawares broke camp and went home.

V ~ Variations

In addition to these consistent features, some accounts include unique features. The area of greatest disagreement is the matter of the locations of the clans within the building. MRH, 87 alone reports sacred fired kindled by a man and a woman. Only CE reports a ritual intensification of the seventh night. NTD and other sources disagreed with the statements that the center post was the Creator's staff (FGS: 87), that eagle feathers were worn during the service (FGS: 97), and that a variety of face paints and designs were worn by men during the [122] rite (FGS: Plates I-IV). NTD also told me that some of the Delaware terms which Webber dictated can be attributable to Webber's Monsi mother, Hannah Stykes Webber. The statement that the Oklahoma Big House building ran north and south (FGS: 85, #2) is plainly wrong. Complete variant rituals include the 6 day Wolf rite (Newcomb 1956: 65), and an 8 day rite using a stuffed deerskin and sweatlodge (MRH: 122).

VI Analysis of the Delaware Big House Rite

The purpose of a structuralist analysis is to seek the order and meaning of a structure, in this case the discrete relationships that make up the Big House Rite, in order to understand Delaware culture and to contribute to our understanding of humanity. The Delaware have been through considerable change and with it went a corresponding loss of traditional interpretations. Numerous are the times that Delaware have warned me about people who are always asking what something means. In most cases they were referring to tourists buying craftwork, but the moral was as much for me as them. Even the contemporary elders insist that many traditional features were meaningless. Yet I know from other more intact Native American societies, especially in the Southwest, that once Delaware society was cohesively integrated by esoteric and exoteric theories of order and meaning. For instance, for the Iroquois, their aboriginal neighbors who have better preserved more of their traditional practices, Speck (1945b: 78) was able to say "Symbolism lurks in almost every material object utilized and every action performed in the course of Iroquois ceremonies. The Long House itself, in which the rites are enacted, is a symbol of the universe of the Iroquois."

While this integrative picture is gone, it is not irretrievable. A subsidiary task of this analysis will be to show some of its former richness. I will recover it by means of a structuralist model that enables me to show the reiterations and internal consistencies in the Big House Rite. The data in the composite description of the Unami rite will be bolstered with comparisons with other Unami and Munsi Big House Rites, with general Delaware ethnography, and occasionally with data from Algonkian and Iroquois sources which are justified by the remarkably close similarities in Delaware and Iroquois societies (Fenton 1951: 48) and the possible significances of features distributed among Algonkian speakers other than the Delaware.

Throughout the previous description, the close ties between myth and ritual were suggested. The interplay of myth and ritual has been carefully explored in contemporary anthropology. Yet the myth for the Big House Rite has never been specified. We are told the rite was renewed during an earthquake, but not how it originated. The Munsi or Minsi Big House Rite began when the Creator came to earth to instruct the people and then dropped 12 prayersticks as he rose into the sky, but we do not know his instructions. I think they can be plausibly outlined based on the symbolism of the Canadian Munsi Big House. The richness of these data is a tribute to the collaborative work of Speck and two Munsi, Nicodemus Peters and

Jesse Moses (Speck and Moses 1945a hereafter S-M). [123] In many respects this text presages structural analysis because of the dualism inherent in the data.

The Monsi Big House represents the universe, specifically a projection of the sky upon the earth (S-M: 30) and the center post, a complete tree trunk, representing the World Tree. Among the Oklahoma Unami the Big House also symbolized the universe, the fusion of sky and earth (FGS: 22), but I can not agree that the center post was the Creator's staff (FGS: 87). It is more likely to have represented the World Tree. What these Munsi and Unami data refer to is the Delaware Genesis or Origin Myth.

According to the myth, the Creator placed earth on the back of the Great Turtle, which rose from the primordial water, and from this earth grew the World Tree, which begot the parents of humanity when a sprout touched the earth to create a woman and another sprout grew skyward to create a man. Miller (1974a) analyzes the myth to show an ultimate manly / womanly contrast mediated by the mind and also expressed as an ocean / land opposition mediated by the Great Turtle, and an earth / sky opposition mediated by the World Tree. The Big House can been seen as a physical expression of the myth. The center post is the World Tree and the clear oval area, the back of the Great Turtle facing west as all life and turtles are said to do. These are the metaphors of the rite, the metonyms *seem* to be the drumsticks, prayersticks, and the turtle shell rattles. Pervading the Big House and the universe is the ubiquitous manly / womanly categorization. A Delaware pointed out the symbolic importance of gender to Speck (1937: 25), who suggested "This leaves no doubt of the latent trend of thought in the basic symbolism of duality based upon sex in Delaware." However, I find that his chart of the emanations of Delaware sexual symbolism contradicts the ethnography. According to Speck (1937: 26) the male or manly is associated with red, life, east, day, right, hunting, and animals while the female or womanly is associated with black, death, west, night, left, cooking, and plants. The majority of this section will explicate the data which supports the subsuming sexual symbolism but which also refutes Speck.

In ordinary Delaware society, the womanly was defined as bound, closed, exclusive, and homogenous while the manly was unbound, open, inclusive, and diverse. Linguists would call the womanly marked and the manly un. The significance is that the manly can include both manly and womanly features, while the womanly excludes all but womanly associations. For example, the Munsi hold a tug-of-war with 12 men, the 6 on the east represent the Munsi women and those on the west the Munsi men (S-M: 67). Among the Unami, only red paint was worn by women, while men could wear red and black paint in religious dances and add yellow paint to these for social dances (NTD, partially FGS: plates 1-111). This means that while Delaware may recognize the red and black sides of the faces as representing respectively life / death (Speck 1937: 25) or good / strength (McCracken 1956: 185), they ultimately represent womanly / manly. Evidence for this comes from the associations of red, blood, and life with women universally (Ortner 1974), an association strangely missed by Speck. Among the Delaware, both blood and life are bound and exclusive in that, for instance, the red paint used in the Big House was specially made of bloodroot by old women (NTD). Black as such was not distinctively manly, except when contrasted with red. Of greater significance for its manliness is its [124] occurrence with other colors, as on the 9th night when a red diagonal is painted on the black (left) side of the faces. While women were symbolically identified with life through birth, men as hunters and warriors were associated with death, directly at this level and indirectly at another level because both men and women die. The associations of the womanly with life and manly with death applied also to the solar passage from east to west. "The Sun and everything else goes toward the west, say the Minsi, in explanation, even the dead when they die" (MRH: 132). Since the Unami were concerned that people live until the next Big House, it is understandable that they would symbolically retard death by sealing the west door, to be opened only for the protective ashes of the dead fire.[65] The Munsi entered by the east door and left by the west one (MRH: 131). Also for these reasons, in the Big House the east fire was associated with the women and the west fire with the men. The report in MRH, 87 of a man and a woman starting the sacred fire would agree with this if the woman kindled the eastern fire and the man kindled the western one. Before the hunters left, tobacco was placed on the west then on the east fire (MRH: 98). Based on the Unami rite, the day seems to be associated with the womanly, secular activities and the night with the manly, religious events. In her experience, NTD said the women recited in the morning before noon. While the earlier accounts suggest that this was a historic change which moved the recitations by women from early evening to early morning, culturally it would have been impossible if the day were not associated with the womanly. It is interesting that the Iroquois also broke the day at noon between the living and the dead (Morgan 1972: 240). Various accounts, especially that of CE, indicate the association of the left with manly and right with womanly. During the nights when men recite, the people raised their left hands; however, when the women reciters entered, the people raised their right hands. In the Big House, the *ashkas* were "using only the left hand in holding the fans, since the left hand is the holy hand, the right hand the unholy" (Speck 1937: 17). Yet when the people lined up outside to pray, they held up their right hands. I suggest this signified that because the inside of the Big House was the sky, it was properly the domain of the manly left while the area outside of the Big House was the earth and the domain of the womanly right. When the women recited they brought their association with the right inside with them, incongruence with the exclusivity of womanly associations. Since the faces were added to the Big House for the people to see the powers and gifts figuratively behind them, it is significant that the left side is black and the right side red. It is also important to mention that the Delaware are one of the few exceptions to the universal priority of the right (Miller 1972). This seems to have been a deliberate reversal of the usual pattern on the part of the Delaware as a means of distinctive self-identification. Kinietz (1940) suggested that this was a historic change by traditionalists to distinguish themselves from Christians emphasizing the right hand; however, it is just as plausible, in the absence of historical documentation, to argue that it was a precontact solution to help distinguish the Delaware from the culturally similar Iroquois, since reversals as boundary markers are well known from analogous cultural situations (Miller 1974b). [125]

While my analysis documents the reverse of most of the associations cited by Speck, I quite agree with him that men were the hunters of animals and women the cookers and tenders of plants. Among the Munsi also, the women cooked during the Big House ceremonies (S-M: 55). These associations are also symbolically recognized in the Unami rite. Old women made the red paint from bloodroot and did not mix this vegetable dye with grease as they would have ordinarily done. Men were sent out on the 4th day to hunt, exhorted by Masing who was patron of game. It is interesting that while the main Unami rite symbolizes animal life with the Masing, the other Unami and the Munsi rites used a stuffed deer. The Masing and deer are very closely associated. Masing is "seen riding about on the back of a buck, herding the deer" (MRH: 33). Yet symbolically Masing is more powerful than the deer. The Masing costume consisted of a wooden mask painted like a Big House face, a bearskin body suit, a walking stick, and a snapping turtle rattle. In the past there may have been more than one Masing (MRH: 36), which

---

[65] Ashes provided protection because in other dimensions, by hostile spirits, they look aflame.

suggests that each of the 12 Sky Keepers may have once been impersonated. Certainly Masing had cosmological symbolism. His mask associates him with the Sky Keepers, his bearskin with animals and his stick with plants (with both related to land), and his rattle links him with water.[66]10 These same elements are represented by the matriclans, Fowl with sky, Canines with land, and Turtles with water. We have already learned that sky is manly and earth is womanly. The Delaware recognize two forms of water, "grandfather water" is free flowing while "mother water" is contained in wells, springs, or vessels. In other words, when water is openly free-flowing it is manly but when bound it is womanly. Water itself is a mediator between sky and earth as in the Origin Myth. In the same way, the Turtle clan mediates between Fowl and Canine clans (Miller 1974a). Because the turtle is omnivorous, it is both herbivorous like fowl and carnivorous like canines. The turtle also lays bird-like eggs but is a tailed quadruped. Its amphibious reptilian ambiguity makes it a suitable cosmic mediator. Because the clans have these elemental associations, I think it likely that the clans did alternate in conducting the Big House Rite--not because each had its own ancestral form which became fused with the others historically, but rather because each in turn could use its mystical association to render special thanks to an element or aspect of the universe. The Big House Rite was anciently charged with world renewal and the maintenance of cosmic order, similar to the Iroquois Thanksgiving Rites (Chafe 1961). It has been historically altered but most definitely not historically originated. Since both the Unami and Munsi (S-M: 38) place the leader on the north side, it is likely that in the past the matriclan of the leader sat on the north side and the other clans on the west and south, as MRH: 93 reported. In alternation, each clan could have held a 12 day rite, but it is equally plausible that the Turtle clan as mediator ran the full rite while the other clans conducted partial rites. An interesting reversal occurs in the seating arrangements. Unlike the social world where the womanly areas were bounded or inside the manly realms, in the Big House the women bounded the men. While the members were separated as clansmen and clanswomen, the clanswomen sat beside the east and the west doors, with the clansmen, Host, and Singers in the middle. This same pattern occurred in Indiana when the women sat behind the men. However, on the last day [126] the social order was reaffirmed when the women formed an inside ring and the men an outside ring around the center post (MRH: 106). During the duration of the rite the complementarity of the sexes was probably represented by the alternating and reciprocal duties of the men and women ashkasak. The ashkasak served as mediators in the rite, they reversed their positions as sweepers from the east and west and their associations with north and south throughout the rite. The 6 ashkasak are another indication of the ritualized cooperation of the clans in the Big House. If each clan had its own rite, only 2 ashkasak should be symbolically paired. Yet each rite seems to have had 6 *ashkasak*. I believe there were 2 per clan because of the supreme importance of the manly / womanly symbolization. In the Munsi Big House the manly / womanly categories are even more prominent because there are no subdivisions like the matriclans, only other expressions of the duality. For the Munsi (S-M: 2l, 54) the associations for the manly are the Turtle or Unami moiety, west, animals, red, and the hide drum with beater

---

[66] 10. Actually the cosmological symbolism of Masing is even more complex. He scares bad children but overly fearful children give him offerings of tobacco, which he places in a pouch, to secure his good will. Bad children are carried off by him in a bag full of snakes (MRH: 32ff). It is more likely that the tobacco represents plant life and the stick, tree life as the Delaware place plants and trees into different taxa. The associations of the snake in Delaware tradition are those of sorcery and evil. It is likely therefore that Masing mediates the contrasts of sky / earth, plant / tree, animal / vegetable, and good / bad. [131]

while for the womanly they are the Wolf or Wapanachki moiety, east, plants, white, and the turtle shell rattle. The first 3 pairs parallel the Unami; however, the color and musical instrument pairs require comment. In the Munsi Big House there were white masks over the east door and on the west side of the center post, and red masks over the west door and on the east side of the center post. In a Munsi myth, red is equated with the blood of a celestial bear, which falls to earth turning the falling leaves red, and white is equated with the grease of the mythic bear, which falls as snow. While there may be more general color associations, it seems that red and white relate to the celestial bear, its blood shed by men and its grease rendered by women. The musical instruments are in the custody of 2 ashkas-like men during the ceremonies, one on the east and the other on the west (S-M: 55). The man on the east and the rattle should have womanly associations and the one on the west and the drum should have manly associations.

Having established this symbolic framework, I can now suggest interpretations for some unexplained features of the rite. Both the Unami and Munsi have the 12 prayersticks. The Munsi say the Creator dropped them from the sky (MRH: 127). This implies he dropped 1 as he passed through each of the 12 sky layers. This suggests to me that the prayersticks were associated with the World Tree linking earth and sky, either as branches or some other metonym. The prayersticks were identified with the prayer words (FGS: 149, #3), which were the cries of innocent children (Speck 1937: 18). I suspect because of the frequency with which it was uttered during the service that "*Ho*" was a prayer to heaven, and its association with the striped prayersticks suggests these stripes represented the sky layers. The prayer "*Ha*" probably referred to the earth and its association with the plain prayersticks is understandable because the plain sticks were "bound" by special concern when they were passed out (MRH: 103). The sexual symbolism of the decorated drumsticks is obvious. Cedar smoke exorcised impurity from the Big House, especially the danger of possible menstrual pollution. Tobacco was offered to the Creator, the Masing, and the Sky Keepers when the hunters left. It was not burnt when the hunters returned. The Iroquois data may explain this, "if the spirit [127] addressed in the ceremonial is thought to live outside the village and its fields, a tobacco invocation is included; but if not, the tobacco invocation is omitted" (Tooker 1970: 25). The Sky Keepers were called with the tobacco, but would already be near the Big House when the hunters returned. In this sacred context then, cedar smoke is womanly and tobacco smoke is manly.

Wampum represents the heart. The Delaware recognize 2 souls in an individual. One is localized in the blood and remains bound to the earth after death, the other is localized in the heart and leaves for an afterworld 12 days after death (FGS: 25). This reinforces the womanly associations of earth with blood and suggests the manly associations of the heart and wampum. Further, as the officials are paid in wampum after the rites, so they are paid with cooked meals during it. Men would have made the wampum and women made the meals.

The significance of the number 12 has been attributed to Christianity (Kinietz 1940: 118) or the annual lunar cycle (Speck 1937: 11). I prefer to see 12 as the resolution of the numbers 3 and 4. The Delaware emphasize these numbers and their combinations. For example, there are 3 matriclans, 4 directions, 7 Pleiades boys, 9 Thunderers, and 12 Sky Keepers. The Big House Rite is structured as 4 sets of 3 day services. The second set involved the hunt for deer. The third set (reported only by CE) began with a new fire and "straight business, wants and wishes." The fourth set was the major refurbishing of the Big House and arrival in heaven. In the process the people had gone through the 12 sky layers, led by the Host who preceded them. If a partial service was held, it ended at the second (MRH: 120) or third (Newcomb 1956: 65) set, which would account for the complete ritual variants. I interpret the progression to show that the first set focused on the earth. In the second set, the hunters were sent out and the Masing (with Sky Keepers) was called to earth to help the hunt. In the *wiltin*, the men whose names were called stood near the meat pole to pray to the Sky Keepers. The meat pole itself may have been a link between animals and their spiritual counterparts or the "bosses" of various species. Also held on the same night, the *mawansi* (gathering) evoked fowl eating berries. This suggests a complex opposition between meat and sky / berries and earth, mediated by the meat pole and low-flying birds. This opposition is strengthened when attention is called to the wooden mortar (*kawhawkn*) that rested near the meat pole. (My attention was directed to the mortar by Dr Jim Howard.) This mortar was used by the female cooks to grind corn meal and some other foods served during the rite. The mortar was made by a man who charred and scraped a deep depression in a section cut from a tree trunk. Corn was ground in the mortar with a double-ended pestle carved from a sturdy limb several feet long. These mortars were considered the chief item of domestic furniture in the past and they were an indispensable part of several special corn recipes. In all, therefore, the meat pole stands opposed to the mortar as meat to vegetables and as sky to earth.

According to CE, the third set was an intensification of the rite as the people moved closer to heaven. [128] In the fourth set the Delaware actually approached the Creator. On the 9th night people prepared to reach heaven and the basic contrast between men and women was affirmed by the drumsticks, prayersticks, paint, etc. The 10th night was the purification and the 11th night the entrance. The 12th and 13th days were spent in thanksgiving. The people wore their finery on the 12th night because heaven is "beautiful, where everything is new and bright" (MRH: 53). On the last day they return to earth. When they arrive, they file out to stand on the earth and to salute the heavens. The secular or social categories are reaffirmed by the dance around the center post and the prayers outside. The Delaware affirmed their unity by praying together until the boundaries of the world were set by men at the ends of the line and each person in turn recognized them until the middle or center was reached. This north and south line-up emphasizing the right side on the last day contrasts with the east and west line-up of the hunters on the fourth day, when they emphasize the left or holy side. Because of its associations with elder brother Sun and the left, the east and west line was manly while the north and south line was womanly. These linear alignments were mediated by the circular dance pattern involving separate lines of men and women behind the reciter on each night of the Big House Rite. The sky associations of these final days suggest how Charles Webber as an infrequent participant in the rite came to associate the rite with festive face paints and eagle feathers. The attribution of the center post as the Creator's staff also satisfies the linking quality of the center post as the World Tree connecting sky and earth, Creator and humans. Thus, while Webber was factually in error according to older traditionalists and other sources, the kinds of errors he made support my interpretation of the meanings lurking in the rite.

VII ~ Summary

The Big House Rite was a dramatization of the Delaware Origin Myth intended to emphasize the complementarity and contrast of the manly / womanly ultimate semantic categories or fundament. Manly was diverse and inclusive while womanly was bound and exclusive. These categories were expressed by sensory, social and cosmic emanations:

Emanations	Manly	Mind (Mediators)	Womanly
Sensory	left	human body	right
	black, yellow		red

	heart		blood
	wampum		meals
	tobacco smoke		cedar smoke
	outside		inside
	(inside for Big House)		(outside for BigHouse)
Social	men		women
	Fowl Clan	Turtle clan	Canine clan
	Religious affairs		Secular affairs [129]
Cosmic	animals		plants
	meat (hunting)		vegetables (cooking)
	forest	stockade	house and fields
	night		day
	air	water	land
	sky		earth
	east-west axis		north-south axis
	manly rituals	Big House	womanly rituals
	(hunt rites)		(corn rites)

In terms of its origin, the Big House was an ancient Delaware cosmic ritual focused on the center post and cleared oval area as representatives of the World Tree and the Great Turtle. Also primary to the rite is the turtle shell rattle as a cosmic mediator, when shaken up and down it seems to have integrated heavens and earth, and when shaken sideways it unified men and women, ocean and land, and the parts of the earth. In addition to the individual variations probably introduced by different chiefs and Hosts, there have been important historic changes. Among these were probably the form and decoration of the Big House building and the shift from sex and clan based duties to gender specific. I have not minutely considered each account of the rite because while they differ on specifics, all agree on the general division by sex. By explicating the sexual principle these recorded differences emerge as variations on a manly / womanly theme. The thrust of the historical changes was an intensification of this core theme. Under the pressures of dislocation, depopulation, missionaries, and White bureaucracy, the Big House and Delaware culture was not so much changed as it was stripped to its essentials with a corresponding loss in the subtleties and interstices that make for a rich system of meaning. Actually, it may be that this richness is not so much lost as ignored. Certainly elder Delaware in Oklahoma recognize the integrative significance of the rite even though it has lapsed. They remember clan affiliations and cosmological details based on the internal arrangements in the Big House. Their memories of the other rituals and myths also contribute to the preservation of the traditional culture in outline form.

Based on manly / womanly concepts and patterns of socialization, especially under grandparents, some members of each Delaware generation discover their culture anew. Structuralism has permitted me to repeat their discovery and illuminate the previous ethnography. This kind of cultural reconstruction and analysis is important for setting the natural constraints on the underlying human similarities. The reconstruction of the structure of Delaware culture is important not only for what it says empirically about the Delaware and humanity, but also for what it says about the natural constraints and theoretical possibilities of Human Culture. [130]

	Woman	Man	Mind
	exclusive	inclusive	inclosive
Sensory			
	right	left	heart
	bloodroot	black	crimson
	charcoal	wampum	sticks
	cedar	tobacco	incense
	laugher	silence	vigil
	sweet	salty	spicy
	1	3	4
	inside	outside	fire
Interpersonal			
	women	men	gifted
	farming	hunting	fishing
	(Winetkok)	Munsee	Unami
	Turkey	Wolf	Turtle
	home	hall	stockade
	Bear	Otter	Doll
	Maize	Football	Masing^{w}
	town	forest	hearth
Cosmic			
	plants	animals	fish
	Thunderers	Sun	Masing
	Pleiades	Comet	Moon
	cannibal	orphan	hero
	Red Snake	Drawer-Under	Turtle
	Tree	Sea	Creator

3/3/96 12 noon

Bibliography

Abbreviations Used

AA = American Anthropologist

AL = Anthropological Linguistics

DIOH = The Doris Duke Indian Oral History Collection, Western History Collections, University of Oklahoma Library

BAE-AR = Bureau of American Ethnology, Annual Report

BAE-B = Bureau of American Ethnology, Bulletin

IJAL = International Journal of American Linguistics

IPH = Indian − Pioneer History, Foreman Collection, Oklahoma Historical Society 1-113 no #45

JAF = Journal of American Folklore

MNE = Man In The Northeast.

Works Cited

Ackerknecht, EH

1943 Primitive Autopsies and the History of Anatomy, *Bulletin of the History of Medicine* 13 (3): 334-9.

Abel, Anna

1904 *Indian Reservations in Kansas and the Extinguishment of Their Title.* Transactions of the Kansas State Historical Society 8: 72-109.

Adams, Richard C

1890 Notes On The Delaware Indians. Report on Indians Taxed and Not Taxed. 1890 United States Census, Volume 10.

1904 Ancient Religion of the Delaware Indians: Observations and Reflections. Washington, DC: Law Reporter.

1906a Legends of the Delaware Indians and Picture Writing. Washington, DC: Law Reporter.

1906b A Brief History of the Delaware Indians. 59th Congress, 1st Session, Senate Document 501. June 22. US Government Printing Office, Washington, DC.

Adams, Robert

1977 Songs of Our Grandfathers: Music of the Unami Delaware Indians. Seattle: University of Washington, Ethnomusicology MA.

Albers, Patricia

1989 From Illusion to Illumination: Anthropological Studies of American Indian Women: 132-170. *Gender and Anthropology*: Critical Reviews for Research and Teaching. S Morgen, ed. American Anthropological Association, Washington, DC.

Anonymous

1772 Box 131, Folder 10, Moravian Archives, Bethlehem, PA.

Babcock, Harold

1971 *Turtles of the northeastern United Slates*. New York: Dover Publications.

Barnes, Carol

1968 Subsistence and Social Organization of the Delaware Indians: 1600 A.D. *Bulletin of the Philadelphia Anthropological Society* 20 (1): 15-29.

Barry, Louise

1972 *The Beginnings of the West*: Annals of the Kansas, Gateway to the American West, 1540-1854. Topeka: Kansas State Historical Society.

Beatty, Charles

1962 *Journals of Charles Beatty 1762-1769*. Guy Soulliard Klett, ed. Presbyterian Historical Society Publications. University Park: Pennsylvania State University Press.

Benedict, Ruth

1923 *The Concept of the Guardian Spirit in North America*. Menasha, WI: American Anthropological Association Memoirs # 29.

1960 *Patterns of Culture*. New York: Mentor Books.

Berlin, Brent, Dennis Breedlove, and Peter Raven

1973 General Principles of Classification and Nomenclature in Folk Biology. *AA* 75: 214-42.

Berlin, Isaiah

1953 *The Hedgehog and the Fox*: An Essay on Tolstoy's View of History. London: Widenfeld and Nicolson.

Black, Mary

1969 A Note on Gender in Eliciting Ojibwa Semantic Structures. *AL* 2 (6): 177-86.

Blalock, Lucy, Bruce Pearson, James Rementer

1994 The Delaware Language. Bartlesville, OK: Delaware Tribe of Indians.

Bloomfield, Leonard

1946 Algonquian: 85-129. Hoijer 1946.

Brinton, Daniel

1888 Lenape Conversations. *Journal of American Folklore* 1: 37-43.

Brinton, DG and Albert Seqaqkind Anthony

1888 *A Lenape-English Dictionary*. Philadelphia.

Brown, Cecil, John Kolar, Barbara Torrey, Tipawan Truong-Quang, and Philip Volkman

1976 Some General Principles of Biological and Non-Biological Folk Classification.

American Ethnologist 3: 73-85.

Callender, Charles

1962 *Social Organization of the Central Algonkian Indians.* Milwaukee Public Museum, Publications in Anthropology # 7: 1-140.

Cannon, Walter

1942 'Voodoo' Death. *AA* 44: 169-81.

Chafe, Wallace

1961 *Seneca Thanksgiving Rituals.* Bureau of American Ethnology Bulletin #183.

Chamberlain, Alexander

1901 Significations of Certain Algonquian Animal-Names. *AA* 3: 669-83.

Cole, Fannie

1912 Pioneer Life in Kansas. *Kansas State Historical Society Collections* 12, 353-58.

Daly, Richard Heywood

1985 Housing Metaphors − A Study of the Role of the Longhouse in the Persistence of Iroquois Culture. PhD, University of Toronto.

Danek, Karel

1975 Some Remarks Illustrating the Dawn of Cardiology. *Nordisk Medicinhistorisk Aarsbok*: 61-70.

Dankers, Jasper

1966 *Journal of a Voyage to New York* (New Netherland) and a Tour in Several American Colonies in 1679-80. Ann Arbor, MI: University Microfilms.

Dean, Nora Thompson

1974 Conversations on the Big House and Ethnotaxonomy.

1984 Remembrances of the Big House Church. *The Lenape Indian: A Symposium.* Herbert C Kraft, ed. Archaeological Research Center, Publication # 7: 41-49. South Orange, NJ: Seton Hall University, Archaeological Research Center.

Deardorff, Merle

1946 Zeisberger's Allegheny River Indian Towns. *Pennsylvania Archaeologist* 16 (1): 2-19.

de Laguna, Frederica

1972 *Under Mount Saint Elias*: The History and Culture of the Yakutat Tlingit. Washington: Smithsonian Contributions to Anthropology, Volume 7, in three parts.

De Schweinitz, Edmund

1870 *The Life and Times of David Zeisberger*, the Western Pioneer and Apostle of the Indians. Philadelphia: Lippincott.

Douglas, Mary

1970 *Purity and Danger*: An Analysis of Concepts of Pollution and Taboo. London: Pelican.

Douglass, Robert S.

1912 *History of Southeast Missouri*: A Narrative Account of Its Historical Progress, Its People, and Its Principal Interests. 2 vols. Chicago: Lewis.

Drake, Benjamin

1852 *Life of Tecumseh and His Brother the Prophet*, with a Historical Sketch.

Cincinnati, OH: HS and J.

Draper, Lyman

1821 Interview of Anthony Shane by Benjamin Drake, November. Draper Manuscript 12YY8. Wisconsin Historical Society Microfilm, Madison.

Dunn, Jacob Pratt

1909 *True Indian Stories*, with Glossary of Indiana Indian Names. Indianapolis, IN: Sentinel.
Edmunds, R David

1983 *The Shawnee Prophet*. Lincoln: University of Nebraska Press.

1984 *Tecumseh and the Quest for Indian Leadership*. Boston: Little, Brown.

Erikson, Kai T.

1966 *Wayward Puritans*: A Study in the Sociology of Deviance. New York: John Wiley.

Esarey, Logan, ed.

1922 *Messages and Letters of William Henry Harrison*. Vol I: 1800-1811. Governors Messages and Letters. Indiana Historical Collections # 7.

Ewing, D

1982 *Pleasing the Spirits*: A Catalogue of a Collection of American Indian Art. Ghylen Press, New York.

Falleaf, Fred

nd Interview by (Catherine Red Corn and JW Tyner. MS on file in the Doris Duke Indian Oral History Collection, Western History Collection, University of Oklahoma # 31: T-299 (7 pp.), T-377 (5 pp.), T-377-2 (30 pp.), T-512 (2 pp.), Y-512-1 (22 pp.), 1968, 1969.

Farley, Alan

1955 The Delaware Indians in Kansas, 1829-1867. Kansas City: Kansas City Posse of the Westerners.

Fenton, Wiliam N

1951 *Symposium on Local Diversity in Iroquois Culture*. Bureau of American Ethnology, Bulletin # 149. Washington.

1987 *The False Faces of the Iroquois*. University of Oklahoma Press, Norman.

Ferguson, Roger

  1972   The White River Indiana Delaware: An Ethnohistorical Synthesis 1795-1867.   EdD: Ball State University.

Fernandez, James

  1974 The Mission of Metaphor in Expressive Culture. *Current Anthropology* 15: 119-145.

Fewkes, J Walter

  1922   Report on the Bureau of American Ethnology.   Annual Report of the Smithsonian Institution 1920: 57-72.

Fliegel, Carl John

  1970 *Index* to the Records of the Moravian Missions among the Indians of North America. New Haven, CT: Research Publications.

Fogelson, R, and Amelia Bell

  1983   Cherokee Booger Mask Tradition: 48-69.   *The Power of Symbols* ~ Masks and Masquerade in the Americas.   NR Crumrine and M Halpin, eds.   University of British Columbia Press, Vancouver.

  1984   Who Were the Ani-Kutani? An Excursion into Cherokee Historical Thought. *Ethnohistory* 31 (4): 255-63.

Foreman, Grant

  1930 *Indians and Pioneers*, The Story of the American Southwest Before 1830. Yale U Press, New Haven.

  1946 *The Last Trek of the Indians*. Chicago: University of Chicago Press.

Foster, George

  1944 *A Summary of Yuki Culture*. University of California, Anthropological Records 5 (3): 155-244.

Galloway, Brent

  1976 Anatomy in Upper Stab Halkomelem, A Morphosememic Study. Paper presented at the 11th International Conference on Salishan Languages. Seattle, Washington.

Gipson, Lawrence Henry, ed.

  1938 *The Moravian Indian Mission on White River*. Diaries and Letters, 5 May 1799 to 2 November 1806. Translated from the original German manuscript by Harry E Stocker, Herman T Frueauff, and Samuel C Zeiler. Indianapolis: Indiana Historical Bureau.

Giesey, Ralph

  1960 *The Royal Funeral Ceremony in Renaissance France*. Geneve: Librairie E Droz, Travaux D' Humanisme Et Rennaissance.

Gilliland, Lula Mac Gibson [130]

  1947 Big House Notes. MS 3873, National Anthropological Archives. Washington, DC.

Goddard, Ives

1971   The Ethnohistorical Implications of Early Delaware Linguistic Materials. *Man in the Northeast* 1: 14-26.

1974   Dutch Loanwords in Delaware: 153-160. *Delaware Indian Symposium.* Herbert Kraft, ed. Harrisburg: The Pennsylvania Historical and Museum Commission, Anthropological Series #4.

1978   Delaware. Handbook of North American Indians. *Northeast* 15: 213-39. Bruce G Trigger, ed. Washington, DC: Smithsonian Institution Press.

1979   Delaware Big House Ceremonial: 104-24. *Native North American Spirituality of the Eastern Woodlands*: Sacred Myths, Dreams, Visions, Speeches, Healing Formulas, Rituals, and Ceremonials. Elisabeth Tooker, ed. Classics of Western Spirituality. New York: Paulist.

Gray, Elma

1956 *Wilderness Christians*. Ithaca, NY: Cornell University Press.

Greenberg, Joseph

1966 *Language Universals*. The Hague: Mouton.

1975 Research On Language Universals. *Annual Review of Anthropology* 4: 75-94.

Grumet, Robert S

1979 "We Are not So Great Fools": Changes in Upper Delawarean Socio-political Life, 1630-1758. Ph.D. diss., Rutgers University.

1980 Sunksquaws, Shamans, and Tradeswomen: Middle Atlantic Coastal Algonkian Women during the Seventeenth and Eighteenth Centuries: 43-62. *Women and Colonization*: Anthropological Perspectives. Mona Etienne and Eleanor Leacock, eds. New York: Praeger.

1989 The Lenapes. Indians of North America. New York: Chelsea House.

1991   The Minisink Settlements: Native American Identity and Society in the Munsee Heartland, 1650-1778: 175-250. *The People of Minisink*: Papers from the 1989 Delaware Water Gap Symposium. David G Orr and Douglas V Campana, eds. Philadelphia: National Park Service, Mid-Atlantic Region.

Hale, Duane K.

1987 *Peacemakers on the Frontier*: A History of the Delaware Tribe of Western Oklahoma. Anadarko: Delaware Tribe of Western Oklahoma Press.

Hale, Duane K., ed.

1984a *Turtle Tales*: Oral Traditions of the Delaware Tribe of Western Oklahoma. Anadarko: Delaware Tribe of Western Oklahoma Press.

1984b *Cooley's Traditional Stories of the Delaware*. Anadarko: Delaware Tribe of Western Oklahoma Press.

Hall, Robert

1997 *An Archaeology of the Soul.* North American Indian Belief and Ritual. Urbana: University of Illinois Press.

Hann, John

1988 *Apalachee: The Land Between the Rivers.* Gainesville: University of Florida Press.

1991 *Missions to the Calusa.* Gainesville: University of Florida Press.

Harrington, Mark R

1913 A Preliminary Sketch of Lenape Culture. *American Anthropologist* 15: 208-35.

1921 *Religion and Ceremonies of the Lenape.* Museum of the American Indian, Indian Notes and Monographs # 19.

1963 *The Indians of New Jersey: Dickon among the Lenapes.* 2d ed. New Brunswick, NJ: Rutgers University Press.

nd Draft on Delaware Social Organization and Ethnography. MS on File at the Museum of the American Indian, Heye Foundation, New York.

Harris, Zellig

1947 Structual Restatements: II ~ Delaware. *IJAL* 13 (3): 175-186.

1966 *Language Universals.* The Hague: Mouton.

Haas, Mary

1965 "Other-Culture" vs. "Own Culture": Some Thoughts On Leslie White's Query. *American Anthropologist* 67: 1556-1559.

1969 "Exclusive" and "Inclusive": A Look at Early Usage. *International journal of American Linguistics* 35: 1-6

Heckewelder, John

1820 *A Narrative of the Mission of the United Brethren among the Delaware and Mohegan Indians*, from Its Commencement, in the Year 1740, to the Close of the Year 1808. Philadelphia:

1876 *History, Manners, and Customs of the Indian Nations Who Once Inhabited Pennsylvania and Neighboring States.* Publications Fund of the Historical Society of Pennsylvania Memoir # 12. Philadelphia. [1819]

Herman, Mary

1950 A Reconstruction of Aboriginal Delaware Culture from Contemporary Sources. *Kroeber Anthropological Society Papers* 1: 45-77.

Hewitt, JNB

1928 *Iroquoian Cosmology* 2. Annual Report, Bureau of American Ethnology # 43. Washington, DC.

Hickerson, Harold

1970 *The Chippewa and Their Neighbors.* New York: Holt, Rinehart, and Winston.

1988 The Chippewa and Their Neighbors: A Study in Ethnohistory. 2nd ed. Prospect Heights, IL: Waveland.

Hill, George

1971 Delaware Ethnobotany. *Oklahoma Anthropological Society Newsletter* 19 (3): 3-18.

Hockett, Charles

1966 What Algonquian Is Really Like. *IJAL* 32 (1): 59-73.

Honigmann, John

1976 *The Development of Anthropological Ideas.* Homewood, IL: The Dorsey Press.

Hoijer, Harry

1946 *Linguistic Structures Of Native American.* Viking Fund Publications in Anthropology 6: 1-423.

Howard, James

1981 *Shawnee! The Ceremonialism of a Native Indian Tribe and Its Cultural Background.* Athens: Ohio University Press.

Howard, Jane
1984 *Margaret Mead, A Life.* New York: Fawcett Crest.
Hunter, Charles

1971 The Delaware Nativist Revival of the Mid-Eighteenth Century. *Ethnohistory* 18: 39-49.
Hunter, William

1971 Correspondence with Nora Thompson Dean, 14 September.

1974a Correspondence with Nora Thompson Dean, 6 May.

1974b Correspondence with Nora Thompson Dean, 29 May.

1974c Correspondence with Nora Thompson Dean, 12 November.

1974d   A Note on the Unalachtigo. *A Delaware Indian Symposium.* Herbert C Kraft, ed. Anthropological Series #4: 147-52. Harrisburg: Pennsylvania History and Museum Commission.

Hyde, George

1974 *The Pawnee Indians.* Norman: University of Oklahoma Press.

Jackson, Jason, and Victoria Lindsay Levine

2002   Singing for Garfish: Music and Woodland Communities in Eastern Oklahoma. *Ethnomusicology* 46 (2): 284-305.

Jameson, J. Franklin, ed.

1967 *Narratives of New Netherland 1609-1664.* New York: Barnes and Noble. [1909]

Jelik, Wolfgang

1974 Salish Indian Mental Health and Culture Change: Psychohygienic and Therapeutic Aspects of the Guardian Spirit Ceremonial. Toronto: Holt, Rinehart, and Winston of Canada, Ltd.

Jones, Ruthe Blalock

1973 Hi'ngwikan: Delaware Big House Ceremony. Manuscript.

Kappler, Charles J.

1903 *Indian Treaties 1778-1883*. Washington, DC: US Government Printing Office.

Kinietz, Vernon

1940 European Civilization as a Determinant of Native Indian Customs. *American Anthropologist* 42: 116-21.

1946 *Delaware Culture Chronology*. Prehistory Research Series 3 (1). Indianapolis: Indiana Historical Society.

Kinzie, J

1901 *Wau-Bun*: The Early Day in the Northwest. Rand, McNally, Chicago.

Kleinman, Arthur

1974 Medicine's Symbolic Reality: On a Central Problem In The Philosophy of Medicine. *Inquiry* 16: 206-313.

Krusche, R

1986 The Origin of the Mask Concept in the Eastern Woodlands of North America. *Man in the Northeast* 31: 1-47.

Landar, Herbert and Joseph Casagrande

1962 Navaho Anatomical Reference. *Ethnology* 1 (3): 70-3.

Laughlin, William

1968 Hunting: An Integrating Biobehavior System And Its Evolutionary Importance: 304-320. *Man the Hunter*. Richard Lee and Irven Devore, eds. Chicago: Aldine Publishing Co.

1972 The Aleut-Eskimo Community: 125-143. *The North American Indians*: *A Source-Book*. Roger Owen, James Deetz, and Anthony Fisher, eds. Toronto: Collier-MacMillian Canada, Ltd.

Leach, Edmund

1967 Magical Hair: 77-108. *Myth and Cosmos*. John Middleton, ed. Garden City: The Natural History Press. American Museum Source-books in Anthropology.

Levi-Strauss, Claude

1944 Reciprocity and Hierarchy. *American Anthropologist* 46: 266-268.

1967 *Structural Anthropology*: 161-201. Claire Jacobson and Brooke Grundfest Schoef, trans. Garden City: Anchor Books.

1968 *The Savage Mind.* Chicago: University of Chicago.

Loskiel, George H

1794 *History of the Mission of the United Brethren among Indians in North America.* London: Brethren's Society for the Furtherance of the Gospel.

Lurie, Nancy

1971 *Mountain Wolf Woman.* Ann Arbor: University of Michigan Press.

Lutz, Rev JJ

1906 The Delaware Mission. The Methodist Missions Among the Indian Tribes in Kansas. *Transactions of the Kansas State Historical Society* 9: 203-7 ~ 160-230.

McCracken, Horace

1956 The Delaware Big House. Oklahoma Historical Society: *The Chronicles of Oklahoma* 34: 183-92.

McCoy, Isaac

1840 *History of the Baptist Indian Missions*: Embracing Remarks on the Former and Present Conditions of the Aboriginal Tribes, Their Settlement within the Indian Territory and Their Future Prospects. Washington: William M. Morrison.

Mahr, August

1949 A Chapter of Early Ohio Natural History. *Ohio Journal of Science* 49 (2): 45-69.

1954 Aboriginal Culture Traits As Reflected in 18th-Century Delaware Indian Tree Names. *Ohio Journal of Science* 54 (6): 380-7.

1955 Eighteenth-Century Terminology of Delaware Indian Cultivation and Use of Maize: A Semantic Analysis. *Ethnohistory* 2 (3): 209-40.

1959 Practical Reasons for Algonkian Indian Stream and Place Names. *Ohio Journal of Science* 59 (6): 365-74.

1960 Anatomical Terminology of the Eighteenth- Century Delaware Indians: A Study in Semantics. *AL* 2 (5): 1-65.

1961 Semantic Evaluation. *AL* 3 (5): 1-46.

1962 Delaware Terms for Plants and Animals in the Eastern Ohio Country: A Study in Semantics. *AL* 4 (5): 1-48.

Maier, Pauline

1971 Review of The Mothers: Three Generations of Puritan Intellectuals, 1596-1728, by Robert Middlehauff. New York Times Book Review Section for June 20, 1971.

Marsh, Gordon and William Laughlin

1956 Human Anatomical Knowledge Among the Aleutian Islanders. *SJA* 12: 38-78.

McClure, Erica

1975 Ethno-Anatomy: The Structure of the Domain. *AL* 17: 78-88.

Michelson, Truman

1912 Ethnological and Linguistic Field Notes from the Munsee in Kansas and the Delaware in Oklahoma, 1912. National Anthropological Archives. Washington, DC: National Anthropological Archives: MS 2776.

1922 Canadian Munsee Linguistic and Ethnological Notes. Washington, DC: National Anthropological Archives: MS 1635.

Miller, Jay

1972 The Priority of the Left. *Man* 7: 646-7.

1974a The Delaware As Woman: A Symbolic Solution. *American Ethnologist* 1 (3): 507-514.

1974b Why The World Is On The Back Of A Turtle. *Man* 9 (2): 306-8.

1974c The Unalachtigo? *Pennsylvania Archaeologist* 44 (4): 7-8. :

1975a Delaware Alternative Classifications. *AL* 17 (9): 434-44.

1975b Addendum On Ethno-Taxonomic Congresses. *AA* 77 (4): 887.

1975c Delaware clan names. *Man in the Northeast* 9: 60-63

1976 The Delaware Doll Dance. *Man in the Northeast* 12: 80-84.

1977 Delaware Anatomy, With Linguistic, Social, and Medical Aspects. *Anthropological Linguistics* 19 (4): 144-166.

1979 A Strucon Model of Delaware Culture and the Positioning of Mediators. *American Ethnologist* 6 (4): 791-802.

1980a A Structural Analysis of the Delaware Big House Rite. University of Oklahoma, *Papers in Anthropology* 21:107-33.

1980b High Minded High Gods in North America. *Anthropos* 75: 916-19.

1980c The Matter of the (Thoughtful) Heart: Centrality, Focality, or Overlap. *Journal of Anthropological Research* 36: 338-42. [132]

1982 People, Berdaches, And Left-Handed Bears: Human Variation In Native North America. *Journal of Anthropological Research* 38 (3): 274-287.

1989a Delaware Traditions from Kansas, Nahkoman to Isaac McCoy. *Plains Anthropologist* 34 (123): 1-6.

1989b The Early Years of Watomika (James Bouchard), Delaware and Jesuit. American Indian Quarterly 13 (2): 165-188.

1990 *Delaware Integrity* ~ The Ritualization of Culture in the Gamwing (Big House Rite). Amazon.

1994a *The Delaware*. Chicago: Childrens.

1994b   The 1806 Purge among the Indiana Delaware: Sorcery, Gender, Boundaries, and Legitimacy. _Ethnohistory_ 41: 245-66.

1996 Changing Moons: A History of Caddo Religion. *Plains Anthropologis*t 41 (157): 243-259.

ms Delaware Public Thought and Culture: The Structure of Its Configurations.

ms A Structuralist Analysis of the Delaware Big House Rite. In possession of author.

** American Humanity and Other Monsters: A Structuralist Analysis of Frankenstein, the Mummy, Dracula, and Wolfman. (Forthcoming).

1971– Delaware Fieldnotes. in possession of author.

Miller, Jay, and Nora Thompson Dean

1978 A Personal Account of the Delaware Big House Rite. *Pennsylvania Archaeologist* 48 (1-2): 39-43.

Morgan, Lewis Henry

1959 *The Indian Journals 1859-1862*. Leslie White, ed. University of Michigan Press, Ann Arbor. Originally published 1859.

1972 *League Of The Iroquois*. Secaucus: The Citadel Press.

Mukhopadhyay, CC, and PJ Higgins

1988   Anthropological Studies of Women's Status Revisited: 1977-1987: 461-495. Annual Review of Anthropology. B Siegel, A Beals, and S Tyler, eds. Palo Alto.

Murie, James

1981 *Ceremonies of the Pawnee*. Part I: The Skiri, Part II: The South Bands. Douglas Parks, ed. Smithsonian Contributions to Anthropology # 27.

Needham, Rodney

1973 *Right and Left*: Essays on Dual Symbolic Classification. Chicago: University of Chicago Press.

Nelson, James David

1963 Herrnhut: Friedrich Schleiermacher's Spiritual Homeland, 2 vols. Ph.D. University of Chicago.

Newcomb, William

1955 A Note on Cherokee-Delaware Pan-Indianism. *American Anthropologist* 57 (3): 1042-1045.

1956a *The Culture and Acculturation of the Delaware Indians*. Ann Arbor: Museum of Anthropology, Anthropological Papers # 10.

1956b The Peyotc Cult of the Delaware Indians. *Texas Journal of Science* 8 (2): 202-211.

Newkumet, Vynola Beaver, and Howard Meredith

1988 *Hasinai* ~ A Traditional History of the Caddo Confederacy. College Station: Texas

A&M University Press.

Olmstead, Earl P

1991 *Blackcoats among the Delaware*: David Zeisberger on the Ohio Frontier. Kent, OH: Kent State University Press.

O'Meara, John

1996 *Delaware-English ~ English-Delaware Dictionary.* Toronto: University of Toronto Press.

Ortiz, Alfonso

1969 *The Tewa World.* University of Chicago Press.

Ortner, Sherry B.

1974 Is Female To Male As Nature Is To Culture?: 67-87. *Woman, Culture, and Society.* Michelle Rosaldo and Louise Lamphere, eds. Stanford University Press.

Parker, Arthur

1912 Certain Iroquois tree myths and symbols. *American Anthropologist* 14.

Pearson, Bruce

nd A Grammar Of Delaware: Semantics, Morpho-Syntax, Lexicon, And Phonology. Ph.D. Dissertation. U of California at Berkeley.

Penick, James Lal

1981 *The New Madrid Earthquakes.* revised. ed. Columbia: University of Missouri Press.

Petrullo, Vincenzo

1934 *The Diabolic Root*: A Study of Peyotism, the New Indian Religion among the Delawares. Philadelphia: University of Pennsylvania Press for the University Museum. .

Prewitt, Terry

1981 Tradition and Culture Change in the Oklahoma Delaware Big House Community: 1867-1924. Contributions in Archaeology #9. Tulsa, OK: University of Tulsa, Laboratory of Archaeology.

Radin, Paul

1970 *The Winnebago Tribe.* Lincoln: University of Nebraska Press.

Randle, Martha Champion

1951 Iroquois Women, Then and Now: 167-175. Symposium on Local Diversity in Iroquois Culture. William N Fenton, ed. Bureau of American Ethnology Bulletin # 149. Washington.

Reichel-Dolmatoff, Gerardo

1971 *Amazonian Cosmos*: The Sexual and Religious Symbolism of the Tukano Indians. Chicago: University of Chicago Press.

Ritchie, William A

1969   The Archaeology of New York State. 2nd ed. Garden City, NY: Natural History Press.

Roark-Calnek, Sue

1977 Indian Way in Oklahoma: Transactions in Honor and Legitimacy. Bryn Mawr College: Anthropology PhD.

1978 The Delaware Moral Economy: Transactions and Transformations in Ritual Exchange. Acts of the Forty-first International Congress of Americanists 5: 327-33.

1980 Delaware Religion and Ethnic Identity: The Last Fifty Years. University of Oklahoma, Papers in Anthropology 21:135-52.

Rohn, Arthur and Mariam Smith

nd   Assessment of the Archaeological Resources and an Evaluation of the Impact of Construction of the Copan Dam and Lake. Army Corps of Engineers, Tulsa District. Contract DACW 56-72-C-0064.

Rossi, Ino

1974 *The Unconscious in Culture*: The Structuralism of Claude Levi-Strauss in Perspective. New York: EP Dutton.

Rountree, Helen C

1989 *The Powhatan Indians of Virginia*: Their Traditional Culture. Civilization of the American Indian # 193. Norman: University of Oklahoma Press.

1990 *Pocahontas's People*: The Powhatan Indians of Virginia through Four Centuries. Civilization of the American Indian # 196. Norman: University of Oklahoma Press.

Sabo III, George

2003 Dancing into the Past: Colonial Legacies in Modern Caddo Indian Ceremony. *The Arkansas Historical Quarterly* LXII (4 Winter): 423-445.

Saunders, Ross and Philip Davis

1974 Bella Coola Head Bone Nomenclature. *Journal of Anthropological Research* 30: 174-190. [p165]

Schultz, George

1972 *An Indian Canaan*, Isaac McCoy and the Vision of an Indian State. University of Oklahoma Press, Norman.

Secondine, Issac

nd   Interview. Indian-Pioneer History. Vol. 9. MS on file in the Foreman Collection, Oklahoma Historical Society, Oklahoma City. [1937].

Schlesier, Karl

1990 Rethinking the Midewiwin and the Plains Ceremonial Called the Sun Dance. *Plains Anthropologist* 35 (127): 1-27.

Siskind, Janet

1973 *To Hunt in the Morning.* Oxford University Press.

Speck, Frank

1931 *A Study of the Delaware Big House Ceremony.* Publications of the Pennsylvania Historical Commission 2. Harrisburg.

1933 Notes on the Life of John Wilson, the Revealer of Peyote, as Recalled by His Nephew, George Anderson. *General Magazine and Historical Chronicle* 35: 539-56.

1937 *Oklahoma Delaware Ceremonies, Feasts and Dances.* Memoirs of the American Philosophical Society 7. Philadelphia.

1945 *The Celestial Bear Comes Down to Earth.* Reading, PA: Reading Museum Scientific Publications # 7.

1945 *The Iroquois* ~ A Study In Cultural Evolution. Cranbrook Institute of Science Bulletin 23.

1946 The Delaware Indians as Women: 377-389. *Pennsylvania Magazine of History and Biography.* October.

1948 Critical Comments on "Delaware Culture Chronology. *American Anthropologist* 50: 723-2.4.

1949 *Midwinter Rites of the Cayuga Long House.* Philadelphia: University of Pennsylvania Press.

APS Collected materials stored in the Library of the American Philosophical Society, Philadelphia. Delaware material in boxes 8 and 9. Manuscript numbers given in the text.

Speck, Frank G, and Jesse Moses

1945 *The Celestial Bear Comes Down to Earth.* Scientific Publication # 7. Reading, PA: Reading Public Museum and Art Gallery.

Spicer, Edward H.

1969 *A Short History of the Indians of the United States.* New York, D. Van Nostrand.

Stocker, Harry Emilius

1917 *A History of the Moravian Mission among the Indians on the White River in Indiana.* Bethlehem, PA: Times Publishing.

Stone, Irving.

1956. *Men to Match My Mountains,* The Opening of the Far West 1840-1900. Garden City: Doubleday and Co.

Straus, Anne

1975 Northern Cheyenne Ethnopsychology. *Ethnos* 5 (3): 326-357.

1976 Being Human In the Cheyenne Way. PhD dissertation, University of Chicago, Chicago.

Swanton, John

1928 *Religious Beliefs and Medical Practices of the Creek Indians.* Bureau of American Ethnology, Annual Report 42 for 1924-25.

1929 *Myths and Tales of the Southeastern Indians.* Bureau of American Ethnology, Bulletin 88.

Tanner, Helen Hornbeck, ed.

1987 <u>Atlas of Great Lakes Indian History</u>. Civilization of the American Indian # 174. Norman: University of Oklahoma Press.

Tantaquidgeon, Gladys

1950 Delaware Indian art designs. *Pennsylvania Archaeologist* 20: 1-2.

1972 *Folk Medicine of the Delaware and Related Algonkian Indians.* The Pennsylvania Historical and Museum Commission Anthropological Series 3. Harrisburg. (original 1942)

Thompson, Charles

1937 *Sons of the Wilderness: John and William Conner.* Indiana Historical Society Publication 12. Indianapolis: Indiana Historical Society.

Tooker, E

1968 Masking and Matrilineality in North America. *American Anthropologist* 70 (6): 1170-1177.

1970 *The Iroquois Ceremonial of Midwinter.* Syracuse, NY: Syracuse University Press.

Torry, Alvin

1871 *Autobiography of Rev Alvin Torry*, First Missionary to the Six Nations and the Northwestern Tribes of British North America. 4th ed. William Hosmer, ed. Auburn, ON: William J Moses.

Trigger, Bruce G, ed.

1978 Handbook of North American Indians. #15 ~ *Northeast.* Washington, DC: Smithsonian Institution Press.

Trowbridge, CC

nd Traditions of the Lenee Lenaupee or Delaware. MS in the Detroit Public Library, Detroit.

Unrau, William

1978 *The Kansa Indians*: A History of the Wind People 1673-1873. Norman: University of Oklahoma Press.

1979 *The Emigrant Indians of Kansas.* A Critical Bibliography. Bloomington: Indiana University Press for the Newberry Library.

Voegelin, Carl F

1939 The Lenape and Munsee Dialects of Delaware, an Algonquian Language. *Proceedings of the Indiana Academy of Sciences* 49: 34-37.

1941a Word Distortions in Delaware Big House and Walam Olum Songs. *Proceedings of the Indiana Academy of Sciences* 51: 48-54.

1941b Proto-Algonquian Consonant Clusters In Delaware. *Language* 17: 143-147.

1946 Delaware, An Eastern Algonquian Language. *Linguistic Structures of Native America.* Harry Hoijer, ed. VFPA 6.

Voegelin, Carl F, and Erminie W Voegelin

1944 The Shawnee Female Deity in Historical Perspective. *American Anthropologist* 46: 370-375.

Walker, Deward E., Jr.

1989 *Witchcraft and Sorcery of the American Native Peoples.* Moscow: University of Idaho Press.

Walker, William

1975 The Proto-Algonquians: 633-647. *Linguistics and Anthropology*: In Honor of CF Voegelin. MD Kinkade, K Hale, and O Wenner, eds. Lisse: Peter de Ridder Press.

Wallace, Anthony FC

1947 Woman, Land, and Society: Three Aspects of Aboriginal Delaware Life. *Pennsylvania Archaeologist* 17 (1): 1-35.

1949 *King of the Delawares*: Teedyuscung 1700-1763. Philadelphia: University of Pennsylvania Press.

1956 New Religions among the Delaware Indians, 1600-1900. *Southwestern Journal of Anthropology* 12: 1-21.

1957 Political Organization and Land Tenure among the Northeastern Indians, 1600-1830. *Southwestern Journal of Anthropology* 13: 301-21.

Wallace, Paul AW

1975 *Indians in Pennsylvania.* Harrisburg: Pennsylvania Historical and Museum Commission.

Watson, James, and Harold Nelson

1967 Body-Environment Transactions; A Standard Model for Cross-Cultural Analyses. *Southwestern journal of Anthropology* 23: 292-309

Chief Waubuno [John Wampum]

1845 *The Traditions of the Delawares.* London: Bowers Brothers.

Weil, Andrew

1972 *The Natural Mind.* Boston: Houghton Mifflin Co.

Weltfish, Gene

1971 *The Lost Universe.* New York: Ballantine.

1977 *Lost Universe ~ Pawnee Life and Culture.* Lincoln: University of Nebraska Press.

Werner, Oswald and Kenneth Begishe

1966 A Lexical Typology of Navajo Anatomical Terms I; The Foot. *IJAL* 34: 247-65.

Weslager, Clinton A

1950 Indians of the Eastern Shore of Maryland and Virginia. *The Eastern Shore of Maryland and Virginia.* Charles B Clark, ed. New York.

1944 The Delaware Indians as Women. *Journal of the Washington Academy of Science* 34 (12): 381-388.

1947 Further Light on the Delaware Indians as Women. *Journal of the Washington Academy of Sciences* 37 (9): 298-304.

1971 Name-Giving Among the Delaware Indians. *Names* 19 (4): 268-283.

1972 *The Delaware Indians*: A History. New Brunswick, NJ: Rutgers University Press.

1973 *Magic Medicines of the Indians.* Signet Books. New York.

1975 More about the Unalachtigo. *Pennsylvania Archaeologist* 45 (3): 40-44.

1978 *The Delaware Indian Westward Migration.* Wallingford, PA: Middle Atlantic. [134]

White, Richard

1991 *The Middle Ground*: Indians, Empires, and Republics in the Great Lakes Region, 1650-1815. New York: Cambridge University Press.

Wilkes, Charles

1845 *Narrative of the US Exploring Expedition*: IV. Philadelphia: Lea and Blanchard.

Williams, Lorraine

1980 *The Delaware Indians*: A Study Combining Archaeology, Ethnohistory, and Ethnography. Trenton: New Jersey State Museum.

Williams, Stephen, and John Goggin

1956 The Long-Nosed God Mask. *Missouri Archaeologist* 18 (3).

Williamson, Ray

1992 The Celestial Skiff: An Alabama Myth of the Stars: 52-66. *Earth & Sky ~ Vision of the Cosmos in Native American Folkore.* Ray Williamson and Claire Farrer, eds. Albuquerque: University of New Mexico Press.

Witherspoon, Gary

1975 *Navajo Kinship and Marriage.* U of Chicago Press.

Witthoft, John

1949 *Green Corn Ceremonialism in the Eastern Woodlands.* Occasional Contributions #13. Ann Arbor: University of Michigan, Museum of Anthropology.

Wood, Philip

1970 Peculiarities of Medical Characteristics for Taxonomic Purposes. *The Classification*

Society Bulletin 2: 23-8.

Wormington, HM

1964 *Ancient Man in North America.* Denver Museum of Natural History, Popular Series #4. Denver.

Wright, Muriel

1977 *A Guide To The Indian Tribes of Oklahoma.* Norman: U of Oklahoma Press.

Zeisberger, D

1885 Diary of David Zeisberger, a Moravian Missionary among the Indians of Ohio. Eugene F Bliss, ed. & trans. 2 vols. Cincinnati: R Clarke for the Historical and Philosophical Society of Ohio.

1887 *Zeisberger's Indian Dictionary.* EN Horsford, ed. Cambridge, Massachusetts.

1910 *History of the North American Indian.* Ohio Archaeological and Historical Quarterly XIX (1-2): 1-189. Archer Butler Hulbert and William Nathaniel Schwarze, eds. Columbus.

On the Web >>

 Origin of the Delaware Woman Dance - Parts One & Two [Xkweyok Enta Naxkuhëmënt Enta Këntkahtit] Told by Lillie Hoag Whitehorn (1902 - 1994) to Bruce Pearson and Jim Rementer in 1977. Lillie was a member of the Delaware Tribe of Western Oklahoma (now The Delaware Nation), and half Caddo through her father, Enoch Hoag, Caddo Chief.

http://talk-lenape.org/story.php?story=44

Sources

73 Triads in Delaware Culture. *Bulletin of the Eastern States Archaeological Federation* 1973.

74 Why the World Is on the Back of a Turtle. *Man* 9 (2): 306-308 1974.

74 The Unalachtigo? *Pennsylvania Archaeologist* 44 (4): 7-8 1974.

75 Kwulakan: The Delaware Side of Their Movement West. *Pennsylvania Archaeologist* 45 (4): 45-46 1975.

75 Addendum On Ethno-Taxonomic Congresses. *American Anthropologist* 77 (4): 887 1975.

75 The Cultural View of Delaware Clan Names as Contrasted with a Linguistic View. *Man In the Northeast* 9: 60-63. (Cf. Nora Thompson Dean (63-65), Ives Goddard (65-67) 1975.

75 Delaware Alternative Classifications. *Anthropological Linguistics* 17 (9): 434-444 1975.

76 The Delaware Doll Dance. *Man In the Northeast* 12: 80-84 1976.

77 Delaware Anatomy: With Linguistic, Social, and Medical Aspects. *Anthropological Linguistics* 19 (4): 144-166 1977.

78 Delaware Terms For Playing Cards. *International Journal of American Linguistics* 44 (2): 145-146 1978.

78 A Personal Account of the Delaware Big House Rite. *Pennsylvania Archaeologist* 48 (1-2): 39-43 1978. (with Nora Thompson Dean).

79 A 'Struckon' Model of Delaware Culture and the Positioning of Mediators. *American Ethnologist* 6 (4): 791-802 1979.

79 Delaware Language and Culture: 23-31. *Papers of the 1978 Mid-America Linguistics Conference.* Ralph Cooley, Melvin Barnes, and John Dunn, eds. Norman: University of Oklahoma Press 1979.

80 A Structural Study of the Delaware Big House Rite. *Papers in Anthropology* 21 (2): 107-133 1980.

89 Delaware Traditions from Kansas: Nakoming to Isaac McCoy. *Plains Anthropologist* 34 (123): 1-6. Feb 1989.

89 The Early Years of Watomika (James Bouchard), Delaware and Jesuit. *American Indian Quarterly* 13 (2): 165-188 1989.

91 Delaware Masking. *Man In the Northeast* 41: 105-110 1991.

91 Delaware Personhood. *Man In the Northeast* 42 (Fall): 17-27 1991.

97 Old Religion Among the Delawares. *Ethnohistory* 44(1): 113-134 1997.

99 *American National Biography*, John A Garraty and Mark C Carnes, eds. Oxford University Press. Teedyuskung 21: 425-426, Mourning Dove 15: 37-38 1999.

96 Changing Moons: A History of Caddo Religion. *Plains Anthropologist* 41 (157): 243-259. 1996.

03 Delaware Colors, Categories, and Culture -- Making The Best Connections. *Archaeological Society of New Jersey Journal*: 22-23 2003.

08 A Birthday Peyote Meeting Attended by Vincenzo Petrullo. *Archaeological Society of New Jersey Journal* 2008.

08 The Last Delaware Doll Dance: An Eye-Witness Account By Vincenzo Petrullo *Archaeological Society of New Jersey Journal* 2008.

08 Enoch Hoag's Suffering And Vision To Make His Own Peyote Moon Altar, As Told By Lillie Hoag Whitehorn, His Daughter *Archaeological Society of New Jersey Journal* 2008.